American Literary Misfits

D. BERTON EMERSON

American Literary Misfits
The Alternative Democracies of Mid-Nineteenth-Century Print Cultures

The University of North Carolina Press *Chapel Hill*

This book was published with the assistance of the Authors Fund of the University of North Carolina Press.

© 2024 D. Berton Emerson
All rights reserved
Set in Arno Pro by Westchester Publishing Services
Manufactured in the United States of America

Complete Library of Congress Cataloging-in-Publication Data for this title is available at https://lccn.loc.gov/2024000480.
ISBN 978-1-4696-7839-9 (cloth: alk. paper)
ISBN 978-1-4696-7840-5 (pbk.: alk. paper)
ISBN 978-1-4696-7841-2 (ebook)

Portions of this book have been previously published in a different form: "'It's Good to Be Shifty': The Local Democracies of Old Southwestern Humor," *American Literature* 85, no. 2 (2013): 273–301, copyright © 2013 Duke University Press (all rights reserved, republished by permission of the publisher); "'This is a strange book': Re-Membering Local Democratic Agency in Bird's Sheppard Lee," *ESQ: A Journal of Nineteenth-Century American Literature and Culture* 61, no. 2 (2015): 222–61, copyright © 2024 Board of Regents of Washington State University; "George Lippard's The Quaker City: Disjointed Text, Dismembered Bodies, Re-generated Democracy," *Nineteenth-Century Literature* 70, no. 1 (2015): 102–31.

To Mom, Dad, and Mandy;
to my children, Samuel and Elizabeth;
and to my love, Jerusha

Contents

Acknowledgments ix

Introduction: Democracies in Parts of America 1

CHAPTER ONE
Philadelphia Protests, Revolutionary Memory,
and Relocalized Democracy 30

CHAPTER TWO
Southwestern Humor, Common Men, and Playful Democracy 61

CHAPTER THREE
Northwestern Settlements, Popular Sovereignty,
and Neighborly Democracy 88

CHAPTER FOUR
Interbellum California, Manifest Destiny, and Contingent Democracy 118

CHAPTER FIVE
Black New York, Antiracist Dignity, and Basic Democracy 147

Coda: Literature, History, Populism, Democracy 173

Notes 177

Bibliography 207

Index 229

Acknowledgments

The challenge of the long-range book project comes down to this: sharing appreciation in a way that is commensurate with the support I've received. Over the decade-plus it has taken to compose, revise and edit, workshop and revise again, pitch publishers, await reviewer reports, wade through a pandemic, and then finally find a publishing home, I have incurred scores of debts. Herein I express my deepest gratitude for the many, many, MANY folks who have shared wisdom, encouragement, insight, feedback, and skepticism with me as I have taken this journey to bring these ideas into a book-shaped life.

My first thanks must go to the person who has been an enduring mentor for more than two decades: Paul Gilmore. Always ready to read a draft or share advice and encouragement, Paul has provided profound guidance since I happened into his classroom for a summer course in American literature at California State University, Long Beach. Although few words remain from its earliest iterations, I benefited enormously from my experience prepping a first rough draft at Claremont Graduate University. Bob Hudspeth is a model of professional excellence, and I will strive to live up to the high standards he has set. Robert Dawidoff offered hours of eclectic conversation and critique, and I am forever grateful for his friendship. Wendy Martin, Lori Anne Farrell, and Martin Griffin provided sustained encouragement throughout my graduate years. I was likewise blessed with amazing peers: Fay Ellwood, Ambereen Dadabhoy, Sharon Becker, and Tyler Reeb. Extra special thanks go to some of the all-time best interlocutors and grad school mates in Michael Contreras, Joseph Coombe, Christopher Farrish, and Brandon Loper. During those grad school years, my work and my life improved dramatically thanks to the joys of academic life shared with David Alworth, Katherine Baxter, Liza Blake, Matthew Boehm, Jane Carr, Yeo Ju Choi, Lindsay DiCuirci, Chris Donaldson, Brigitte Fielder, Erica Fretwell, Perla Guerrero, Brian Hochman, Nisha Kunte, Lori Leavell, Rob McLoone, Julie Orlemanski, Alpen Razi, Lindsay Reckson, John Reuland, Kelly Ross, Kacy Tillman, and Jonathan Senchyne. To those who participated in the School of Criticism and Theory 2008 at Cornell and the Futures of American Studies 2010 at Dartmouth, the revelry and camaraderie made all this work so much more enjoyable. Before finishing out my graduate experience, I was incredibly blessed to gain the wisdom and advice of some of the best Americanists around: Dana Nelson, Christopher Looby, Elizabeth Maddock Dillon, Jeaninne DeLombard, Lloyd Pratt, Kyla Tompkins, Ivy Wilson, Kyla Schuller, Emily Satterwhite, Keri Holt, John Funchion, and Greg Jackson. Likewise, I owe many thanks to Tam Carlson, Tim Caron, and Rob Pearigen for their insights and encouraging words throughout these years.

A National Endowment of the Humanities Summer Stipend offered substantial time and resources in the revising stages of the project. Research fellowships at the Library Company of Philadelphia, the Bancroft Library at UC Berkeley, the Huntington Library, and the American Antiquarian Society made archival research possible. Special thanks to Jim Green, Connie King, Juan Gomez, and Paul Erickson for the added bonuses of tremendous advice and community building.

I'm grateful to faculty colleagues and students at all the different Los Angeles universities and colleges where I held contingent posts: the writing programs at Woodbury University and UC Riverside; the American Studies department at Cal State Fullerton; and the English departments at Cal Poly Pomona, College of the Canyons, Pomona College, and Redlands University. Adjuncting is tough sledding, but these places gave me time and place to hone my craft.

In my LA years, I picked up many more fellow travelers. Christopher Hunter, Sarah Mesle, and Aaron DeRosa were stalwart friends and colleagues. In the summer of 2014, I caught the bug to resuscitate the Southern California Americanists Group (SCAG 2), which was graciously hosted by the Huntington Library. To date, ten scholarly books (I think) have emerged from this group, and this one is number eleven! One would be hard-pressed to find better scholars and friends than Michelle Chihara, Aaron DeRosa, Mark Eaton, Rebecca Evans, Chris Farrish, Glenda Goodman, Chris Hunter, Carrie Hyde, Evan Kindley, Tom Koenigs, Greta LaFleur, Leila Mansouri, Sarah Mesle, Michele Navakas, Sharon Oster, Siobhan Phillips, Lindsay Reckson, Christian Reed, Shirley Samuels, Stella Setka, Stefanie Sobelle, Derrick Spires, and Caleb Spencer. The project further benefited from workshopping with two marvelous scholarly communities in LA: the Americanist Research Colloquium at UCLA and the scholars who come and go at the Huntington Library. Profound learning opportunities and friendships also came with folks like Sari Altschuler, Ben Beck, Sarah Blackwood, Hester Blum, Carrie Bramen, Chris Castiglia, Russ Castronovo, Michael Cohen, Daniel Couch, Peter Coviello, Joe Dimuro, Betsy Duquette, Duncan Faherty, Travis Foster, John Funchion, Greg Laski, Koritha Mitchell, Matthew Rebhorn, Sarah

Salter, Caleb Smith, Michele Speitz, Jordan Stein, Claudia Stokes, Nafissa Thompson-Spires, and Caroline Wiggington.

Moving to Spokane to take up a post at Whitworth University, I found a splendid institutional home. Special thanks to department mates Casey Andrews, Jake Andrews, Courtney Barajas, Laura Bloxham, Vic Bobb, Karly Bosma, Jessica Clements, Fred Johnson, Lori Lamon, Peter Moe, Kari Nixon, Leonard Oakland, Pam Parker, John Pell, Nicole Sheets, Allie Shook, and Doug Sugano; and to the broader humanities community: Tony Clark, Amanda Clark, Aaron Griffith, Davey Hendrickson, Elise Leal, and Dale Soden. I am so grateful as well for incredible students who have helped me refine ideas in this book, and for teaching me so much beyond it.

As someone who spent too much time in sports, I never thought I would pursue a career in academia, but lessons of hard work and perseverance learned on the field have proven essential. Thanks to John Tatum, David Bethea, Tim Bethea, Ronnie Elmore, Robert Black, John Windham, Scott Baker, and Tom Flynn. In my career change from coach to academic, I owe so much to my colleagues and administration at Palmer Trinity School in Miami and Sage Hill School in Newport Beach—at PTS, Susan Patterson, Laura Walker, and Michael Zavada; at Sage Hill, Chris Ellsasser, Fiona Fraser, Chris Irwin, Chris Marshall, George Pratt, Arlie Parker, Liz Resnick, and Clint Wilkins.

My professional life would be pretty limited without the support of friends beyond academia. To my faith communities at Bel Air Presbyterian Church in Los Angeles and New Community Church in Spokane, thank you for the sustenance. To the Allen family, I owe an enormous debt; special thanks to Byron and Jane, to Matt, and to Emily, who first planted this seed. To Louie and Courtney, Jeff and Shelly, Michelle and Austin, Julian and Debra, Rondal, Scott, Campbell, Stroup, Robin, Tug, Parker, Swiney, Jarrett, Jay, Ted, Tripp, Bobby, and Costa; Nordan and Morgan, Kittie and Nick, Zach and Kelly, Jon and Kristy, John and Sarah, Jake and Chris, Russ and Shannon, Aaron and Wendi, Dave and Bri, and Dani and Lewis: thanks for the faith, encouragement, lessons, neighboring, and lifetimes of endlessly rewarding friendship.

Thanks to the folks connected with the University of North Carolina Press, especially Lucas Church and Thomas Bedenbaugh, as well as Alyssa Brown, Kylie Haggen, Liz Orange Lane, Iris Levesque, Abigail Michaud, and Lindsay Starr.

Most importantly, thanks to my family. In the last decade I have become a Hoffman. To Roger and Ava, John and Alice, Hannah and Ben, Nathanael, Sarah, and all the nieces, nephews, cousins, and extended family, thank you.

In my own clan, I am blessed to have the best big sister ever. To Mandy, her husband Brent, and my three precious nieces—Mary Kate, Abby, and Emmy—you have always been the bright lights in my world. Love and thanks to you, Aunt Peggy. And whatever good I've done in my life, it has come because I have the two best parents of all time. My dad has modeled the life of faith, hope, and love for me, and I will always strive to make him proud. And my mother, who regrettably did not get to see the culmination of this chapter of my life, nevertheless guides my steps. I miss you deeply. I think you'd find this book pretty neat.

And finally, to my children, Samuel and Elizabeth, and to my wife, Jerusha, through you I have learned what grace means in wholly new ways. I'm humbled daily with the blessings of sharing this life with you, and I'm ever motivated to do my part to make this world better for you and with you. Y'all are my love.

American Literary Misfits

Introduction
Democracies in Parts of America

In most European nations, the initial movements of power resided with the upper echelons of society and passed gradually and always in a partial manner to the other sections of the society. By contrast, in America we can state that the organization of the township preceded that of the county, the county that of the state, the state that of the Union. In New England, townships were fully and definitively constituted from 1650. The individual township was the place where local interests, passions, duties, and rights clung together, and it fostered at its heart real political activity which was active, thoroughly democratic, and republican.
—Alexis de Tocqueville, *Democracy in America, Volume 1* (1835)

Considered in its entirety, literature of democratic times could not possibly present, as it does in aristocratic times, a picture of order, regularity, science, and art; its formal qualities will normally be disregarded and sometimes despised. Style will often appear quickly, incorrect, inflated, flabby, and almost extreme and violent. Authors will aim more at speed of execution than perfection of detail. Writing on a small scale will occur more often than weightier books, wit more often than scholarship, imagination more often than profundity.
—Alexis de Tocqueville, *Democracy in America, Volume 2* (1840)

Democracy in America, Tocqueville's celebrated account of American politics, traces the origins of US democracy to the New England towns of the seventeenth century. Tocqueville contends that the sociopolitical system he witnessed in Jacksonian America thrives because of its ongoing, heartfelt commitment to "real political activity." Taking the local-scale history of the colonial New England township and mapping it onto the larger body of the nation, he elides any distinction between (local) democracy and (national) republicanism. This rhetorical move is also an aesthetic one: he champions ideal forms in New England towns, proclaims their representativeness with personifying metaphors, and establishes a standard for quality and achievement in the political life of the young nation. Tocqueville's second observation, however, argues that local origins and democratic energy do not offer the same kind of value in the aesthetic domain of literary culture. He doubts the possibility of quality literary production in US democratic culture, specifically with regards to the formal categories of order and style. Tocqueville punctuates his dour assessment by predicting an abundance of "writing on a small scale": quick, witty, and imaginative, perhaps, but neither scientific nor artistic. Considered together, the two passages imply that US citizens could take pride in local roots that foster a vibrant democracy; however, small-scaled, flabby writing would be one of the costs.

For nearly two centuries, proponents of a distinguished US literary culture have worked to rebut this unflattering assessment. They have done so by employing some of the same rhetorical and aesthetic moves Tocqueville made in *Democracy in America*: identifying an idealized figure on a local scale and ebulliently proclaiming its representativeness on a national one. Unlike Tocqueville, they believed a distinguished, national literary culture and democracy could and should be co-constitutive. Nineteenth-century texts like Ralph Waldo Emerson's *Representative Men* (1850) and Walt Whitman's *Leaves of Grass* (1855) helped initiate and deepen this intellectual-political-aesthetic tradition, proclaiming their productions to be representative of the growing nation, nourished primarily by its egalitarian political system. F. O. Matthiessen's *American Renaissance* (1941), which practically framed the field of pre–Civil War US literature in the mid-twentieth century, championed the aesthetic achievements of Emerson, Thoreau, Hawthorne, Melville, and Whitman precisely because they shared what he called "a devotion to the possibilities of democracy."[1] For Matthiessen, their writing was "good" in no small part because it addressed the nation's potential as a democratic collective. Scholars have since poked, prodded, and reconstructed Matthiessen's canon, establishing different standards for artistry as well as inclusiveness, often in the name of democracy. Yet, a national scale of reference and lofty standards for representation and achievement have persisted. And this is understandable, given that, as Sacvan Bercovitch has claimed, the US nation was built on capacious symbols that produced a quasi-religious affinity for representative selfhood, "a tyranny not of the majority but of a liberal-symbolic system of thought."[2] When literary texts have not fit in this liberal-democratic framework of synecdochic representativeness—that is, certain highly esteemed parts standing in for the whole—they have typically been displaced from the national canon, cordoned off as regional or local, and deemed less valuable in both cultural and political spheres.

This common critical maneuver in US literary history raises an important question: can flabby, despised, small-scale literature be good for the study of democracy? In the years when Tocqueville praised the foundations for real democratic activity while also maligning literary culture in the United States, inhabitants were experiencing profound shifts in key areas of their political, material, and cultural lives—changes to the reputation of the term *democracy*, the technologies of material production and circulation of printed texts, and the measurements for literary and aesthetic value. A term Loyalists and Federalists had once used in derogatory fashion, *democracy* had become the name of the new political vanguard on the national stage as white men saw nearly all restrictions removed from their opportunities to exercise voting rights. These positive connotations of a previously spurned political concept coincided with new imaginings of national cohesion bolstered by material developments like railroads, telegraphs, and high-speed printing presses that facilitated an interstate market economy and a burgeoning mass culture. Literary texts like transcendentalist essays, historical romances, and sentimental novels emerged with a recently established sense of aesthetic autonomy and performed the cultural work of tying readers to a national community.

But what if this pursuit of *national* cultural achievement and increasing attention paid to *national* politics cleaved democracy from the very site where it arguably should exist, where Tocqueville paradoxically claimed "real political activity" actually did exist: rooted in the localities that fostered political activity and vibrancy? To be sure, standard-makers of national literary achievement privileged texts promoting a liberal, deliberative version of democracy, the very form that worked in concert with the well-ordered checks and balances of the constitutional nation. But what varieties of democratic thinking lie hidden behind the master narrative of the liberal tradition and Whiggish faith in the progressive advance of deliberative democracy? And how should we understand the texts—especially literary ones—that posit alternatives to the predominant political and aesthetic norms of this period?

Approaching these questions from a different angle, consider a minor episode in a little-known political novel of this era, *The Adventures of Col. Gracchus Vanderbomb* (1852), by John Beauchamp Jones. The discordant, often incoherent narrative follows the campaign of the self-absorbed, monomaniacal titular character who thinks himself fated to make a run for the presidency and to unite the polarized sections. The narrative slowly and awkwardly reveals the absurdity of his quest, while also leaving open the possibility that the charade might actually work. Midway through the novel, during one of Vanderbomb's campaign speeches, readers encounter a clear and likely familiar national vision. Directly addressing sentiments of secession, Vanderbomb offers a commonsense rebuttal imbued with classical republican rhetoric: "But the greatest security for the Union . . . will be the elevation to the presidency of an individual whose private interests lean neither to one side nor the other; one who is, from birth, from education, and from interest, just as much inclined to the North as to the South." Expecting praise and adulation from the crowd, Vanderbomb is disappointed. The crowd shouts back, "'We don't understand you,' cried several; 'you're getting dull. Give us something spicy.'"[3] The satirical novel of course takes this moment of obstinacy and misunderstanding to score comedic points. To what degree, though, should we take these auditors' comments at face value as legitimate questions about their democracy? Although some might assume that the unthinking herd merely seeks entertainment at a political spectacle, might we also see their comments as demonstrating a longing for something that more effectively delivers the type of empowerment that often gets conjured in the language and practice of democracy? Instead of condescendingly presuming the crowd's ignorance in the face of deliberative consensus, though, I want to start by taking their comments seriously. No matter how awkwardly it is articulated in their speech or in the broader narrative apparatus in which they are represented, I aim to wade through varieties of democratic thinking that have not always been obvious to those trained in literary and cultural studies.

This book thus takes these kinds of complaints sincerely and pursues a democratically inclined criticism that pushes not only beyond Tocqueville's general assessments, Matthiessen's field-establishing "possibilities," and Bercovitch's "liberal-symbolic system of thought," but also beyond mere recovery—often nominally democratic—of representative writers connected with peoples originally excluded from legitimate participation in the US demos. Such an approach requires not only a new catalogue of literary texts but also alternative critical sensibilities with which to read them. This book makes the case for an eclectic set of pre–Civil War literary texts that have long defied the more orderly values associated with the liberal tradition of US literary history and its preferred version of an individualistic, contract-oriented, rights- and property-protecting, managed form of democracy. Prose narratives like George Lippard's *Quaker City* (1845), John Rollin Ridge's *Adventures of Joaquín Murieta* (1854), and Metta Fuller Victor's *The Backwoods Bride* (1860), although wildly popular in their respective days, have rarely if ever been celebrated as meditations on democracy, much less as representative of the nation, largely due to their presumed aesthetic flaws, political unsavoriness, and local peculiarities. Less widely circulating texts like Robert Montgomery Bird's *Sheppard Lee* (1836), Louise Clappe's *The Shirley Letters* (1854–55), and William J. Wilson's *Afric-American Picture Gallery* (1860) have seldom been cited as key texts of literary history, much less as important for the cultivation of a democratic citizenry. Whatever their popularity in their day or since, the assignment of such texts to regional or local subcategories has impacted their relevance to the study of democratic and literary cultures in the United States. Such critical framing plausibly makes sense for post–Civil War texts that appeared when regionalism and local color developed generic coherence within an interconnected nation-state. It makes less sense in the three decades before the Civil War. In some—not all—locales, a materially and ideologically networked nation was developing thanks to the time- and space-altering transportation and communications revolutions. These early yet uneven developments of national cohesion led to many political and cultural analyses that assumed the scale of the nation (Tocqueville's treatise on American democracy, for instance). But not all peoples and their conceptions of democracy, nor the imaginative literature that represented them, fit neatly within these narratives oriented to the nation. US literary criticism has typically *fit* these texts into regional subcategories, regardless of time period. I contend that these *misfits* require a rewriting of US literary history.

INTRODUCING THE CRITICAL TERM *misfits* calls for some clarifications. For those familiar with US literary history broadly, it might initially summon the brutally murderous antagonist of Flannery O'Connor's "A Good Man Is Hard to Find" (1953), a man simply known as "the Misfit." Although O'Connor is most assuredly known for being a regional (i.e., southern) writer, and her story featuring the Misfit carries a strong regional (i.e., southern) flavor, O'Connor writes in an historical moment when regionalism had very much become a functioning element in the broader story of the nation's literature as well as its political system. Instead, I am interested in an earlier, more transitional historical moment when literary culture and material culture, the nation and its people's conceptions and convictions about democracy, were all changing. In this era, the term *misfits* might conjure well-known iconoclasts like Edgar Allan Poe and Henry David Thoreau, yet these nineteenth-century authors have hardly suffered in obscurity or been understood primarily as regional writers. And I do not mean socioeconomic groups from this era that many assume to be misfits—poor white people, for instance—as a negative comparison useful for identifying the traits of an emerging middle class.[4] Rather, for the purposes of my arguments, I use the term *misfit* to capture three overlapping issues: the unruly characters and communities that are frequently represented in such texts; the narrative incoherence and structural flaws that have long compromised their valuation in their historical moment; and their too often mistaken temporal and spatial locations in US literary history.

Although US literary history might be widely populated by eccentric types, the characters and communities represented in this book's entourage of literary misfits are valuable for reevaluation because they lack the genteel qualities and deliberative sensibilities of more distinguished types. Characters like Simon Suggs and Sut Lovingood in the frontier Southwest, Mary Clavers's village-building neighbors in rural Michigan, and members of the crowd attending Gracchus Vanderbomb's speech have rarely been appreciated as emblematic participants in the work of democratic self-governance. By the 1830s, generations had passed since founding figures like George Washington and John Adams presumed that social deference would ensure the proper grounds for a governing hierarchy to which ordinary folks would proffer a nominally democratic consent. But old prejudices lingered. To many, several characters and communities represented in these stories appear as unqualified and highly uncivil political subjects, as figures of the very excesses of Jacksonian-era democracy that threatened the changing yet enduring expectations of a deferential social order. In other instances, misfit characters materialize as more rank-and-file types who reject the idea that democracy would be managed by someone else, whether by elected or appointed officials or by enduring institutions like schools and churches. Both of these types prove poor fits for the work of a traditionally engaged, deliberative, democratic citizenry. And yet, I will show, these misfits possess significant value for the ongoing development of cultures that foster radical democratic empowerment.

Along with representations of these indecorous and run-of-the-mill types who have either been offensive to tastemakers or unwitting tools of policymakers, the narratives they inhabit typically defy the formal qualities of order, form, and style that have served as the bedrock of critical sensibilities since the Romantic era. They appear in precisely the type of "inflated" or "flabby" literary works that Tocqueville expected from a democratic culture. This combination of unseemly content and compromised form not only offends literary sensibilities, but also runs counter to the aesthetic orderliness of national standards developing in this era: the fundamental symmetry of governmental checks and balances, a narrowly framed two-party system, the rule of precedent, procedure, and law. Prominent critics desiring an elitist and nationalistic literary culture disparaged these literary representations. To whatever degree literary culture supported the development of democratic muscles, such denigration correlatively discouraged both unseemly and more middling types from cultivating cultures and skill sets valuable for a democratic society. Such norms, I contend, have had long-term repercussions on everyday people's understanding of their opportunities in a democratic governance.

The literary misfits assembled herein are likewise valuable for their contrast with more popular antebellum, nation-oriented texts like sentimental novels and historical romances that have appealed to national symbols and employed progressivist orientations, often in the name of democratic reform. Whether contributing to the consolidation of a white, male, liberal polity—like, for instance, James Fenimore Cooper's Leatherstocking Tales—or prompting revised collective identities purged of blights like slavery—Harriet Beecher Stowe's *Uncle Tom's Cabin* is a famous example—such texts assumed the telos of the nation. Literary misfits like August Baldwin Longstreet's *Georgia Scenes* (1836) and James McCune Smith's *Heads of the Colored People* (1852–1854) were not only dislocated spatially from the national to the regional or local but also disjointed in time. In one sector of US democracy, the presumably democratic reform movements of these decades generated what Christopher Castiglia has dubbed "institutionalism," a discourse that redirects citizens from democratic opportunities in the present with the promise that some combination of abstract, corporate entities like churches, schools, or associations would eventually deliver the long-deferred pursuit of happiness.[5] As progressive as this alignment might seem, and as important as institutional anchors are to the endurance of thriving democracies, this temporal orientation compromises democratic activities exercised by ordinary people in the present, a compromise the literary misfits assembled in this book appear disinclined to accept.

Misfits in their own day, such texts have proven incompatible within the canon-building work—and its revisions—of the twentieth century. For the most part, midcentury New Critics rejected such works due to their formal incoherence and their failure to achieve a full-fledged totality topped up with intellectual ambiguity. Later critics of a New Historicist or cultural studies bent have come to appreciate such texts as windows into broadening senses of social and cultural history, but few have wrestled with the complications of aesthetic malfeasance. And even as scholars with transnational inclinations have decentered the nation as the default scale of reference in literary studies, and as book historians have more copiously mapped the print networks through which literary cultures circulated in the pre–Civil War decades, our predominating narratives about US literary history have continued to situate these kinds of texts in otherwise reductive configurations.

A reexamination of select misfits starts with an appreciation for the often dismissed or abstracted people making up the demos. It continues with more openness to a broader variety of literary expressiveness, whatever the intellectual and formal qualities. With refined literary sensibilities comes the need to understand that more radical variations of democracy—or better said, *democracies*—do not necessarily connote orderly political systems. Combining these three filters, we can see in these literary misfits the projection of alternative democracies that surfaced in common across a range of geographic and demographic sites. Emerging from long-settled urban areas and rural frontier sites from coast to coast, the literary misfits considered in this book—all published between the election of Andrew Jackson in 1828 and the days before civil war engulfed much of the country—demonstrate people working through the challenges and possibilities of democratic ideas and practices outside the contours of liberal, deliberative paradigms. They do so on more localized scales via an unassimilable linguistic mode that I call *vernacular aesthetics*. In multiple ways they differ markedly from literary texts that complemented nation building by heralding a representative part, claiming that it stood in for the whole, erasing or rendering abstract local exceptions, and performing a type of cultural work that affectively tied both characters and readers to the nation and its imagined community. Exploring such misfits reflects an inclination not only to rethink predominating values in literary criticism but also to mine the political knowledge they disclose. Such literary misfits, I contend, offer some of the nineteenth century's most radical and understudied representations of democracies in the United States.

Sequence and Scope

Because the eclectic group of texts that make up the primary objects of study are less well known than many contemporaries, I will start with a general outline of the chapters and their arguments and then return in this Introduction to the conceptual framework of literary misfits, their vernacular aesthetics, and the alternative democracies they imagine. This book explores five constellations of pre–Civil War literary misfits that have typically been fit into separate categories organized by geography, demography, or genre: Philadelphia novels of satire and social protest, old southwestern humor, settlement narratives from the Old Northwest, California gold rush myths and epistolary sketches, and African American periodical writing in New York. I juxtapose readings of these misfits with traditional representatives of a national literature—George Bancroft, Davy Crockett, Harriet Beecher Stowe, Bret Harte, and Frederick Douglass—along with liberal democratic themes and movements of the era: Revolutionary legacy, rise of the common man, popular sovereignty, manifest destiny, and abolition.

The sequence of chapters follows some different yet related logics. The general architecture of the book on the surface appears spatial due to arrangements anchored to places. Launching from the concept of critical regionalism, I demonstrate the ways that these tendencies toward alternative democracies appear in specific locales and go on to defy the arbitrary boundaries of more broadly conceived geography and demography.[6] (Here I note that *The Adventures of Col. Gracchus Vanderbomb*, although sharing many misfit qualities with the texts considered herein, assumes a national scale of reference and thus lacks this element of adherence to democracies in specific locales.) Underlying these spatial constellations is a temporal trajectory working from origins to new beginnings. Starting at the birthplace of radically democratic ideas as well as the nation, and then moving south, then north, then west, then back east, the chapters engage different emphases in time, from backward-facing to present tense to future possibilities. Substantively, the first two chapters take up texts written by and largely about the experiences of white men, who gained the franchise in these decades even if they did not always find their democratic empowerment to be satisfactory. The latter three chapters broaden their scopes to engage the literary productions of and conditions pertaining to women and people of color. To be sure, these general trajectories do not address all the included and excluded of the era. Yet, the sequence engages a range of challenges that have long vexed those who want democracy to sort itself out.[7]

The first chapter, "Philadelphia Protests, Revolutionary Memory, and Relocalized Democracy," investigates the original site of nation building in the United States and the ways its local culture evolved in an era of increased investments in the history of the American Revolution. I evaluate how Bird's *Sheppard Lee* and Lippard's *Quaker City* deploy an alternative aesthetic that challenged official accounts of the Revolution and the myths that came with it, allowing both authors to explore the consequences of democratic power being transferred from city streets to the distant removes of national governance. Bird's satire criticizes the way a Federalist system of governance abstracts power from the local and the individual through its innovative use of a popular post-Revolutionary genre, the picaresque. Lippard's exploration of disempowered people living on the margins of Philadelphia society reveals the horrifying costs of a national democratic system that provides no recourse for nonelite peoples. Together, they imagine a version of urban democracy that extends beyond the labor movements of early industrialization.

Chapter 2, "Southwestern Humor, Common Men, and Playful Democracy," examines the fictions that have long been understood as representations depicting the movement of backward frontier cultures toward more progressive national forms. Juxtaposing Longstreet's *Georgia Scenes*, Johnson Jones Hooper's *Simon Suggs* (1845), and George Washington Harris's *Sut Lovingood* tales (1850s) with the popular almanacs of Davy Crockett, I show how myriad tales present a vernacular-tongued character operating on the fringes of national experience according to the dictates of something I dub *democratic play*: a two-part action in which authors first highlight the disconnects between national ideologies and their local sites, which then enables rank-and-file types to participate in the ongoing games of self-rule. Along with close readings of these primary texts and their politics, I track the circulation of a few examples in print culture across the country and their subsequent impact on the democratic imaginary in the nation.

Whereas the first two chapters focus on writers who self-consciously work to counter or to abjure national norms, the third chapter, "Northwestern Settlements, Popular Sovereignty, and Neighborly Democracy," settles in a region that readily assumed an identity aligned with the nation's dictates. Harriet Beecher Stowe's first short story, "A New England Sketch" (1836), published in Cincinnati but set in a New England village, offers a compelling example of a literary construction of abstracted democratic space complicit with national norms and forms. The misfit in the Northwest is Michigan, whose democratic push for statehood suffered numerous setbacks due to imbalances within national politics. These setbacks prompted a variety of reactionary norms that become apparent in Caroline Kirkland's narrative of settlement, *A New Home, Who'll Follow?* (1839) and Victor's *The Backwoods Bride*. With Kirkland's narrative, I track its rejection of an inevitable merger of eastern and western sensibilities—themes often misunderstood by critics and locals represented therein. I then move to Victor and her first contributions to the newly born Beadle Dime Novels series. Victor's novels demonstrate ambivalent engagement with national standards and assess the value of neighborly democracy.

John L. O'Sullivan's coining of the term *"manifest destiny"* in 1845 and the subsequent acquisition of California in the US-Mexican War suggest the consolidation of a vision of expansion that tied the nation together coast to coast. The discovery of gold immediately after only reinforced the providential rhetoric. Early stories from the California borderlands before the Civil War, however, demonstrate that the imposition of national frameworks on the vast yet isolated space produced violence and a destiny that was anything but manifest and inevitable. To see this, chapter 4, "Interbellum California, Manifest Destiny, and Contingent Democracy," juxtaposes the post–Civil War stories of Bret Harte with two texts published in 1850s California, Ridge's *Joaquín Murieta* and Clappe's *The Shirley Letters*. Both texts demonstrate the radical altering of the nation's spatial and temporal dimensions amid the booms and busts of the gold rush era. Ridge's messy portrayal of the notorious hero-outlaw dramatizes the difficulty early Californians had with negotiating the awkward establishment of the liberal dictates of law and order across vast space. Clappe's serialized letters exhibit the failure to produce anything like Kirkland's village democracy while implicitly calling for a more flexible and engaging democratic form.

The concluding chapter, "Black New York, Antiracist Dignity, and Basic Democracy," returns from more recently established locales of the West to Philadelphia's heir as economic and cultural center. Here I assess midcentury African American literary history, its presumed investments in national scales of reference, and the growing alternatives to nationalist orientations. Unlike Frederick Douglass's paean to heroic individualism in his one work of fiction, "The Heroic Slave" (1852), Smith's serialized *Heads of the Colored People* and Wilson's installments making up *The Afric-American Picture Gallery* offer a more complex case of democracy before liberalism. Through their depictions of Black vernacular voices—Smith in the experimental essays that transgress their declared intention of innocently representing everyday lives, Wilson in his meditations on aesthetics in a variety of ekphrastic, dialogic, and narrative writing—both texts prioritize the conferral of dignity on all peoples as preconditions for American democracy.

A Global Literary Republic, Its National Subsidiaries, and Local Literatures

Certain literary texts of the modern era have been linked to specific times and places, while others have achieved a status that disentangles them from historical particularity. Pascale Casanova's sociological account of the operations of this "world republic of letters" distinguishes between the perishable and the immortal in this way: "Work is condemned to become dated unless, by achieving the status of a classic, it manages to free itself from the fluctuations of taste and critical opinion.... Literarily speaking, a classic is a work that rises above competition and so escapes the bidding of time."[8] Along with this temporal definition, Casanova assesses these texts in spatial terms. Imaginative texts that possess the ability to transcend time carry a universality that unmoors them from any specific locality. Through a combination of internal rhetoric and extratextual critical investments and extrapolations, the classic becomes far removed from the delimiting, often pejorative labels of *local* or *regional* and lands on a categorical plane with other literary classics that have achieved similar status. As one illustration in US literary history, although Mark Twain's *Adventures of Huckleberry Finn* (1885) is memorably set before the Civil War along the Mississippi River, the novel-become-classic has come to be recognized as transcending its deictic temporality and spatial boundedness. When an imaginative text falls short of this achievement, it remains enmeshed in its particularity, not necessarily conceived as a failure, but certainly less than extraordinary. And in a US culture that has long privileged extraordinary achievements, such a designation could be considered a condemnation.

Casanova claims that this world republic of letters—a rarely questioned metaphorical conflation of the literary and the political world—emerged in the sixteenth century with the privileging of vernacular languages in the Renaissance and the growing political rivalries between emerging nation-states; in later centuries, a center-periphery relationship formed.[9] The belated entry of the United States into this geopolitical order meant that a distinctive national character could be forged in its literary production.[10] As a relative latecomer to the international scene of the Atlantic world, the territorially expanding and materially evolving United States of the mid-nineteenth century needed fuel for its cultural fire to support its claims to power in the global domain. As part of the formation of its internal political identity, many in the consolidating nation looked to literature. This cultural project was no doubt important to many after the nation's inception, but it took on a heightened urgency from the so-called Era of Good Feelings (1817–1825) into the Jacksonian era (1825–1849) and up until its presumed achievement in the 1850s.[11] US literary history in these eras is littered with such calls by both individuals and corporate groups to make a mark in the global literary community. James Fenimore Cooper's career legendarily started after his wife challenged him to prove good on his claim that he could produce fiction better than any English novel. Corporate culture makers, including the *North American Review*, the *Knickerbocker Magazine*, and the Young America movement, variously sought and organized the criteria for a distinctive and exceptional national literature that would counter an old-world tradition defined by monarchic and aristocratic ideologies. On a national scale of different dimensions, southern literary journals became the sites for contested debates between those who would be advocates for a national literature, those who bemoaned such ambition (mostly due to a perceived lack of audience), and later on, those who saw literature as being a key element for fomenting identifications of a Southern nation. On yet another scale, David Walker's *Appeal* (1829) inaugurated a Black nationalism that he hoped would thrive in the global marketplace. In each case, calls for a national literature had far-reaching political ramifications, since nearly all were infused with democratic rhetoric.[12]

Among these many calls, William Ellery Channing's lecture "Remarks on National Literature," delivered to the American Philosophical Society in 1823, offers a representative sample. Throughout his remarks, the foremost Unitarian preacher of his day draws on conventional Enlightenment discourse privileging reason and assuming the inevitability of progress. Consistently peppering his call for a national literature with a heavy serving of classical republican ideology, he declares that a nation's first responsibility involves cultivating "superior men." Channing believes literature readily serves this purpose, especially in a political and social environment that privileges, at least nominally, liberty and equality. Assuming a materially networked public, he contends that "the influence of literature is perpetually increasing," because "reading, once the privilege of a few, is now the occupation of multitudes."[13] The theologian acknowledges the value of producing superior minds via education of all classes, but this effort should not supplant the pursuit of literary excellence, something that would both satisfy international audiences and cultivate a particular form of national feeling. Fortunately, Channing finds an abundance of literary resources available to writers in the United States. Here he sees the same associative qualities that Tocqueville witnessed in abundance, but envisions far different results in the effects of high-quality literary production: "Here the different classes of society flow together and act powerfully on each other, and a free communication, elsewhere unknown, is established between the gifted few and the many."[14] While Channing cites liberty as the primary contributor to literary production, he also believes that equal exchange pays dividends as well, especially in light of the tendency of Europe's historical and contemporary institutions to ignore the needs and offerings of all persons. By combining institutional infrastructure with a call for geniuses to produce important aesthetic works, Channing registers a sense of inevitability that this national literature will come to pass. However romanticized his rhetoric, the establishment of the United States as a sovereign nation stands as Channing's primary goal, and quality literary production, dissemination, and consumption are crucial elements for producing the social and political norms that would make this happen.

This appropriation of democratic rhetoric for national purposes was hardly new in Channing's time, even as he privileged grand achievements first and foremost. His top-down, nation-first approach to cultivating a democratic citizenry vis-à-vis literary excellence promoted democracy, albeit a particular kind. It assumed only one scale on which democracy might be imagined and experienced as well as a version of well-ordered democracy that merged classical republican doctrine with emerging liberal values. A quarter century later, these calls continued, but the rhetoric became less deferential even as it grew more delimited. For instance, in his introduction to *The Prose Writers of America* (1840), Rufus Wilmot Griswold prefaces his anthology of US writers with a savvy argument against the doubters of a distinguished national literature. "The commonly urged barriers to literary advancement supposed to exist in our form of government, . . . the restless and turbulent movements of our democracy, and the want of a wealthy and privileged class among us" matter little, Griswold writes. To the contrary, "Tumult and strife, the clashing of great interests and excitements, are to be regarded rather as aids than as obstacles to intellectual progress."[15] For Griswold, great literature will come, and the only two requisites in the meantime involve an international copyright to protect American writers in the marketplace and stronger institutions that cultivate the talents of the elite: "We need a great university, into which only learned men can enter, where there can be a more thorough literary and scientific culture, . . . giving form and authority to the first order of understandings which in them are brought to light."[16] With a copyright protections and higher education, Griswold fuses together the presumption of economic order in the marketplace, a belief in institutions that serve the best first, and the conviction that form and authority and order will deliver national achievement.

Defaulting to the nation as scale of reference and relying on democratic rhetoric to justify the predominant socioeconomic order has long been the trend among literary critics, intellectuals, and tastemakers like Channing and Griswold. It has also been problematic. Much of this tendency has resulted from the typical take on the constitution of democracy in the United States. As Dana Nelson has argued, the US nation—particularly as it was formulated and defined by the Constitution—has effectively limited our capacity to imagine ways that the political can take shape according to democratic ideals practiced by its inhabitants, a collective phenomenon often characterized as the "democratic imaginary." Nelson contends that "the Constitution created a new, abstracted, and antipolitical national identity that worked to sublate what it cast as the confusions, unpredictability, and inefficiency of local democracy. . . . The Constitutional nation persistently draws our attention toward its containment promise, its promise to manage democracy for us."[17] Embedded in Nelson's critique is the Constitution's privileging of the national over the local, order over disorder. Deference to national principles in the political sphere has led to a powerful, well-functioning nation-state, one that has been bolstered by the emergence of renowned cultural achievements that have effectively represented the nation in the global order. But it has also resulted in a struggle to recognize democratic activity outside of the terms prescribed by the nation whose very existence depends on managing people. Channing's and Griswold's insistence on a national framework and adherence to more deferential—and in time, more individualistic—versions of democracy poses serious problems for the chances of literary culture fostering any sort of alternatives beyond a version that combines elitist republican and classically liberal doctrine (much as Tocqueville would dismiss the chances of a distinguished literary culture in a democratic United States).

If democratic ideals balancing liberty and equality provided material for writers, who would then develop literary productions that would cultivate even greater senses of liberty and equality (and thus produce "superior men" and their submissive followers), then the intellectuals' and tastemakers' insistence on a great literature of nation-scaled achievement leaves little room for a significant number of noncontenders and leftovers. This critical neglect might work if the notions of liberty and equality remain in the abstract and are determined by individual experiences. But if they are intended to be made manifest in forms of collective action in which all have a legitimate say, and are combined with crucial yet less famous elements of democracy like reciprocity, pluralism, and dignity, then critical standards should provide allowances and justifications for such oversights. US literary culture and history have often gone a different route, continuing to be built by calls on the grandest of scales and being narrowly represented by more genteel sectors of the general population.

While Channing's and Griswold's aggrandizing calls and Casanova's descriptive account contribute to the idea of a national-global republic of letters, what might we do about the material leftovers? How do we reconcile the one-offs and the offshoots, the remainders and the excesses, especially in a nineteenth-century society made up of an expanding and more diverse population, which produced and circulated more printed texts than ever before, which fostered a wider variety of local and semiautonomous literary cultures? And how do we do so in the wake of a profoundly successful, two-decade critical response to the conflation of the historical US nation-state with imperialist ambitions?[18] Moves toward transnational studies have dislodged the nation as the default scale of reference in many instances, providing valuable alternative frameworks for understanding nineteenth-century culture and affiliations.[19] While productively recalibrating investigations of a variety of human activities along with the development of a global republic of letters, this move to the transnational—or the oceanic, the hemispheric, the planetary—similarly produces leftovers and misfits. From a different direction, the critical invention of regional literatures within the United States has provided a more secure place for some less distinguished texts. And yet, as scholars have shown, the institutionalization of regional literatures has typically followed trajectories similar to the genealogies that David Shumway has highlighted in the context of US national literature.[20] Yet again, there are remainders, material that does not quite fit into our conventions and categories. For many, an easy answer has been to roll these local and regional misfits into the narrative of progress. As Lloyd Pratt has suggested, though, traditional assessments that regard the local as something inevitably absorbed by the national in the pre–Civil War decades warrants reconsideration. "If the national is thought to follow the local and replace it," he argues, "then this is because history is often thought to have only one track. It follows that in order for the national to realize itself, the local must ipso facto yield to the nation."[21] History should bear a multitude of tracks. So should democracy. Neither should suggest inevitability (hence my avoidance of the term *antebellum* when contextualizing many of my own arguments situated in this era). So the question remains: How should we understand these misfits, especially in the context of uncovering more varieties of democratic thinking—more democracies—in the nineteenth century?

A Nation, Its Misfits, and the Idea of a Vernacular Aesthetics

It seems unlikely that literary texts by less familiar nineteenth-century authors like Bird, Harris, or Smith—much less their literary creations: Sheppard Lee, Sut Lovingood, or select "heads of the colored people"—would provide a satisfying answer to Channing's call for the cultivation of "superior men." (One admission: Bird, at least, made the cut in Griswold's anthology.) Whatever the reputations of these authors in their day, none are well known outside circles of nineteenth-century scholars; even then, such texts are rarely if ever esteemed as aesthetic masterpieces. Moreover, the characters in these literary productions more closely resemble the types that made elites not only blush but also doubt the plausibility of universal participation in democratic society, much less the project of collective self-governance. And this makes sense, given prominent foundational thinking in the political sphere that a great nation, however democratic in name, would succeed once leaders established the formal structures that would ensure sufficient distance between the governing and the governed. Best captured by James Madison in Federalist 10, this plan would be much more efficient and, paradoxically, more democratic—at least in one kind of thinking about democracy that prioritized the avoidance of tyrannical majorities—for government to establish greater separation from the people it would virtually represent.[22]

Both state and federal governments had taken to deepening this divide two generations after the publication of the *Federalist Papers*, in spite of the obstinacy of local figures regularly asserting claims of democratic interest as well as agency. Their persistence, in actual life as well as in the often unceremonious literary representations of it, has typically been papered over by the archive-saturated, top-down productions of more familiar canonical writers like Edgar Allan Poe, Nathaniel Hawthorne, and Herman Melville, in assessments cast by historical commenters like Channing, Griswold, and Tocqueville, and in the progressive historiographies of subsequent generations. Simply put, founding figures like Madison and Alexander Hamilton and later politicians and writers—from Andrew Jackson and Abraham Lincoln to Harriet Beecher Stowe, Frederick Douglass, and Walt Whitman—have left historians a thicker archive of written materials than everyday, less writing-prolific people. It makes sense that stories about other kinds of democracy—ones that prioritize the arrangements of power not from the top down but from the bottom up—have rarely been captured by the record-keeping types. In addition to fewer articulations of democratic thinking, these archival limitations and absences likewise have consequences for scholarly understandings of aesthetic values for these types, both in terms of production and reception.

Difficult as they may be, bottom-up histories, at least in the area of alternative political practices, have nevertheless appeared. An especially relevant example can be found in Laura Edwards's legal history *The People and Their Peace* (2009), which demonstrates the persistence of contingency-based local rule as a viable system under extensive attack from state leaders who pursued an alternative revolutionary vision in the construction of the new republic. That vision? A streamlined code of law that would protect a rights-based legal economy (primarily for the sake of protecting property rights).[23] According to Edwards, advocates for localized legal systems that privileged (the somewhat antiquated) demonstration of democratic participation known as "keeping the peace" persisted well into the middle years of the nineteenth century. That these legal battles have been overlooked in most historical accounts has chiefly been a consequence of the rhetoric of the primary contributors to the written archive. "Recognizing the importance of history to [their] task," Edwards contends, nineteenth-century legal officials "compiled documentary sources and crafted narratives that cast localized law as an archaic throwback, which inevitably gave way to progressive change as laws were standardized and rights were uniformly defined and applied."[24] The progressive nature of these sources and narratives—invoking the same kind of rhetoric that Tocqueville had—has led to a legal studies historiography that increasingly assumes a singular narrative scope.

One could draw a readily apparent correlation between the actions of legal officials developing a streamlined, state-based code of law that would limit the disruptive inconsistencies of local contingencies and the cultural tastemakers calling for a literary culture built on "weightier books" that would cultivate superior men. Beyond the unapologetic nationalist boosters, even a writer like the iconoclastic Poe could be said to have contributed to the standardization of aesthetic values, especially in his critical essays that championed unity and coherence in poetry and short stories.[25] And all this advocacy came in the two generations just following the general establishment of principles now characterized as "aesthetic autonomy." Prompted largely by those experiencing the tumult of revolution and its reactions, artists and arts advocates promoted opinions about imaginative writings that would protect them against potential suppression and censorship. In the words of Nancy Glazener, "Guarding a space for imaginative experimentation under governments wary of revolution—and among citizens weary of polarization—seemed to require stipulating that the aesthetic subject was completely separate from the citizen capable of rabble-rousing."[26] By declaring imaginative writing to be outside the explicitly political realm, advocates like these created a safer harbor for verbal art while also protecting it from the negative effects of commodification.[27]

Despite the doubters and the critics, standards like streamlined legal codes and aesthetic autonomy have largely won out across history, delivering to us the democratic, legal, economic, and literary norms already sketched out. That said, their victory was far from assured in the United States during its awkward age of adolescence between 1830 and 1860. In these decades of diversifying population growth, territorial expansion, and transformations in printing technologies as well as transportation and communications networks, more literary texts met the eyes of an increasingly heterogeneous and dispersed population. Many of these offered the opposite of Channing's and Griswold's and Poe's declared preferences. They could hardly be valued for their craftedness. They appeared in unruly narratives that lack unity and cohesiveness, challenging conventions of literariness that were ossifying transatlantically since the start of the nineteenth century. As for their positioning in a developing discourse of aesthetic autonomy, often the misfits themselves, or the readers who encountered them, had not subscribed to the notion that imaginative writing had foresworn its political power. That said, and often problematically for their political efficacy, many of these texts displayed—and at times, made a case for—boorish behavior in formally awkward ways that raised serious concerns about the writers' or their represented figures' capacity for assuming the responsibilities associated with social, economic, and political life—all elements, I contend, of collective, democratic self-rule. Whereas formally coherent texts like *The Scarlet Letter* (1850) and *Huckleberry Finn*—texts that fit snugly within the confines of aesthetic autonomy—could shave off the rough edges of less attractive sociopolitical figures in well-ordered narratives, the combination of deficiencies in these literary misfits proved more challenging to overcome. Whether spurred on by anxious and self-conscious cultural critics and promoters in the nineteenth century who desired esteem in a world republic of letters, or by twentieth-century scholars who formed, challenged, revised, and championed a variety of literary canons, formal excellence in literary studies has long been valued and privileged.

And yet, these texts remain. However rude or informal or artistically compromised, these texts regularly capture voices of people. And not in the abstract, as a national politician might acknowledge in a widely circulated speech filled with platitudes, but rather in the concrete. In the everyday. In ways that are important to those who see in these texts a legitimate representation of their selves and their communities, no matter how refined or formally excellent that might be. And so they are important to me. Following the suggestion of Toril Moi, I see value in suspending suspicion and reading these texts anew.[28] In order to avoid the pitfall that made them misfits in our critical histories, we need some new terms. Hence, vernacular aesthetics.

The term *vernacular aesthetics* accounts for the ways that politically charged discourses in this era's literary misfits resist the collapsing of local events and individual characters into national narratives of incorporation that were coming to amalgamate a diversifying cultural and political scene and have become benchmarks in US literary histories. Such misfits register the good, the bad, and the ugly of democratic life in spite of attempts by paratextual forms like prefaces and framing devices to contain them. Often these flaws result from a narrative that starts with one set of preoccupations and then steers into something brand new by the end. Other times, the narratives are more poorly conceived, filled with loose threads and unresolved plot lines, tangled grammar and gnarly syntax. Generically, they draw from many traditions, often mashing them up into unrecognizable new forms that deny easy categorization and complicate readerly expectations. When integrating the voices of represented people, often in dialect, they do not devolve into acts of literary tourism but rather celebrate the people represented in their vernaculars. In their refusal to be rendered abstract and then folded neatly into nation-oriented or even region-oriented modes of consensus, they imagine and articulate new modes of belonging, recognition, dignity, and agency that work through the possibilities of alternative democracies.

This initial description calls for some immediate qualifications, especially given the history of aesthetic criticism in literary studies. Since the emergence of cultural studies as a discipline and its challenges to nationalistic chauvinism and political elitism in literary studies of the mid-twentieth century, continued adherence to formal and substantive standards through the lens of aesthetic criticism has rightly been attributed to upper- and middle-class hegemony and the politics of European and US imperialism. Yet, engaging aesthetic criticism becomes useful as we acknowledge that these literary misfits work against conventional representations of docile, bourgeois citizens who are receptive to the dictates of national management and imperial ambitions, often while celebrating the irreducible voices of everyday people speaking in their own languages and dialects. Cultural studies has opened up literary criticism and literary history and importantly has brought new voices into the conversation. A closer look at these contributions, however, will demonstrate ways that my arguments differ.

For a variety of purposes, Americanist literary scholars have expanded their scope beyond the midcentury canon and reintroduced texts formerly deemed less than worthy of academic study. They have shown how a variety of previously dismissed genres—the sentimental novel, the gothic, the historical romance—performed important cultural work. As valuable as these studies have been, nearly all have cited a common, national feeling within these texts or highlighted the ways they folded local episodes synecdochically into a national whole, and thus contributed more and more to national cohesion.[29] While these scholars have rarely been fussed by the aesthetically unruly or formally incoherent, I would still contend that their work shows that our critical vocabulary has some deficiencies for literary texts that do not cater to national cohesion. Even when we broaden scales of reference with correctives like world-systems analysis or transnational rubrics, I am concerned that we risk missing relevant literary texts. The books I am calling *literary misfits*, to make it plain, fail to fit neatly within highly esteemed formal conventions as well as the broader US nation-state framework. Employing a term like *vernacular aesthetics* begins the process of bringing these imaginative expressions out of an orientation structured by the nation and the homogenization of a national body politic, and it returns these literary texts to actual people living their lives and telling their stories. More often than not, this approach involves a privileging of words articulated in literary texts that represented and were read by everyday people, rather than a focus on authors, publishers, and literary marketplaces.

Beyond circumventing the framework of the nation by going local, there might be something even more basic. Not all have agreed that aesthetics are necessarily political.[30] My arguments, on the other hand, see them so. In *Lectures on Kant's Political Philosophy*, Hannah Arendt argues that the experience of a seemingly purposeless aesthetic object—it does in fact have the purpose of "pleasing men, making them feel at home in the world"—prompts operations of judgment. When readers or viewers experience an aesthetic object and interiorize that experience by means of imagination, they by necessity discriminate between choices that would determine the experience to be pleasing or displeasing. This discrimination leads to a second operation of reflection, a move to determine approval or disapproval, and the requisite for this operation is "communicability and publicness."[31] The aesthetic experience thus moves from a seemingly privatized, interior space back to a public one that is a site of the political. This linkage between aesthetics and judgment and the political realm has unavoidable repercussions for the history of political thought and the varieties of democracies that all types of people have imagined and at least aspired to practice.

If Arendt's definition is right—that aesthetics are inevitably political—then we readily find an abundance of recent work on aesthetics that has brought invaluable insights to literary studies as it pertains to understanding the history and politics of aesthetics. Oftentimes, aesthetic judgments in literary history have tended to focus on the beautiful and the sublime. Sianne Ngai's multibook project on more negative and ambivalent aesthetic categories—the ugly, the cute, the zany, the interesting, the gimmicky—has added extraordinary range to understandings not only of aesthetic criticism but also of the ways that these more rarely considered aesthetic categories have worked powerfully to foster the conditions of late capitalism.[32] Similarly, US literary scholars have revisited aesthetic concerns through the lens of cultural studies and historicized accounts, frequently making the case for the democratic and oftentimes politically subversive possibilities of aesthetic criticism.[33] The historian

Jason Frank has demonstrated how antidemocratic rhetoric has drawn on discourses of disgust in response to the apparent disruptions and disorder of democratization, and prodemocratic critics should address this tendency head-on.[34] Importantly, too, as Edward Cahill and Edward Larkin have argued, the dominance of historicism in literary studies' corpus of "frequently strange, ungainly, fragmentary, anxious, and even paranoid texts" has effectively led to the "reduction of literature to merely another form of discourses—and thus discourages attention to its particular qualities, rules, and expressive capacities."[35] Literature as specialized language and aesthetic enterprise, Cahill and Larkin remind us, calls for this distinctive consideration.

In light of these various approaches, I add the category of *vernacular aesthetics* to account for the aesthetics of storytelling in all its various guises and in ways that it might be made legible, particularly those that are more generative even as they are less than pleasing or beautiful. Some content might simply be deplorable to those pursuing progressive politics (for instance, works that promote racist, misogynistic, or homophobic slurs). Conversely, expressive material often displeases due to its violations of long-running, top-down literary sensibilities like those espoused by Tocqueville, Channing, Griswold, and Poe. It has always been easy to blame democracy for aesthetic offenses like structural incoherence, formal deviations, and stylistic flaws. When these so-called flaws coincide with the representation of voices belonging to ordinary people seeking recognition and dignity as full-fledged participants in democratic societies, both in terms of procedural politics and other elements making up democratic culture, democratically inclined critics should hesitate before dismissing such narratives for failing to satisfy critical protocol. Whatever judgments might ensue, such combinations call for a recalibration of literary sensibilities in the vein of the anthropologist Kathleen Stewart's theorization of a late twentieth-century "cultural poetics in an 'other' America."[36] Such insights are crucial when assessing the cultural forms that have paralleled the abstracting work of distancing power away from the polity, like that which occurs in representative national government under the US Constitution.

Vernacular as a critical term has most commonly been used in scholarship on language, visual art, and architecture. The mid-twentieth-century scholar John A. Kouwenhoven has argued that an exceptional vernacular tradition in the United States was born from distinctive technological innovations that left an indelible mark on all types of cultural art forms, literature included.[37] In the rare moments when it has entered the literary critical lexicon, however, the term has largely been used to focus more on the political representation of writers rather than the artistic objects they produced, whatever their aesthetic qualities might be.[38] More recently, Dana Nelson has employed the term synonymously with the *commons* in examining early American literature for its representation of everyday, nonprocedural democratic practices. Like Edwards's description of the contingent-based peace-keeping legal systems, Nelson highlights the traditions and customs of commoning as being "informal, seldom codified, and function for the well-being of a self-defined community.... [Commoning] has always been like human language, a communal labor in communication, sharing, and meaning-making.... Commons are produced, regulated, and maintained both in and *as* local vernaculars."[39] Whereas Nelson's study of commons or vernacular democracy "differs from other studies of democracy and American literature" because she is not trying "to make a general theory about American literature," I am interested in both the "political knowledge" that can be recovered as well as the formal features in which it was relayed.[40]

Neither National nor Counternational: Misfits as Alternative Democracies

Local political histories have received increasing critical attention in recent years, notably from historians of the early national period who have uncovered a wider range of voices in debates over the meanings of popular democratic governance and the kinds of culture and society that undergirded it.[41] Few studies, however, have taken a sustained look into mid-nineteenth-century print culture and the persistence of localism in the face of national compression coinciding with the transportation and communications revolutions, the consolidation of the market economy, and competing cultural nationalisms arising in the era.[42] In the political arena, the near-realization of universal white male suffrage and the mobilization of political parties on a national scale helped foreclose some possibilities of democratic action contrary to a developing national standard and its historical record.[43] From the materialist perspective of print culture, the explosion of published texts, the enhancement of distribution networks across railroads and canals, and high literacy rates all contributed to a sense of simultaneity and the production of national imagined community. Scholars such as Benedict Anderson, Lauren Berlant, and Trish Loughran have offered various accounts of the ways that, in the face of these changes, individual and collective identifications were wrenched free from local spheres and rechanneled into mobilized bodies and imagined communities of broader, supralocal proportions.[44] At stake in these transformations was the capacity for rank-and-file individuals to merge democratic aspirations in theory with the lives they lived. A cosmopolitan citizen transcending locality and nationality might serve as the idealized democratic identification in the twenty-first century, as Kwame Anthony Appiah has asserted.[45] But prior to the Civil War, in the face of the material and ideological forces that challenged conventions undergirding political activity in general and democracy more specifically, there remain a range of alternative yet imaginable varieties of democracy circulating alongside or in the shadows of what would become the national norm.

A major challenge in finding alternatives to the predominance of liberal versions of democracy in America is developing a vocabulary and a methodology to see it. First efforts begin with rethinking typical scales of reference along with long-held critical and aesthetic conventions, as already discussed. An additional step involves rethinking conventional wisdom on democracy, a political system typically rendered in the singular. In Douglas Lummis's project to revive the concept of democracy in its root, or "radical," sense of the term—that is, "a political form in which the people have power"—he contends that advocates of democracy must repeatedly rehabilitate the word *democracy* because it has so frequently been misused or misinterpreted.[46] Among a plethora of "misunderstandings and disfigurements of the word"— which include misconstrued definitions of "the people," pairings with governance that "cares for the people" or rulers "supported by the people," and assertions that it is "the free market," "free elections," "allowing the people to have their say," or "vicarious power"—Lummis addresses two mistakes especially relevant to my arguments. First, "democratic centralism," often at the nation-state level, may have practical benefits for the sake of management, and perhaps even in certain stages of democratic revolution. Yet, we should be caution about pairing *centralism* with the qualifier *democratic*, Lummis argues, for "democracy depends on localism: the local areas are where the people live. Democracy doesn't mean putting power some place other than where the people are."[47] Second, democracy is too often confused with the ideas and institutions of the US constitutional system. While the US system possesses laudable aspects, Lummis admits, the supposedly governing people (or majority) "have not solved the problem of economic democracy, ... have not found a way of overcoming their country's antidemocratic imperialism." They have neither "solved the problem of the massive and growing power concentrated in Washington" nor "rid themselves of their forlorn dreams that their problems will be solved by the next in their long line of elective kings."[48] While the latter two issues seem more relevant to the postbellum decades and the twentieth century, the substance of these problems all took deeper root in the three decades from 1830 to 1860. Taken together, Lummis's catalogue of misrepresentations about democracy addresses many of the rather narrow or even inaccurate formulations that literary critics have articulated, especially when giving US literature pride of place in the cultivation of a democratic society.

To address these shortcomings, I pursue the idea of alternative democracies by starting with a conventional definitional taxonomy that the political historian James Kloppenberg has identified. Historical ideas of democracy since the seventeenth century have been built around "three contested principles, popular sovereignty, autonomy, and equality; and three related, but less visible, underlying premises, deliberation, pluralism, and reciprocity."[49] While tracking the evolution of these ideas across the Atlantic as well as the centuries, Kloppenberg's intellectual history demonstrates how difficult it has been for any democratic society to materialize these ideas harmoniously. And while few if any historical societies have pulled off the perfect combination, which has led to the inaccuracies that Lummis's book addresses, there also appears a limited appreciation of the moments when these different elements get bundled together in rather odd formulations drawing on a variety of philosophies, only some of which are typically categorized as political. In the pre-Revolutionary American context, for instance, Kloppenberg notes that 1760s rabble-rousers like James Otis and Samuel Adams did not "differentiate between the traditions of civic republicanism, as articulated by a thinker such as [James] Harrington, the tradition of liberalism now usually associated with [John] Locke, and the doctrines of Christianity." In practice, "they drew on all three traditions, and on eighteenth-century ideas of reason and common sense, to forge wide-ranging and supple arguments that they deployed against the threats of British authority."[50] Democratic thinking has often cropped up in such stitched-together forms. In fact, one thread of argument running through this book is that some of the most interesting and challenging conceptions of democracy in the nineteenth century appear in texts that lack coherent, well-articulated theories and instead present a dynamic, ever-moving account of how individuals develop cultures that lend themselves to people being empowered together, ruling themselves together, engaging in collective decision making that addresses local concerns, whatever their success, together.

The democracies that emerge in the misfits gathered in this book offer a wide variety of alternatives to the national norm. They evidence local decision making existing alongside or outside the abstracting, normalizing tendencies of elitist republican doctrine and its presumption that the best should rule.

Through their unassimilable vernacular voices, the variously represented people and their communities often prove unreceptive to traditional social hierarchies, civic institutions, and bootstraps individualism that undergird the constitutionally managed nation-state. They engage in more commons-oriented versions of democracy characterized by dialogical negotiations in immediate spaces and temporalities. Resistant to efforts that would fold them into some form of national consensus and its telos, they instead promote the recursive agency not of a single, coherent, or unified voice but of a messy cacophony of voices unified only in their commitment to a political ideal of inclusive and empowering democratic life.[51]

While these varieties of democratic practice were surfacing in various parts of the country, the tenets of the more regularly celebrated brand of US democracy were likewise shoring up in the form of a streamlined codes of law, mass party politics, and political action—all powerfully cohering to liberal principles. This combination, grouped together with highly influential narratives like Tocqueville's *Democracy in America* along with the presumption that the Jacksonian era represented the high-water moment in participatory democratic politics in US history, has often occluded alternative democracies imagined, articulated, and practiced in these moments.[52] From a cultural vantage point, scholars have pursued some such representations in literary texts, commonly emphasizing the rational public sphere or more emotional participation in publics, participatory public spectacles or counterpublic expressions, print culture or oral culture, deliberative or radical practices.[53] Such studies have largely remained tethered to the volitional, consensual norms of liberal democracy that dominated the era. As Stacey Margolis has asserted, though, these assessments potentially pay too much attention to democracy as it was recorded in intentional speech-acts alone, thus failing to account for the ways that democratic thinking and activity often manifest in the ephemeral and the affective, in unintentional and nonconsensual ways (for instance, when misunderstood gossip sparked the Panic of 1837).[54] In addition to Nelson's work on literature of the democratic commons, cited earlier, Cathy Davidson and Christopher Castiglia have both argued that imaginative literature of the early national period and the pre–Civil War decades became a prominent source of alternative political imaginings, not only working through the ways that democratic politics could take place in their historical moment, but also serving as an archive of what might have been.[55] Following these leads, we can better see how variations of democratic thinking have long extended beyond the procedural realm of politics and attend to theories of democracy that play out beyond the predominant registers of deliberative and agonistic. Pursuing more localized frames of reference helps address how well democracies have done in the historic challenges to achieve, as Richard Brown has shown, the elusive goal of equal rights not just in voting and representation, but also in more enduringly unequal political places like hereditary private property law and the criminal justice system.[56]

The democracies in these literary misfits, as we will see, operate quite differently than the canonical contemporaries that have been lauded for their imaginings of democratic possibilities. In contrast to assumptions that the most noteworthy of US literary texts have pushed the envelope on democracy—that is, paved the way for a more perfect union built on a more inclusive liberal democracy—Nina Baym has convincingly argued that Hawthorne's and Thoreau's and Whitman's literary works—along with the twentieth-century critics who have heralded them—might best be read as offering a "consensus criticism of the consensus."[57] The literary misfit thus becomes valuable for rethinking the cultural history of democracies in the United States, for the misfit holds a different position from the two principal figures typically understood as democratic movers and shakers. Regarding the first figure, misfits like Devil-Bug of Lippard's *Quaker City*, Ethiop of Wilson's *Afric-American Picture Gallery*, and Susan Carter in Victor's *The Backwoods Bride* do not share the same status or approach to the collective as more famous US literary figures like Natty Bumppo, Hester Prynne, and Ishmael, who famously became heroes of liberal individualism by shunning the collective and asserting the values of liberty in a society that came to terms with their self-positioning. These types share a democratic legacy with post-Revolutionary examples highlighted by historians like Gordon Wood and Joyce Appleby: men and women asserting their individualism and demanding commercial opportunity, and thus promoting a version of democracy built on self-interest and voting for presumed equals to manage the politics.[58] Regarding the second type, the misfits differ from those who have historically occupied the constitutive outside on which democracies have been built, the disfranchised underclass as well as nondemocratic others excluded from the nation-state.[59] (In an 1858 speech, US senator James Henry Hammond of South Carolina dubbed this group the "mud-sill of society."[60]) Such "radicals" have offered more provocative, progressive, and protest-oriented assertions within the political public sphere, all very intentionally and courageously, as cultural historians like Seth Cotlar and Holly Jackson have demonstrated.[61] As alternatives to these predominating consensus and subversive types, the misfits studied herein occupy a more ambiguous middling sphere, as something I might risk calling not so much a "silent" but rather an "insignificant majority." Removed from the realms of both elites in power and the disfranchised vociferously demanding recognition and inclusion, these figures occupy a more perilous middle ground that all too often gets dematerialized into abstractions of population, or, when political, either public opinion or singular mass democracy.

The distinctions could potentially be legion, but the ones I draw out in this book demonstrate the remainders and excesses of democracies that rarely get told, yet still offer illustrative imaginings of people-empowered democracies that could be. More specifically, whereas the politics of pre–Civil War cities tended to adhere to the issues related to labor relations, the social protest gothic novels of Philadelphia, for example, came to see the chief problems with the accumulation of disempowerment that accompanied a newly emerged devotion to old Revolutionary monuments in national lore; by extension, the misfits considered herein call for an investment in relocalized democracy. In more rural places, literary misfits demonstrate reactions to national narratives of progress, playfully making cases either against the presumed atavism of their represented cultures (as in the case of southwestern humor) or more soberly recognizing the limitations of uniform assumptions of popular sovereignty (as in the case of settlement narratives in the Old Northwest), offering new imaginings of their constituents' capacities for self-rule. In the future-oriented projects of a nation all grown up, the misfits of the Far West—gold rush California, specifically—further challenge national narratives of progress by recognizing that the only thing manifest about national destiny was not the presumption of expansion under the aegis of abstract self-governance but the more contingency-filled complications resulting from trying to map national norms onto new, recalcitrant spaces. And finally, with African Americans in New York City, instead of presuming that the only causes in town were abolition and emigration and the self-elevation of the formerly disfranchised, readers might see a more basic form of democracy built first and foremost on the principles of dignity.

Lest I sound too celebratory, I state here that the alternative political imaginings articulated within these literary misfits—the democracies in parts of nineteenth-century America—do not necessarily promote well-oiled political machines, and they often do not deliver better prosecutions of distributive justice. They look a lot different from many of the primary texts that scholars have explored to work through the challenges and paradoxes of democratic ideals and possibilities at play in the United States.[62] They likely feed much of the current doubt about the chances of democracy in the United States and around the world in the early twenty-first century.⁶³ They also might risk overdoing democracy, as political philosophers Nancy Rosenblum and Robert Talisse have contended.⁶⁴ But they do register an important history of political possibility. When many people in the fledgling United States—wealthy merchants on the coasts and backcountry farmers alike—threw off the virtual government of British imperial rule, they believed in the fiction that that they would possess the democratic power of actual self-rule. As Danielle Allen has noted, many have understood the Founders' intentions to establish a republic, but the vast majority insisted on democracy.⁶⁵ As we will see, these misfits' democracies contrast sharply with that which appears under the abstract heading of "We the people" in the Constitution and its merging of classical republicanism (the best shall rule) with classical liberalism (prioritization of protecting property rights and corresponding contracts).⁶⁶ They also diverge from national narratives of a homogeneous imagined community united through representative, procedural government and abstracting cultural forms. Rather, they offer democracies that involve the less formal, more localized instances of direct political experience, playing out in works that explore the possibility of local peoples working out power relations outside the legal, judicial, and executive maneuverings of the US nation. Unyoked from the nation and its norms, these literary misfits project senses of affective empowerment brought about by people having the power. They help reframe, historically as well as today, the terms through which we understand political action, which, according to Jacques Rancière, is consistent with the logic of democracy.⁶⁷

CHAPTER ONE

Philadelphia Protests, Revolutionary Memory, and Relocalized Democracy

Robert Montgomery Bird's *Sheppard Lee: Written by Himself* (1836) features a first-person, satire-laced narrative and picaresque plot that is a retrospective depiction of a metempsychotic journey through a variety of nineteenth-century lives in and around contemporary Philadelphia. Midway through his journey, the eponymous protagonist wishes to use his supernatural powers to escape the unhappy life of his third inhabitation, the body and life of Abram Skinner, yet he struggles to locate a spare corpse. His dilemma leads to a Swiftian proposal for a more profitable way to dispose of dead bodies: instead of burying them, convert them into manure (incidentally, a proposal that would in no way help Sheppard's current plight). After calculating the conversion rate of bodies to manure and reckoning economic profits, his ruminations turn to the political sphere: "A similar disposition (to continue the subject) of their mortal flesh might be ... required, in this land, of all politicians and office-holders, from the vice-president down to the county collector; who, being all patriots, would doubtless consent to a measure that would make them of some use to their country. As for the president, we would have him reserved for a nobler purpose; we would have him boiled down to soap ... to be used by his successor in scouring the constitution and the minds of the people."[1] The initial musing—syntactically awkward and littered with distracting punctuation—considers useless all local and national officials with the exception of the chief executive, but also jocularly declares these representatives to be "patriots" who would readily lend their "consent" to having their dead bodies converted to manure. The narrative's alternative proposal for the president's dead body and its action on "the constitution and the minds of the people," however, eschews distinctions of scale and disregards the need for compliance from either presidents or people. In the first sentence, the narrative favors concrete and agency-filled terms: these politicians and office holders are the "mortal flesh" collectively possessing patriotic feelings that lead to willful consent. The second transacts in more abstract registers and passive phrasing; a royal "we" stands ready to "have [the president] boiled down into soap" and expects the successor to carry out the regenerative cleansing not only on a specific document but also on the minds of a generalized "people." As a whole, the narrator thinks little of politicians at any level (and critics might think the writing itself little better). Yet the distinctions between the two sentences—concrete bodies, animated by collective or fellow feeling and actively participating in acts of regeneration, versus a nationalized political economy that relies on deferral to individualized, corporatized abstractions that simply recycle the status quo—betray the novel's more specific concerns with prevalent dysfunctionality in 1830s democratic politics. The problem, the passage implies, can be found in the tendency for local agency and contingency in the broader metropolitan area to be subsumed in the abstractions and passivity of national life.

Just a few decades prior to the novel's historical setting, these tendencies were quite different, at least reputedly. As the local site of an official declaration of independence and the formulation of the nation's first (and only) two systems of government, Philadelphia held center stage in the early days of US nation formation.[2] All three founding events occurred in the city that, at the time, served as capital of the most radically democratic of the original thirteen states.[3] Presumably, in this one site the revolutionary democratic aspirations of both local and national entities commingled. As such, Philadelphia would seem to be the node where the local and the national came together, where the vision of a united, coherent confederation would be made manifest in local conditions and politics. In the decades following the Declaration of Independence, Philadelphia would serve as a crucial testing ground for competing visions of both local and national identifications through an archivable print culture as well as through more ephemeral phenomena of oral traditions, parades, and ceremonies.[4]

Philadelphia's status as the national metropolitan center, though, proved temporary. In the same years that writers and printers circulated texts and "perpetual fetes" demonstrated popular affinity for democratic activities throughout Philadelphia's streets—merging myriad constituencies and their competing interests—the city saw institutions of procedural political power leave town: the federal government relocated to Washington, D.C., in 1800, and the state government moved temporarily to Lancaster in 1799 and a decade later took up permanent residence in Harrisburg. Such moves perhaps seemed to be the new tendency. In 1790, Pennsylvania replaced its radically democratic 1776 state constitution—which is credited to the agitation of disenfranchised peoples who goaded a recalcitrant state delegation to endorse independence from British rule—with a much more conservative one that looked a lot like the US Constitution.[5] The physical relocations thus worked in concert with constitutional changes to literally and politically distance the sites of state and federal governments from diverse peoples, their everyday experiences, their inclinations for collective participation, and the reality that competing interests would not necessarily be resolved. With the deaths of the Revolutionary generation, the aging of the first generation of US Americans, and increasing mobility and immigration, democratic principles and nation-building rituals took on a more abstract, more symbolic cast in the very place they had first been enacted.

As the former national center, nineteenth-century Philadelphia and its cultural history thus offers a valuable if unexpected first case study of the impact of literary contributions on nationalization and democratic cultures in a rapidly transforming urban scene. In the fifty years after the US Constitution instituted a more powerful centralized government, the nation increasingly became the default scale of reference for all things cultural and political, and many Philadelphians felt the pinch. This development likely led Samuel Otter, in a 2004 review essay of cultural histories of Philadelphia, to contend that scholars should take special care to resist the nationalist pull. Philadelphia, Otter writes, "is a part that is not the whole. [It] pose[s] a challenge to critics who reduce the local to the national or the global or fold text into context."[6] In *Philadelphia Stories* (2010), however, Otter takes a different tack and nominates the city for equal standing among more established US literary cities—Concord, Boston, New York—due to two distinctive yet critically selective features: its geographical position on the border between North and South and its having the largest free African American population in the country. Importantly to Otter, "Verbal performance and social behavior assumed the weight of race and nation, as a new national literature was shaped by debates around key terms—character, conduct, narrative—that were both political and literary."[7] Recognizing the convergence of literary and political discourses, Otter maps the immediacy of Philadelphia events across seventy-plus years of history, both literary and political, as national synecdoche.[8]

Unlike Otter, in this chapter I scale back, or down, to explore articulations of non-nationalistic democratic thinking found in two very different misfits set in and around Philadelphia: Bird's *Sheppard Lee* and George Lippard's *The Quaker City* (1844–45). Although formally and substantively quite different, and enjoying wildly different commercial success, the anonymously published satire and the sensational book-in-parts seem both less willing and less able to assume the weight or scale of the nation and its increasingly abstract form of democracy. Moreover, juxtaposing these two misfits gains critical value for several reasons. They appear in a new period of national fervor, one which was developing novel versions of Revolutionary memory and history. Both set out to recycle post-Revolutionary literary materials and forms to take up problems in their respective political moments, but deviate in key ways that register alternatives from their predecessors. In these deviations appear what I am calling their vernacular aesthetics, which differ from forms that were becoming national norms—historical, literary, and political—thus making them misfits both then and now. Both stake their political critiques of nationalized democracy in the 1830s and 1840s on the very site where radical democratic ideas had been debated and enacted but now were undone. Unlike contemporary works that have often been praised for their radical politics, they expand their concerns well beyond a predominant focus on labor movements and into more affective and everyday experiences of peoples collectively addressing systemic issues in their local place.[9] In contesting the memorialization of the Revolution as instituting the nation rather than fueling democratic culture locally, these two literary texts, in formally messy ways, deploy alternative stories that enable the imagination of a less refined but more democratic past and future. And finally, as far as their fit in our critical histories, both stand outside the canon, and even when they have received increasing attention in the last few decades, they are typically categorized as Philadelphia gothic, as exemplary sensational novels that inspire the larger scope of US fiction while doing little for real political life.[10]

Determining whether these texts fantasize nostalgically of a past that never was or seek to revive a real democratic fervor shared by a vast majority of everyday participants matters less to my arguments. Historical remembering in this period, as I will show, had robust affective power, often in concert with national interests that increased the distance between government and the governed. *Sheppard Lee* and *The Quaker City* criticize the dominant grain of nationalization via memorialization for promising yet failing to address local, systemic issues. They thus imagine a regrounding of democratic empowerment in the everyday rank and file, albeit in a rather unclean and nonorderly and nondeliberative fashion. Drawing these threads out in these two misfits, I contend, reveals an alternative genealogy of democratic thinking that returns to the Revolutionary era, not in the era's tendency to monumentalize the achievements of a now-distant governmental power on a national scale, but in working through the benefits and costs of everyday democratic activity in the local 1830s and 1840s urban scenes.

Philadelphia, Revolutionary Memory, and Democracy in the City

Before discussing these two misfits, it is valuable to establish the general context of Philadelphia and the predominant cultural movements of these transitional decades, particularly in relation to national founding and contemporary thinking on democracy. A good starting point comes in a letter by the English travel writer Frances Wright, addressed to a friend and dated May 1819. Within, Wright offers ambivalent reflections after her encounter with the ground zero of US nation formation, the building that came to be known as Independence Hall.[11] Early in the letter, she asserts that the "statehouse, state-house no longer in anything but name, is an interesting object to a stranger, and, doubtless, a sacred shrine in the eyes of Americans." At the time of Wright's visit, the building had been repurposed to house the "stuffed birds, and beasts, and mammoth skeletons" of Charles Willson Peale's natural history museum, which causes her some offense. Philadelphians apparently did not share such objections, for "every friend or acquaintance that ever passed it with me paused before it to make some observation. 'Those are the windows of the room in which our first Congress sat.' 'There was signed the declaration of Independence.' 'From those steps the Declaration of Independence was read in the ears of the people.'"[12] Their collective pride situates the State House at the intersection of past and present, a fixed monument to the nation's history, one aptly demonstrating a reverence for continuity with a past and fuel for nationalistic pride in the present. Following this documentary account of local feelings about the statehouse, Wright joins in the collective nostalgia, describing the historical actors from the Revolutionary period as "that little assembled senate, who, in the name of a young and unskilled people, there set at defiance the power of a mighty empire." Wright's history becomes a paean to deliberative action by distinguished representatives acting in concert with the represented, couching legislative actions in aesthetic terms: "I know not, in the whole page of human history, any thing more truly grand and morally sublime than the conduct of the American Congress throughout the unequal contest.... How admirable was the moderation which marked their earlier deliberations."[13] She goes on at great length, twice quoting David Ramsay's *History of the American Revolution* (1789) to praise the extraordinary steadfastness and unity of the leading actors in the Revolutionary period, to extol their contributions to democratic thinking, and to express hope that their legacy would prove exemplary for generations to come. Wright thus presents a harmonious relationship between the exceptional leadership of Congress and the consent of the people.

In sum, Wright's nostalgic account effectively expunges internal conflict from the Revolutionary era and demonstrates the power such erasures have on the political present. Her comments thus raise important questions about memory and forgetting, about abstract narratives of the past versus the concrete sites and experiences of those living in the present in a city, in a nation, and in a democracy. They demonstrate, as Catherine Holland has contended, that the transformation of the old State House into a museum full of stuffed beasts threatened a living, breathing democracy through "the normalization of a fixed and constraining nature that overcomes history and suffocates politics."[14] As potent as the transformation of the physical building is, though, so too is Wright's historical narrative. An aesthetic invention akin to that of the constitutional nation, it elides the stark civil discord within the colonies that dominated the Revolutionary era.[15] Wright was far from alone in this aesthetic—and anesthetizing—venture, as her borrowings from Ramsey's version of Revolutionary history evidence.[16] Such maneuvers nevertheless had significant consequences for the Philadelphians that Wright observed in 1819.

Over the next few decades, this reverence for—and aesthetic representations of—a formally coherent but also conflict-free past would contribute mightily to an even more suffocated politics and a democracy in name if not in actual practice, especially in local places. A large majority of literary, historical, and political writers followed Wright's trend in building democracy-stifling monuments to the national past. As one result, in the decades following independence, the US nation increasingly assumed a key paradox of modern nationalism pointed out by Benedict Anderson, that no matter how recently a modern nation has been born, its origins are carefully cloaked in antiqueness.[17] The paradox stretches even further in a nineteenth-century US context in which citizens were simultaneously fixated on the nation's break from the traditions of the past while also inscribing an ever-growing archive of historical significance. Michael Kammen has marked the 1820s as the initial decade for a new national reverence for the traditions of the Revolution.[18] He also identifies key ways that the 1830s and 1840s saw a watering down of Revolutionary conflict, impacting the possibilities for democracy-in-practice: "The nation shifted its interest and emphasis . . . from the Declaration of Independence to the Constitution, from the more radical principles of 1776 to the consolidation of power that occurred in 1787."[19] Familiar names like James Fenimore Cooper, Ralph Waldo Emerson, and Nathaniel Hawthorne contribute to Kammen's assessment thanks to their various imaginative invocations of Revolutionary lore. Fittingly, these writers and their works have achieved a secure fit within US literary history.

In concert with the imaginative narratives of canonical writers, Kammen ascribes a key complementary function to the official custodial care of historians like Jared Sparks and George Bancroft.[20] Sparks was one of the key contributors to Alexis de Tocqueville's impressions of democracy and its alleged roots in New England towns.[21] Bancroft and his multivolume *History of the United States* did perhaps even more cultural work to fold the more unseemly democratic conditions of the Revolution into a well-tamed package. Take, for instance, the exemplary passage kicking off the volume covering the years 1774 to 1776. Bancroft starts with the strike of a single drum: "The hour of the American Revolution was come. The people of the continent obeyed one general impulse.... Beyond any other nation, [Americans] had made trial of the possible forms of popular representation, and respected individual conscience and thought.... In their political aspirations they deduced from universal principles a bill of rights, as old as creation and as wide as humanity."[22] In triumphant tone, Bancroft's opening gambit unifies the people under "one general impulse" and thus erases any divisions of a differently interested population. Like Wright's account, trial and error and clashing perspectives are set aside in favor of a now-harmonious and unmediated relationship between individuals and representative government. And more than a decade before the first Congress under the Constitution would propose the first ten amendments to the states for ratification, a unified people in Bancroft's rendering created a universal bill of rights. Bancroft thus fuses together a national population under the figureheads of democracy, even as it changed the terms by which readers might understand the challenges and complications of historical democracy in the Revolutionary era.

Even if Wright's, Sparks's, and Bancroft's versions of Revolutionary politics occluded the conflict-ridden experiences of the Continental Congress, theirs is the story of the leaders and the elites who have left paper trails in archives. What about everyday folks? Were they democratically inspired enough to enter into the political fray? Around the time Bancroft published the first volume of his multivolume *History* in 1834, a local Bostonian shoemaker named George Robert Twelves Hewes rose to celebrity status thanks to the recently born popular reverence for the Revolution. In the mid-1830s, Hewes became the subject of not one but two separate biographies as well as a public celebration that took place in Boston on 4 July 1835.[23] Hewes's rise to fame, though, came concurrently with a highly tendentious social and political culture in Boston, aggravated by interests ranging from labor and abolitionist movements to stark conservative reaction—all of which were slowly subsumed in the mass-party folds of Jacksonian Democrats and Whig opposition. And yet, all partisans, as Alfred Young asserts, claimed to be the true heirs of the Revolution. Among several Revolutionary events in which Hewes had participated, the December 1773 destruction of the tea rose to prominence, thanks in large part to the recently born appellation "tea party." Young speculates that though it never made it into print prior to the 1830s, the term was most likely used for decades by "ordinary people in their everyday speech, that is, the vernacular," while "the genteel considered it a vulgar expression, [meaning] that authors who were trying to reach audiences avoided it."[24] The new moniker "tea party" and esteem for its participants cannily demonstrates the 1830s political climate in that the term worked for both conservatives and radicals, by either "mocking a genteel custom or as a playful way of making the most revolutionary event of the era 'safe.'"[25] Thus, whether in the everyday language and culture of Boston locals or in the more aestheticized work of imaginative writers like Hawthorne or custodial historians like Bancroft, the Revolution and its more unruly democratic impulses were transformed into nostalgia and abstraction and reined in to fit the national prescriptions of order, form, and consensus. Local problems in cities and towns across the country, and in Philadelphia specifically, nevertheless remained in need of some kind of remedy.

One further observation from Young's assessment of Hewes bears mentioning. As the historian pieces together some sense of Hewes's interior makeup, Young speculates that his Revolutionary transformation from deferential colonial subject to impassioned, discriminating, politicized, democratic citizen came not from reading *Common Sense*, nor from the influence of a charismatic leader like James Otis or Samuel Adams. Instead, Hewes "was moved to act by personal experiences that he shared with large numbers of other plebeian Bostonians."[26] Despite the lack of archived evidence to account for the changes in others, Young's conclusion seems right: Hewes's Revolutionary "experiences transformed him, giving him a sense of citizenship and personal worth. [Famous Revolutionaries like Samuel] Adams and [John] Hancock began with both; Hewes had to arrive there."[27] This sense of empowerment would no doubt be appealing to everyday figures in any era that appreciated a sense of recognition, stood ready to act with others against oppression, and harbored a desire for democratic action. And it seems less likely that inspiration would come from weighty books rather than from more vernacular exchanges with neighbors and, perhaps, a few items here and there that one came across in print. And yet this kind of transformation seems a surprise to Young. Why?

The propensity to build monuments to Revolutionary memory that gained steam in the second quarter of the nineteenth century came at the same time as a transformation of the terms by which democratic activities were characterized in cities like Boston and Philadelphia. For Sean Wilentz, the rapidly changing world of industrialization and immigration reduced democratic action largely to labor movements.[28] Other histories of urban democracy in this period have cast city life in more sanguine terms; for instance, Mary Ryan has emphasized "relative urban contentment" in cities, making them valuable incubators for democratic cultures.[29] Beyond such takes lie threads of alternative democratic thinking that played out in vernacular expressions of less highly esteemed imaginative literature. Such texts often looked to the Revolution for the type of empowerment that everyday figures had seemingly enjoyed in that era, but not in the predominating nostalgic fashions that had removed democratic conflict from the Revolutionary narrative. George Hewes was an historical curiosity for Alfred Young, a misfit who demanded a rewriting of Revolutionary history and its descent through the early nineteenth century. Similarly, in the first misfit work I read, we see a return to a revolutionary form, an assessment of politics emphasizing affect over labor, and a search for democratic empowerment.

Parody and Apathy in *Sheppard Lee*

The passage on transmuting bodies into manure quoted at the opening of this chapter, and *Sheppard Lee* more broadly, play on the tensions of a democratic politics operating across a range of scales. Satirical, disjointed, and messy, the novel is an exceptionally dodgy misfit, especially for critics both then and now who aspire to pin down a clear political message.[30] Several contemporary reviews heralded its entertaining qualities.[31] But the novel sold very poorly.[32] One contemporary reviewer offers an explanation for the poor sales with this poignant complaint: "This is a strange book. The first volume is to us unreadable; and the second very little better.... We cannot see the aim or object of the writer—the book being neither a novel, nor romance, nor, indeed, story of any kind."[33] Both then and now, *Sheppard Lee* has been a tough fit in US literary histories.

The strangeness and imperceptibility, I contend, were signs of the novel's critical concerns with suffocating democratic conditions in America generally and in Philadelphia specifically. To stage these concerns, Bird has Sheppard

Lee transmigrate through a range of figures and social scenes of the Jacksonian-era nation. This feature has led Christopher Looby to identify the novel as "a satire on politics, and a meditation on the bodily basis of political life" and to argue that it pursues this objective while providing "a map of the American society, and a taxonomy of American social types and roles."[34] Indeed, the picaresque plot yields intimate encounters with a diverse set of figures ranging up and down the socioeconomic ladder. The protagonist's body-jumping journey takes readers across demographic and sectional lines—he travels from the New Jersey suburbs into Philadelphia proper, then south into Virginia before making a hasty return to New Jersey—to offer multiple varieties of American locales and people. In this journey, however, readers confront numerous inconsistencies: the discrepancies noted in the bodies-into-manure quotation, a distinctive twist on the conventional picaresque plot, an unstable monologic consciousness, frequent narrative interruptions, ever-shifting targets of satire, doubts cast on the verity of the protagonist's adventures, and dissensus in the final interpretive act. In these inconsistencies lie marks of its vernacular aesthetics, which perhaps proved unappealing to contemporary audiences in a couple of ways.[35] On one level, they make for a challenging, "strange" read that led to reviews like the one cited above. On another level, and more subtly, these particular inconsistencies, as I will show, repeatedly work to undercut the coherence building of a depoliticized national collectivity so prominent in the literary and historical writings of this era; that is, rather than representing the nation through a relatively depoliticized and therefore undemocratic exploration of its constitutive types (à la e pluribus unum), the novel instead critiques national unity and consensus building, along with its version of liberal democracy and the likelihood of deliberative models, to provide remedy to an increasingly suffocated political scene at localized levels.

Prior to embarking on his body-jumping adventure, Sheppard shares that he is the sole heir of an enterprising sausage manufacturer in the New Jersey suburbs of Philadelphia, and that he suffers from a "natural disposition [that] was placid and easy.... [In] all those qualities that are necessary to the formation of a great man, I had not the slightest desire to be one" (*SL*, 11). He fails at numerous occupations to pass the time—breeding racehorses, seducing a wealthy widow, trying local politics—and soon finds himself cheated of his inheritance by a hired overseer. Digging for a legendary lost treasure, he strikes his foot with a mattock, falls into a reverie, and awakens as a spirit bereft of his body. The transmigrating begins. He assumes in succession the bodies of the wealthy brewer John H. Higginson, the penniless dandy I. Dulmer

Dawkins, the miserly moneylender Abram Skinner, and the Quaker philanthropist Zachariah Longstraw. Kidnapped and taken to Virginia, he inhabits two more bodies: an enslaved man named Tom and an aristocrat named Arthur Megrim. In this final body, he happens on his original one, now mummified and on exhibition, then reassumes the prototype and hastily runs back north. In the conclusion, Sheppard undercuts the narrative reliability of his far-fetched tale even more by citing his brother-in-law's explanation for the narrated events: Sheppard has been quite ill and dreamed up the whole adventure. Sheppard less than assuredly denies these claims and concludes with a trite moral: "Be my body what it may, hardy or frail, stiff or supple, I am satisfied with it, and shall never seek to exchange it for another" (*SL*, 425).

The local, contemporary setting and picaresque plot of *Sheppard Lee* deviated from the preoccupations and tone of Bird's first three novels, which variously explored far-off places and distant pasts. He located *Calavar* (1834) and *The Infidel* (1835) amid the sixteenth-century Mexican conquest; he set *The Hawks of Hawk-Hollow* (also in 1835) closer to home in rural Pennsylvania, but decades earlier, in 1760. With *Sheppard Lee*, Bird turned his novelistic focus toward the present, anchored it largely in the city, assumed a more satirical tone, and recycled a generic tradition employed by many writers of the early republic: the picaresque. According to Cathy Davidson, the picaresque provided significant flexibility for authors who wished to explore the heterogeneity of American types by having a central character range across various locales.[36] These engagements often led to satirical criticism of mainstream, respectable types and to celebrations of the bawdier elements of misfit life. "The writer," Davidson asserts, "could explore a full range of contradictory impulses within the new nation."[37] Davidson thus identifies a form of bottom-up democratic maneuvering inherent to the genre; that is, in the face of aristocratic or oligarchic attempts to enact governmental controls against the presumed confusion of democratic society, both content and form of the picaresque "countered the official attempt to homogenize the *polis* with a rambunctious heterogeneity."[38] By the 1830s, though, the nation was even more populous and heterogeneous. Nationalizing narratives like Wright's travel narrative, Hewes's biographies, and Bancroft's histories eschewed the picaresque form for genres and aesthetics that focused less on diversity and radically democratic politics than on the assent of the many to a unified vision, as Bercovitch notes. In this historical moment in which so many politically oriented writings were reaching back to the Revolution and its exemplary forms and norms, Bird made a similar reach, yet the picaresque is a rather unconventional choice. While the picaresque could explore a variety of types, as Looby contends, Bird's adaptations resist an easy fit within the national narrative.

The narrative delivers its heterodox position in the opening when it presents material that recalls and parodies one of the most famous exemplars of life-writing in the post-Revolutionary nation: Benjamin Franklin's *Autobiography*. With the title itself, "The Author's Preface,—which the reader, if in a great hurry, or if it be his practice to read against time, can skip," the narrative follows literary protocol by opening with an authorial preface, yet undercuts that adherence to form with a sarcastic, perplexing excuse for the reader to skip reading this portion of the text. Misfit behavior ensues, targeting Franklin's famous self-effacing opening, "From the poverty and obscurity in which I was born, and in which I passed my earliest years, I have raised myself to a state of affluence and some degree of celebrity in the world."[39] Sheppard strikes a similar chord when he admits that it "sometimes happens that circumstances conspire to elevate the humblest person from obscurity," pushing him to share his tale that would ideally "instruct the ignorant and inexperienced" (*SL*, 7). Instead of following Franklin's confidence in the unquestioned verity of his narrative, though, Sheppard focuses on readerly expectations and acknowledges that the fascinating events to be narrated would likely prove dubitable to skeptics. Sheppard does himself no help when he weaves a tangled web that admits his lack of evidence ("It is impossible I should have laid up proofs to satisfy any one"), scoffs at would-be doubters ("Doubt, and be hanged"), apologizes to the offended ("not . . . meaning any offence to anybody"), and closes with the following: "I write for the world at large, which is neither philosophic nor skeptical; and the world will believe me: otherwise it is a less sensible world than I have along supposed it to be" (*SL*, 8). The ambiguity of Sheppard's closing lines, along with the circular and entangling gestures of punctuation and syntax, not only create constant qualification and deferral but also make for a rather frustrating read. The narrative repeatedly denies any stable ground on which a reader might stand. Herein lies evidence of what I am calling the vernacular aesthetics of the text. While it represents a clear moment of flabby writing that offends literary critics wedded to formal norms, it also presents an alternative to the rather narrow track that Franklin's self-narrative traverses. Between the syntactical instability of the prose and the fact that Sheppard heaps doubt after doubt on the verity of his entire experience, Bird's narrative sharply contrasts with the deeply deliberated truth production and justification of Benjamin Franklin's opening salvo.[40] The satirical swipe at a sacred Founding Father (intentional or not) invites a reconsideration of Revolutionary monuments.[41]

The shoddy writing plays on throughout the text, but becomes especially relevant in the most disconcerting and most political moment of the novel: the slave insurrection appearing late in the narrative. The staging of this episode invokes a kind of formal resistance similar to that in the opening preface, while also recalling sacred national history in ironical and disturbing ways. In the early phases of Sheppard's inhabitation of an enslaved man named Tom, the narrative establishes its temporal present in the posttransmigrating Sheppard describing his experience in the form of retrospective, sarcasm-rich commentary interspersed with dialect-laden quotations from other slaves. The observational distance created by this narrative strategy decreases after the arrival of an abolitionist pamphlet. For a brief time, the narrative oscillates between a reflecting Sheppard emphasizing the pamphlet's targeted audience as the enslavers rather than the enslaved and reading the contents aloud to his enslaved companions. After Lee-as-Tom voices the lines that the slave should be "as free as the master himself," the temporal shiftiness ends: "Here, I paused for breath; my companions looked at me with eyes staring out of their heads. Astonishment, suspicion and fear were depicted in their countenances. A new idea had entered their brains." The enslaved men are nevertheless ready to dismiss the pamphlet's arguments until they hear the opening "quotation from the Declaration of Independence, that 'all men were born free and equal,' which was asserted to be true of all men, negroes as well as others."[42] Shocked that "Gen'ral Jodge Washington, him make dat; and Gen'ral Tommie Jefferson, him put hand to it," Lee-as-Tom's auditors demonstrate that the Revolutionary figures had been misrepresented to them in less than revolutionary ways (*SL*, 353). The radicalism of the Revolution, which had been sanitized in cultural narratives fashioned for the enslaved, now reemerges and politically empowers the group.

From here to the bloody ending of the revolt, the narrative suspends sarcastic commentary, inserts only occasional retrospective comments in terms more sober than at any other point in the narrative, and removes its judgmental stance. To some critics, the shiftiness of narrative perspective evidences a lack of authorial control (which was one of Poe's negative criticisms of an otherwise positive review).[43] And yet the formal shift narrows the distance between the reader and any narrative device that would maintain a safe distance in this moment of intensively revolutionary uprising. A less mediated version of the conflict means it cannot so easily be reduced to abstraction, nor can it be folded into a consensus-driven, national narrative. Ending in violence and bloodshed, the uprising fails to bring about revolutionary change in this fictive world (freedom for the enslaved), and its chances for engendering revolutionary change beyond the text, antislavery or otherwise, seem slim. Some might think the violence of the failed insurrection justifies the conflict-free versions of the Revolution. Some might think the writing lacks sufficient order and control. But thanks to the formal slippage and the recasting of the Revolutionary figures, readers more directly see that democratic ideas spurring revolution can inspire collective democratic action in people who, like George Hewes and his rank-and-file peers, had formerly been thought to be disinterested or had thought themselves unqualified.

After one more inhabitation, Sheppard returns to his original body and sets about writing his adventures. As he does so, the narrative shifts from a mode of recollection to one of interpretation. For Davidson, "picaresque novels are *about* interpretation—about how experience is transformed into a narrative." Coming from a national frame of reference, the picaro becomes "a representative man and a commentator on the most diverse, contradictory, obscure, and idiosyncratic elements of the Republic."[44] This may be the case in post-Revolutionary picaresques, but not in *Sheppard Lee*. As in the disjointed author's preface, the narrative repeatedly disrupts meaning-making interpretation in its closing sequences. In the final chapters, Sheppard quotes his sister and brother-in-law, who both suggestively and then explicitly tell him that he has dreamed up every event. To counter, he essays a meager scientific explanation for his travels and writes his narrative anyway. The disputed interpretations combine to form a cascade of doubts crashing down on the denouement. Instead of presenting a representative man punctuating his tale in a mode of collective consensus making, the narrative delivers an unresolved, tension-filled anti-interpretation that paradoxically remains open to contest. While this conclusion does not speak directly to national politics, it nevertheless fails to do the work of promoting national identifications that so many novels, travel writing, and histories were performing in this historical moment.

Bird's notes held at the University of Pennsylvania indicate that he apparently conceived a wide variety of potential character types for Sheppard Lee to inhabit—an archival treasure that Looby examines at some length in his introduction to the most recent edition.[45] Also among Bird's notes is a document that suggests Bird entertained a substantially different conclusion to the novel: a carefully prepared copy of the table of contents of *Sheppard Lee* based on the characters the body-jumping protagonist would inhabit. This alternative table of contents explicitly names the first four characters and their chief plights as they appear in the final narrative—for instance, "J. H. Higginson—gout and scolding wife" and "Skinner, the Miser—avarice, remorse, and dissipated children." After Longstraw, the route deviates through three alternative figures: Hampden Jones, a congressmen (who does appear in the final narrative, though not as one of Sheppard's inhabitations); Tommy Tumble, a schoolboy (absent from the published narrative); and Dionysius Murray, "schoolmaster and author."[46] At some point during composition, Bird not only reconceived the bodily inhabitations to take his picaresque plot outside the Philadelphia area and across sectional boundaries, but also ensured that the narrative voice would return to its original body. The decision to expand the geography of the narrative certainly extends the scale of the novel beyond Philadelphia to more nationalized dimensions. This invites a greater degree of heterogeneity among the nation's inhabitants as well as its political issues. Moreover, bringing the voice back to the body of Sheppard Lee suggests that his story cannot be *re-presented*—that is, presented again—by another figure; even if the voice seems the same, a virtual representative cannot be substituted in this case. It is unlikely that Bird would promote any notion of direct democracy, but the narratological decision to return Sheppard to his original body to tell his story betrays some measure of discontent with the nation's emphasis on representation distanced from the represented.

AS THE VERNACULAR AESTHETICS of *Sheppard Lee* works in concert with Bird's twist on past forms and principles of the Revolution to express discontent with representation distanced from the represented, so too does it target the failure of nationalized politics in the present. The chief culprits are the recently mobilized mass parties, which are democratic in name yet fail to deliver the affective empowerment that facilitates collective self-rule. Unlike the active and inspired citizenry in the vein of George Hewes and fellow rank-and-file Revolutionary actors, three nondemocratic types have come to dominate the 1830s political scene in *Sheppard Lee*: those crippled by apathy, those driven by exploitative self-interest, and those unthinkingly riled up into mass frenzy.[47] While many politicians thought that deliberative practices would ensure a functional representative democracy on a national scale, the novel portrays nonelite figures and situations that reveal the limited chances of such forms to filter down to everyday people, as Sandra Gustafson has shown.[48] The narrative thus suggests the untenability of current democratic practices—both the thoughtless brand of mass-party politics and more deliberative variations—to work with the fluctuations of affective experience and implies the need for localized alternatives to the dictates of national constitutional management.[49]

The opening chapters establish the pretransmigrating Sheppard Lee as repeatedly failing to take advantage of opportunities to build on his privileged upbringing. His incapacity to pursue a profitable occupation contrasts sharply with the example set by his father, a farmer who became "famous for [his] excellent sausages[,] ... converted his whole estate into a market-farm[,] and ... became a rich man" (SL, 9). For a protagonist whose soul moves from one fleshy encasement to another, having a father who is a sausage maker is apropos. More subtly, this detail suggests that Sheppard is familiar with the amalgamating processes that associate capitalist gain with success in the political life of the nation for those in the first generation in the early republic.[50] On his father's death, Sheppard is the only remaining male heir, yet he lacks any interest in growing his inheritance. Aware of his anomalous behavior, he describes his condition within a national frame of reference: "I was so indifferent of the game of greatness which was playing around me, that ... there was a President of the United States elected to office, and turned out again ... without my knowing any thing about it" (SL, 11). That he would miss chances not only to capitalize on his inheritance but also to participate in the "game of greatness" indicates a disconnect between the so-called national mood and Sheppard's experience. That he would confess ignorance of electoral politics illustrates that his apathy extends beyond private life and into the public responsibilities of a participating citizen.[51] In due time, his apathy leads him to turn over the management of his property to an overseer, who eventually cheats him out of his estate.

Now impoverished, Sheppard desires some occupation that proves sustainable, something that would both address his flagging finances and retain his attention. Nothing proves lasting, however, and all the while, his economic situation grows dire. Once again, his private inclinations and the public sphere of politics are conjoined, for after coming up short on several money-making ventures, Sheppard "resolve[s] to turn politician, with the hope of getting some office or other that might afford [him] a comfortable subsistence" (SL, 23). Given the expansion of partisan-led government appointments during Jackson's tenure—known as the spoils system—this choice seems a plausible one.[52] Sheppard conversely sees political work as something more than means to secure income, for he follows his announcement with revelations that suggest that his motivation is as much affective as it is economic, "reflect[ing] one day, that of my old school and college mates ... there was not one who had not made some advance in the world," and also observing "the same things with dozens of people whom I remembered as poor farmers' boys." Consequently, he not only finds himself "discontented" but also acknowledges that his "dissatisfaction was increased by discovering with what little respect [he] was held among these happy people" (*SL*, 24). His decision to pursue formal politics at this point is prompted less by rational solution to financial problems than by a desire to secure some sense of empowerment that he had previously bequeathed.

Sheppard's pursuit of local office thus contains a scathing indictment of contemporary political culture driven by the new mass-party politics. An idealized conception of the rational play of impersonal, representative politics turns out to be riddled with problems, and readers see that feelings and emotions more aggressively drive the behavior of political agents. Starting out with the judicious enterprise of studying the "principal office-holders, candidates, and busybodies" in his local precinct, he soon finds himself swept up by the allure of party affirmation and begins making speeches on issues that he can only partially recollect (*SL*, 25). This new role proves empowering as he discovers "a degree of industry that surprised myself" (*SL*, 26). He pours his energy and his money into electioneering, confesses his limited understanding of the issues he promotes, and admits that he converts no one to his party's message, and yet he brims with confidence that his party will win and that he will be rewarded with a lucrative appointment. The democratically active Sheppard finds his political engagement quite fulfilling right up through election day. Just after his party wins, though, someone else is awarded the office promised to him, leaving him suffering from the winner-take-all nature of US democracy that is antithetical to its declared ideals. He self-interestedly resolves to join the rival party, but fate intervenes and sets him on his transmigrating journey. Before taking this route, the narrative has portrayed an apathetic figure who initially does not share in the national program of politics and self-improvement as a result of his satisfaction with having others manage the system for him. Yet, when he takes it upon himself to claim some measure of democratic agency and affective empowerment from participation, he finds that the local politics—democratic in name only—is rife with corruption in this new era of nation-scaled partisan politics.[53]

Mass-party politics receives an even harsher rebuke in the one other scene focused on procedural politics, when Lee-as-Longstraw is kidnapped and nearly lynched in a small town in Virginia in a raucous election-day scene that portrays a local, affectively charged sociality that would seem to be the democratic idealist's worst nightmare. This locality is hardly immune to mass-party discourse and the national politics it attempts to represent, especially amid the hubbub of a national election in which people would ostensibly exercise their greatest instrument of democratic self-rule, the vote, and "return a representative to Congress" (*SL*, 319). Lee-as-Longstraw's party arrives at an assembly gathered to hear the speech of the incumbent Hampden Jones, but immediately the "independent freemen of that district... deserted their orator... to join in the nobler sport of Lynching" (*SL*, 321). The capitalization and repetition of the term "Lynching" throughout the scene seems especially significant. A curious term for extralegal justice, its origins go back to the Revolutionary period to one Charles Lynch, whose treatment of Tories in Bedford County, Virginia, in 1780 likely exceeded the order of due process (and thus drew a carefully worded directive from then-governor Thomas Jefferson to operate within the law).[54] In May 1836, Edgar Allan Poe published "Lynchers' Character," an alleged transcript dated 22 September 1780 of the original agreement among residents of Pittsylvania County, Virginia and their leader, William Lynch, who had previously claimed to be the original "Judge Lynch."[55] Whether William or Charles merits the eponymous honor, "Lynching" became popularized in the same moment when other elements of Revolutionary history and memory were gaining attention.[56] *Sheppard Lee* once again highlights an element from the Revolution (democratic in one register, if democracy is defined in popular interest, but not in terms of collective empowerment).

With "Lynching" dropping from so many tongues, Congressman Jones, determined not to lose his platform, exhorts the crowd to stop and listen. Deliberative decision making and leadership from a national representative seem plausible for a moment. The speech turns out to be a "sublime exordium with prodigious earnestness and effect" on the love of virtue, law, order, and justice as an American rather than an old-world trait. As with Sheppard's mindless speech making in his pretransmigrating days, confusion ensues, for the auditors think that Jones might be talking the crowd out of hanging the abolitionist. Immediately, though, the congressman reassures the crowd that he only urges an "orderly and dignified" approach to execution (*SL*, 323). Here Jones pays lip service to order and form, demonstrating that they can be employed even in the most nondemocratic of moments. Clearly, the scene bears no resemblance to the carefully measured harmony between citizens and Senate articulated in Wright's recollection or Bancroft's representation of the Revolutionary moment. Ever critical of current operations, the manipulative narration thus spurs doubts concerning remedy for the confusion of the 1830s political scene.

Although correctives to these aberrant democratic politics seem unlikely, two possibilities do emerge in the text, and both eschew the orderliness of constitutional appeal and instead show faith in the relocalized democratic empowerment of all the people in the vein of Hewes and his Revolutionary compatriots. Just before the election-day scene in Virginia, the narrative pauses to reflect on Longstraw's disappointments with unappreciated philanthropy in an extradiegetic chapter titled "A remark, in which the Author appears a politician, and abuses both parties" (*SL*, 305). Touting an economic determinism that accepts the inevitability of rich people and poor people—a premise that cost the Federalists from 1800 on, and which was completely out of vogue by the Jacksonian era—the narrative reckons the United States faces a much greater conflict between these two types due to its "political complexion," which is described in affective terms rather than procedural ones.[57] Pointing the finger at "the folly of the richer classes," the narrative explains that "the poor man in America feels himself, in a political view, as he really is, the equal of the millionaire; but this very consciousness of equality adds double bitterness to the sense of actual inferiority, which the richer and more fortunate usually do their best, as far as manners and deportment are concerned, to keep alive" (*SL*, 305–6). The "double bitterness" comes with poor people's familiarity with democratic ideals, the democratic elements of equality and autonomy, and the misalignment of reality and vision. This bitterness subsequently prompts "all those political evils which demagoguism, agrarianism, mobocracism, and all other *isms* of a vulgar stamp." Subscribing to a political determinism, the narrative nevertheless entertains the idea of nonreactionary politics in a concluding paragraph—one that awkwardly reassumes Longstraw's idiomatic diction in yet another demonstration of vernacular aesthetics—returning to the procedural realm and acknowledging the leveling potential of democratic politics: "Reader, if thou art a rich man, and despisest thy neighbour, remember that he has a thousand friends of his class where thou hast one of thine, and that he can beat thee at the elections" (*SL*, 306). This short chapter undoubtedly bears the marks of contemporary debates about the changes taking place with the election of Andrew Jackson and the supposed elevation of the common citizen. Despite the elitist and deterministic acceptance of class difference, the conclusion nevertheless acknowledges the presence of democratic mechanisms to provide recourse, which does not occur at the far remove of national politics. Instead, Lee-as-Longstraw's language explicitly states that the democratic remedy takes place in the more immediate sphere of the local neighborhood.

As one other potential corrective, I return to the political intent of the passage in which the narrative recommends transfiguring the remains of the president into soap that can be "used by his successor in scouring the constitution and the minds of the people" (SL, 229). In the decade following the anonymous publication and commercial failure of *Sheppard Lee*, Bird became an active member of the Whig Party, the Jacksonian opposition that borrowed an old appellation to cast themselves as the true heirs of the Revolution. Among his notes are several undated drafts of letters and speeches expressing his disdain for what he deems the self-interested politics of Andrew Jackson, Martin Van Buren, and the laissez-faire Locofocos; also included are notes for speeches, including one titled "Whig Apathy," which express his consternation with those of his current party who lack earnestness in their exercises of democratic self-rule.[58] His notes are critical of the two predominant national parties, revealing frustration with politics driven by self-interest or muddled by apathetic disinterest, and the whole system—politician, constitution, and people alike—needs some cleansing. It seems unlikely that he wanted to do away with the Constitution in favor of a more direct democratic system, but his narrative betrays increasing frustration with a US democratic politics riddled with contradictions and ambiguities. The suggestion to boil down a dead president to soap and scrub the Constitution and the minds of the people, like the rest of the sardonic picaresque of *Sheppard Lee*, might have simply led to an unreadable, nonsensical, strange book for contemporary readers as well as later critics. Conversely, this use of the chief body of the nation's body politic stages a desire for some radically imagined renovations, even as the narrative repeatedly demonstrates how difficult that might actually be. Less than a decade later, the Philadelphia scene, as imagined by George Lippard, would offer an even starker appeal for democratic reform.

The Ad Hoc Qualities of *The Quaker City*

Whereas Robert Montgomery Bird wove his criticism of contemporary politics into an old post-Revolutionary form that resisted easy folding into the newly developing national narrative of the 1830s—and sold very few copies—George Lippard made his complaints much more explicit in the decade that followed and reached a much larger audience. Lippard bears a long-standing reputation for his radical urban politics, most notably in his late-career work in the labor movement known as the Brotherhood of the Union.[59] Lippard's politics across his career, though, were a more complicated story, especially given his nationalist boosterism in frequent public lectures that fictively manipulated numerous Revolutionary stories. Credited with myth-producing tales like the striking of the Liberty Bell at the reading of the Declaration of Independence on the steps of the State House on 4 July 1776, Lippard found significant success in the rise of interest in stories of the Revolution.[60] Dustin Kennedy has convincingly demonstrated the ways that Lippard's combination of a revised version of the Revolution with his radically progressive 1840s politics developed working-class solidarity across divisive lines of ethnicity and race.[61] Lippard's larger oeuvre thus worked to overcome a new variety of problems associated with the nation's brand of democracy, primarily through the lens of labor, and specifically in terms of the increasing ethnic and racial discord in large cities like Philadelphia.

That said, Lippard's combination of imaginative writing and radical politics throughout his career depends on the coherence of both of those visions, in his head and on paper. As Michael Denning and Christopher Looby have noted about Lippard's politics, in the early stages of his career, coherence was an elusive achievement.[62] This was also true of his writing. A case in point: in a letter dated 18 February 1844, Edgar Allan Poe offered George Lippard some mixed feedback after reading the younger writer's first romance, *Ladye Annabel* (1842). He wrote, "You seem to have been in too desperate a hurry to give due attention to details." Despite the faulty prose, though, Poe proclaimed "the work . . . indicative of *genius*."[63] Mixed reviews of this variety followed Lippard into the twentieth century. In a 1935 essay, Joseph Jackson breathed new life into the reputation of the once popular but by then forgotten writer. Before praising Lippard's work, Jackson accounts for the same stylistic issues that had irked Poe: "We have it on the authority of one of his friends . . . that he never read his manuscript after penning it, and seldom took the trouble to glance at a proof." After providing romantic explanations for Lippard's "carelessness," Jackson eventually confesses that few modern readers "could read with pleasure or satisfaction, any of Lippard's novels." Like many critics with literary sensibilities committed to order and form, Jackson was also working from a nation-scaled framework, which meant fitting Lippard's deviations from the era's romantic norms like this: Lippard "was the product of the world in which he lived," and amid the chaos of the 1840s, "the stage was set for the realist in fiction, [and] Lippard was the only writer to appear in that character."[64]

After Lippard had spent much of the twentieth century as a minor footnote, his most famous literary production, *The Quaker City*, received renewed critical interest in the 1970s and 1980s in relation to the nation's canonical literature of the same era.[65] More recently, critics have gauged the novel on its own merits as popular literature and for the cultural work it performed.[66] Scholars have acknowledged (at times) its distinctive publication in parts—ten serialized installments published on an irregular schedule across a nine-month period and later gathered into a single binding. *The Quaker City* contains many elements like those in contemporary popular generic fictions—the sentimental, the gothic, the sensational—that have been said to have affectively and imaginatively tied individual readers to the nation as a community. Reputedly the most popular nineteenth-century novel prior to *Uncle Tom's Cabin*, *The Quaker City* draws from all these types, making it a potpourri of generic elements that would conceivably work together to prompt national identifications. Given Lippard's deep investments in Revolutionary history as well as his supposed convictions about the ideals of the US nation, one could understandably assume as default a national scale of reference.

Conversely, attending to the disrupted production of the serialized text and Lippard's aversion to editorial revision, I argue that the narrative's disjointedness more indelibly works against the fantasy of totality, cohesiveness, and imagined community as it gradually discovers that national prescriptions fail to cure local ills. *The Quaker City* achieves this narratological feat through its unrevised, vernacular expression that not only refuses to fit neatly within the confines of a singular novel but also resists critical tendencies to force it into a national narrative of consensus (like the ones institutionalized by Wright, Bancroft, and others). The result is an unfinished trial-and-error experiment with local as well as global solutions to systemic problems.[67] Across the production, what we see is not the abstract idea of global revolution emerging from the working classes of the world, but rather something more concrete, more localized: a disjointed literary performance that articulates several democratic alternatives. Far from foreclosing the messy realm of democratic politics with a coherent master narrative, its vernacular aesthetics exceed the framework that Lippard's published intentions and paratextual apparatuses sought to enclose. Anchored in the city but lacking the labor movement politics that would become central to Lippard's later career, the novelistic work in progress grapples with the pros and cons of local democratic action as antidote to the sociopolitical ills in Philadelphia.

The composition and publication of *The Quaker City* has garnered limited attention other than scant accounts celebrating its impressive sales and recognizing its publication in parts.[68] Although the figures are likely exaggerated due to Lippard's own self-reporting, the first numbers (or installments) of *The Quaker City* no doubt reached a large audience, thanks in large part to its cheap serial publication process. But Lippard failed to follow through on an initially promised biweekly schedule in the fall of 1844; the early publication plan was later expanded after a four-month lapse between the fourth and fifth numbers, and a final flurry appeared in the late spring of 1845.[69] Closer attention to the irregular publication schedule suggests a shift in focus, a feature belied by the disjointed narrative. Rather than being evaluated as a coherent novel, *The Quaker City* is better understood when divided into three general sections: the first three numbers, the interlude of Number 4, and the more improvisational six numbers of what Lippard early on dubbed "a sequel" to the first four.[70] Numbers 1 through 3 focus tightly on two interwoven triads: first, a seduction plot involving the innocent Mary Arlington, her seducer Gus Lorrimer, and her brother Byrnewood Arlington; second, an adultery plot involving the social-climbing Dora Livingstone, her betrayed husband Albert Livingstone, and the con man Algernon Fitz-Cowles. Both plots revolve around the concern detailed in an 1849 preface: "*That the seduction of a poor and innocent girl, is a deed altogether as criminal as murder. It is worse than the murder of the body, for it is the assassination of the soul. If the murder deserves death by the gallows, then the assassination of chastity and maidenhood is worthy of death by the hands of any man, in any place.*"[71] Pairing the seduction plotline with occasional diatribes against a libelous periodical press, in these early parts Lippard seems interested in resuscitating gauges of national health in the early nation; in other words, reclaiming the radical democratic energy of the Revolution requires dredging up old cautionary tales to provoke more virtuous behavior.

In Number 4, the narrative moves into the next day and gradually expands its scope, showing initial signs of discarded faith in national remedies to local ailments.[72] Among the new features, none is more impressive than the reform of a character initially crafted as one of the corrupt Monks of Monk Hall, Luke Harvey. A recently discovered playbill of a cancelled theatrical performance of *The Quaker City* scheduled for 11 November 1844—an event that plausibly led Lippard to change course in his narrative starting with Number 4—describes Luke as "a consummate Scoundrel, who betrays everybody under the guise of Friendship," a description consistent with Luke's relatively minor, supplemental role in Numbers 1 through 3.[73] In Number 4, however, Luke assumes a central and more dynamic position as he peripatetically pops up all around Philadelphia. His characterization as a "scoundrel" appears less apropos after his speech concerning "*Justice* in the Quaker City." In this passionate diatribe, Luke makes concrete allusions to specific events in Philadelphia, the theatrical performance included, to critique the city's injustice: "One day [Justice] stands grimly smiling while a mob fires a Church or sacks a Hall, the next, ha, ha, ha, it hurries from its impartial throne, and places its placards over the walls of a Theatre, stating ... that THE TRUTH must not be told in Philadelphia."[74] Most likely composed after publication of the first three numbers, the narrative signals Luke's new role as moral compass instead of the "scoundrel" of the early numbers and the playbill.

Beyond the transformation of Luke Harvey and his allusion to the cancelled play, Number 4 includes numerous conflations of local and national cultures, importantly in a variety of dialect expressions that conjure the vernacular in more familiar yet no less distinctive ways. A physician confesses an inability to distinguish his horse from a prominent politician, both of whom are named Henry Clay: "Seen my blood horse Henry Clay? Splendid creature, capital action, glorious gait. . . . Make a good President: in favor of the Tariff" (QC, 178). Sharing details of his career, a former officer jumbles up political policies of the pro-internal-improvements, pro-tariff Whig Party: "I've been perambulating the continent. Part of the time, . . . I carried the chain on the railroad. Part of the time I . . . drove the horse on the canawl. I attributes the present depression of my funds to the cursed Whig tariff of '42" (QC, 181–82). Luke Harvey, disguised as Brick Top, spouts similar remarks about national politics, like "Hurray for Tippeycanoe" and "Go up stairs boys, and Remove the Deposits! We're the rale Dimmycrats" (QC, 196, 199). As these dialect-soaked allusions accrue, there seems to be a strong invocation of national presence to correct more than just the criminality that makes the seduction of Mary possible; that is, the invocation of national points of reference, even in jest, seems like an anxious appeal to some higher power to cure Philadelphia of its ubiquitous ailments.

Readers waited four more months before learning that the "sequel" had finally appeared. Almost immediately, they discovered that appeals to national symbols had been replaced with something else. Shortly into Number 5, a return to local priorities appears when F. A. T. Pyne stirs up his Patent-Gospel audience to send a committee to take down the pope of Rome. Lippard is clearly lampooning the anti-Catholic sentiment with an over-the-top narrative about shipwrecked sailors being captured by Vatican officials and then turned into sausages. But then enters an old man, who cites his credentials as a Revolutionary War veteran and asks, "Are there no hideous moral sores to be examined and healed by the Missionary of Jesus in this our moral heart of Philadelphia?" (QC, 226–27). The veteran aims to yoke the passions of the collective body into addressing the malfeasances located in their immediate vicinity. But Pyne's congregants will not have it, and they throw him out into the streets. Having coerced the crowd into doing "benevolent work" in some far-off place, Pyne directs the attention of his public away from his (and his Monk Hall accomplices') abuses of power and onto a site far removed from his locality. Lippard's dramatization presents a heavy-handed critique of the hypocrisy of this spiritual leader. But it also highlights how easily attention can be taken away from the concrete actualities of suffering people in their local spaces, punctuating the missed opportunities for individuals to come together and make collective decisions to improve quality of life in a democratic spirit.

TO SAY THAT LIPPARD'S SEQUEL DEVELOPED a set of more radically democratic solutions to the local problems in Philadelphia ignores the reality that his editorial aversion made a coherent solution less than feasible. We know that it took more than four months to bring out the "sequel" to *The Quaker City*, and in his sole acknowledgement of the shifting design, Lippard admitted in the 1849 preface that as he "progressed in [his] task, other ideas were added to the original thought" and that he became "determined to write a book which would describe all phases of a corrupt social system, as manifested in the city of Philadelphia."[75] To work through his depiction and evaluation of this corrupt social system, he needed more time. Juxtaposing the early parts, which recycle literary devices from the post-Revolutionary era, with material in the latter six numbers, we see evidence of a more radicalized if experimental approach to addressing local needs. The narrative's most imaginative reforms would address two key constituencies of his sociopolitical milieu: print culture and the body politic.

The early parts of *The Quaker City* issue many complaints against fictive books as tools put to use in acts of seduction and moral degradation. Such complaints recycle warnings against novel reading in the post-Revolutionary era. In the 1790s, these concerns grew out of assumptions concerning the weaknesses of female sexuality—the key issue at stake in Lippard's earliest conception of *The Quaker City*—and carried the weight of the young nation and its identity-forming citizenry.[76] Lippard drew from these late eighteenth-century sensibilities and restaged them amid mid-nineteenth-century urban culture, presumably to educate and to reform. With Lorrimer's initial seduction of Mary, the narrative bestows on romances much of the credit for enabling the libertine to defile the emblem of innocence. Rationalizing the far-fetched events leading to her pending secret marriage with Lorrimer, Mary esteems her experience as both fantastic and yet believable: "All this is very strange—how like the stories we read in a book!" (*QC*, 74). Mary's relationship to books merges the early nation's fears of seduction with antebellum reading practices elucidated by Gillian Silverman, which recognize the capacity for books to spawn new forms of communion in the face of more limited interpersonal experience.[77] Although more culturally reputable in the 1840s, fictive books, in Lippard's depiction, still produce credulous women and pave the way for victimization.

A related anxiety in the early republic concerned the role of libelous material in the periodical press, and here again, in the early stages, Lippard plays on such fears in hopes that national rhetoric would provide correction. At the center of this critique are two representative types of contemporary periodical culture: Buzby Poodle, the editor of a sensational penny paper named *The Daily Black Mail*, and Sylvester Petriken, the editor of the sentimental *Ladies Western Hemisphere*. Early on, these two figures appear as the targets of Lippard's thinly veiled attacks on his personal enemies in the Philadelphia periodical scene.[78] More broadly, the narrative suggests such figures responsible for the proliferation of duplicity and ethical compromises of 1840s periodical culture. Near the end of Number 3, the narrative stages a conversation between Poodle and Fitz-Cowles in which Poodle discloses the self-interest driving the salacious articles of his penny paper. He admits to ginning up stories in order to have slighted figures pay for retractions. Not always seeking monetary gain, he often uses his paper to facilitate other indulgences, most often to slander women who spurn his sexual advances. The narrative rebukes Poodle's unscrupulous practices when he turns to one of the nation's most cherished elements as a viable referent of correction: "Oh, glorious Liberty of the Press, let us take the opportunity . . . [to] chant a psalm in your praise! Oh, glorious Press, what a comfort it must be to you, to think and feel in your inmost heart, that Buzby Poodle . . . is no reality, no fact; but a mere fictitious impersonation" (*QC*, 140). Although dripping in sarcasm, the narrative nevertheless appeals to a national standard to lament the faults in this local instance of a penny paper editor.

Subsequent moments in the sequel show less confidence in the reform potential of national rhetoric, most notably when Poodle and Petriken share the stage in Number 8—a clear implication that Poodle's offensiveness and Petriken's sentimentalism are two sides of the same coin.[79] Staged in front of Independence Hall, where "giant trees, whose massive trunks had been young sixty years earlier, when the Proclamation of Independence rang from the steps of the ancient Hall" (*QC*, 361), the conversation makes clear that old ideals have been abandoned. In their place, these two print culture criminals now thrive, "the one fattened on the garbage of the town; the other lived on stolen literature . . . the one living on Murder, Suicide and Bloodshed of the town, the other thriving on the fruits of various adroit literary robberies" (*QC*, 361–62). Subsequently, the two men gloat over related ambitions. First, Petriken proclaims his pending status in language that appears almost presidential: "And so you see we'll have a great Magazine! . . . To-morrow morning all the Intellects of the land will meet in my office to talk the matter over.

I, Sylvester J. Petriken, will become the Focus of American literature." Poodle follows with similarly sweeping and prophesy-laden language: "Won't the name of Busby [sic] Poodle be known all over the country" (QC, 362). They shake hands, sealing their bond as future leaders of a nationalized print culture. Set in the shadows of the very site of nation founding, the unflattering portraits of these two figures clash sharply with the presumably noble aspirations of those responsible for the "Proclamation of Independence." Unlike in Number 3, in this part the narrative's appeal to a national symbol seems powerless to make corrections, nor does a reassuring narrator step in to insist that it could.

In the concluding portion of Number 10, we see a representation of print that no longer appeals to national standards as social correctives and instead imagines a scene in which local oversight might make amends. The fallout of the primary events is summed up in a newspaper dated six months after the fact. An article curiously praises two figures that the narrative has taken great pains to condemn: Pyne, the anti-Catholic minister who also tried to drug and rape his adopted daughter Mabel, is initially praised as a "worthy and eminent divine"; and the counterfeit Algernon Fitz-Cowles, who is cleared of rumored ill conduct "by an undeniable manifestation of public opinion" (QC, 490). Readers would presumably be appalled by the injustice of these two getting away with their crimes. The narrative, though, corrects this injustice in the same newspaper in two addenda that retract the praise of Fitz-Cowles and Pyne by stating that the former has just been arrested for forgery and the latter has been accused of "a most daring and atrocious act of perfidy [against] the daughter of one of our wealthiest merchants [Livingstone]" (QC, 491). The multiple reports apparently can coexist in the same paper.[80] Such is the possibility of print to publicize a more just outcome, at least eventually. The narrative no longer reckons the agents and instruments of print culture will be protected and rendered democratic by defaulting to a national standard like "Liberty of the Press" or by placing faith in the sacred site where the "Proclamation of Independence rang." Only an honest, forthright, ad hoc action like the newspaper's immediate retraction can do the democratic work of addressing the contingencies and exigencies of local life.

Even more pervasive than concerns with print culture are the frequent references to leftover bodies and body parts. These come in the form of carefully curated corpses employed for medical education and experimentation, body parts dismembered and carelessly strewn about, or spectral presences that haunt the living. For Dana Nelson, *The Quaker City*'s attention to bodies is a highly gendered operation, one that displaces the anxieties of white male fraternity in this historical moment—what she terms "national manhood"—onto the bodies and sexualities of women. This definitely seems to be the case with the seduction plots that dominate the first three numbers. As the narrative shifts from its previously avowed faith in national remedies, though, the increasing number of references to bodies in parts and spectral hauntings plausibly do more than register what Nelson describes as a collective "fear of dissolution . . . of a bounded nation, city, and manhood."[81] The revised focus from women's bodies to more generalized bodies in parts indexes the consequences of the predominance of abstracted national politics divested from material bodies; additionally, the numerous spectral bodies register a desire to reanimate a more radicalized and contingent form of democracy embraced by everyday people in the Revolutionary era.

In the early numbers, descriptions of women dwell on their tempting yet unguarded bodies. Mary has a beautiful face that lacks a "remarkable manifestation of thought, or mind, or intellect," which seems a serious weakness when paired with her "well-developed bust . . . slender waist, and the ripening proportions of her figure" (QC, 16). Dora likewise cuts a dangerous figure: "Her form was full, large, voluptuous . . . swelling with the full ripeness of womanhood" (QC, 117). While these women are displayed as objects that simultaneously prompt sexual desire and call for (national) protection, the men's bodies are often marked as unhealthy. Fitz-Cowles sartorially supplements his counterfeiting activity with calf-enhancing boots and prosthetic hips to give "a voluptuous swell to the outline of [his] figure" (QC, 133). Livingstone's ailment is less visible: he is "For years the victim of a secret and insidious disease [that] ossifies the main arteries of the heart" (QC, 157). Even Luke Harvey briefly suffers from a painful toothache before having the tooth pulled (QC, 167). And as the abject underbelly of these more public figures, the doorman of Monk Hall, the villainous Devil-Bug, possesses a ghastly body and single eye, which garner repeated references. The female bodies suffer as objects of the narrative gaze, and the physical ailments of the male bodies register the failing health of the social body. While never explicitly calling for national symbols and slogans to redress these physical afflictions (as we see in the depictions of print culture), Lippard's treatment relies on recycling seduction tropes and compromised bodies—hallmarks of early national literature—with the implicit sense that a cautionary tale might produce a cure.

In the backgrounds of these early numbers there are few references to dismembered parts and spectral hauntings, yet they abound in the latter parts. In the transitional Number 4, bodies in parts appear more conspicuously, most notably when Livingstone visits Dr. McTourniquet's "Museum" and finds jars containing "dead men in fragments, in great pieces and little, [including] a grisly skeleton, one hand placed . . . with fingers stuck in the cavity of the nose, performing the stale jest, common with boys along the street" (QC, 179–80). Receiving no extra comment, the discourteous treatment of leftover body parts earns explicit rebuke in the sequel. In Ravoni's "Dissecting Room," the narrative lingers over tables on which "lay the remains of woman and child and a man. Here was a grisly trunk, there an arm, there a leg, and yonder a solitary hand" (QC, 370). Medical students chatter profanely about the plausible histories of the bodies, often using them as macabre puppets to make obscene jokes in stilted, necrophiliac, disturbing ways. McTourniquet delivers the ironically barbed moral corrective: "There my boy you see the respect paid by living dust to dead ashes!" (QC, 372). A representative (if flawed) man like Byrnewood might avert his glance from the desecration of everyday bodies, but the narrative's increasing concern with their representation, along with its explicit rebuke, disperses the attention from the materially symbolic act against a single woman's body and looks more expansively on offenses to all varieties of bodies.

More indelible than these comments on bodies in parts are the repeated appearances of ghosts—victims of various types of violence who simply refuse to go away. The most haunted figure is Devil-Bug, who near the end of Number 4 laments, "Why can't a feller kill his man or woman and have done with d'em?" (QC, 205).[82] His haunts belabor him in both novel and sequel, and Devil-Bug's psychic torture seems a logical consequence of his individual actions. Yet his experience with spectral hauntings takes on a whole new meaning in his dream that occurs midway through the sequel. Cast 100 years into the future, Devil-Bug witnesses an apocalyptic phantasmagoria depicting the final demise—or allegorically, the death of freedom—in Philadelphia. Accompanied by an unnamed ghost, Devil-Bug watches as "the lordlings of the Quaker City . . . tear down Independence Hall and raise a royal palace on its ruins" (QC, 316). Reduced to an empty sign of Revolutionary ideals, Independence Hall gives way to its antithesis—a royal palace that heralds inequality and repression. National symbols like a monument to George Washington have been torn down and replaced with repressive state apparatuses—a jail and gallows. On the day preceding the crowning of the new monarch, Devil-Bug sees the resurrection of countless dead bodies that "mingled with the gay throngs of the side-walk . . . yet [they] beheld them not" (QC, 318). Interspersed among the passive living bodies, the dead proceed unnoticed. The next day brings the coronation of the king. Amid the great crowds, the dead suddenly become visible; the king is struck dead by the sight of a ghost, the city starts sinking into the earth, and the land convulses. As the scene closes, Devil-Bug witnesses the city reduced to ashes, to the refrain of "Wo unto Sodom" (*QC*, 331).

The fantastic scene has received frequent attention from literary critics.[83] Removed from the landscape, Devil-Bug sees what the living cannot: legions of dead bodies that register the invisible victims of nominal yet immaterialized democracy, a common nineteenth-century condition that Russ Castronovo has dubbed "necro citizenship."[84] With this scene depicting a total, inescapable finality in all-destructive terms, there seems little hope for regeneration. But we witness, interspersed within this apocalypse, key elements that underscore Lippard's shift away from thinking calibrated to the scale of nation. First, nowhere in the dream do these events map onto the rest of the nation. Unlike with the biblical destruction of Sodom, there's no other city, like Gomorrah, that is also destroyed for its sins, much less any national or global doom. This event is purely local. And although national symbols have given way to signs of a reborn monarchical tyranny, it seems that the expansion of national imagery has created the conditions that brought an end to sociopolitical ideals born in the radicalism of the Revolution. So it appears when Devil-Bug meets an old antiquarian on the day of the king's crowning. The antiquarian presents Devil-Bug with a "relic of the past" that is now criminal contraband, "an old banner with thirteen crimson stripes, and twenty-nine white stars, emblazoned on a blue field" (*QC*, 327). While the tattered flag prompts a lamentation from the antiquarian over the demise of the nation, Lippard's description of the flag numbering twenty-nine stars is telling. Number 7, the issue in which this dream appeared, was first advertised on 3 May 1845. Two months prior, on 3 March, the United States admitted Florida as the twenty-seventh state of the Union, the first new state since Michigan's admission in early 1837 (a conditional one, to be addressed in chapter 3). The twenty-eighth state, Texas, joined in December 1845; a twenty-ninth star was needed when Iowa entered the Union in December 1846. Lippard's prognostication of the fall of democracy after the addition of the twenty-ninth star conceivably implies that an expanding nation was the primary source of the pending crisis. With greater investments in the expansion and consolidation of the nation, the seeds for an antidemocratic counterrevolution were sown, all to the detriment not of the nation, but of the city alone. All this occurs as ghostly bodies return to stake their claim on the political events of the moment.

OVERLOOKING THE DISJOINTED SERIAL PRODUCTION of *The Quaker City* and assuming novelistic coherence follows a logic similar to that of nationalizing imperatives buttressed by an orderly story of the Revolution. Lippard seemingly discovered during the process of writing that nation-oriented principles and symbols were not delivering good changes in Philadelphia. The sequel at times suggests he had discovered that the nation and its cultural accoutrements were contributing to rather than correcting local problems, yet he also experimented with revolutions on a global scale. The narration of the mysterious Ravoni and the potential for world revolution under his mystical sorcery includes significant emancipatory rhetoric, but Ravoni ends up being more demagogic than democratic, and his magnetized followers are described as fanatics who blindly follow his bidding. Whatever Lippard's imaginative attempts, the unrevised vernacular aesthetics of the novel and sequel register ideas on contemporary politics that were more radical than what the author himself might have conjured. Moving from the banal seduction and adultery plots to a broader assessment of the people in the city, the narrative provokes a new, more profound response from its readers and posits a more contested literary space in which more alternative democracies—then, now, and in the future—might be imagined.

Lippard and Bird no doubt had a variety of aims in their literary productions. To what degree the texts we now read as *Sheppard Lee* and *The Quaker City* achieved their author's intentions and claims cannot be fully known. For more than a century, both texts have largely remained on the margins in US literary history, for different reasons. And yet, in their respective moments, they both took up the contemporary issues plaguing their city by looking backward to and recycling Revolutionary forms and ideas. Perhaps their motivation was nostalgia, but their final products seem dissatisfied with memorials that offer little remedy. Despite the stark differences in content, production, and commercial success, they both betray concerns about the ways that egalitarian democratic practices had seemingly left the very city in which the nation was formally produced. Though they offer few practical solutions to the loss of popular democratic empowerment, the few that do appear share traits in common with the democratic imaginings of the misfits yet to come. Next up are narratives that struck a pose far different from that of their Philadelphia counterparts—texts from what came to be known as the old southwestern humor tradition.

CHAPTER TWO

Southwestern Humor, Common Men, and Playful Democracy

Midway through Johnson Jones Hooper's *Some Adventures of Captain Simon Suggs* (1845), the narrative declares its arrival at the "most important moment in the history of [the titular] hero," but then digresses, issuing the following apology:

> And we beg the reader to believe, that we approach this portion of our subject with a profound regret at our own incapacity for its proper illumination. Would that thy pen, O! Kendall were ours! Then would thy hero and ours—the nation's Jackson and the country's Suggs—go down to far posterity, equal in fame and honors, as in deeds! But so the immortal gods have not decreed! Not to Suggs was Amos given! Aye, jealous of his mighty feats, the thundering Jove denied an historian worthy of his puissance! Would that, like Caesar, he could write himself! Then, indeed, should Harvard yield him honors, and his country—justice!

In the next sentence, the narrative changes tone in an awkwardly punctuated sentence: "Early in May of the year of grace—and excessive bank issues—1836, the Creek war was discovered to have broken out."[1] In this compressed introduction to a fictionalized episode set during an actual historical war, the narrative makes numerous allusions to national politics: the most famous of southwesterners to date, Andrew Jackson, along with his campaign biographer Amos Kendall; Jackson's honorary degree from Harvard; Jackson's contentious political war on the US Bank; and the heated politics of Indian removal and land redistribution. On the face of it, such references glorify Jackson while associating Simon Suggs and his humble aspirations to be county sheriff with the era's prickly symbol of popular democracy. The ironic, even mocking tone, however, suggests that these allusions might take aim at something other than the would-be sheriff's provincialism. Instead, the conceit highlights the gaps between local and national scales of reference. Rather than neatly fitting into the national framework evoked by the allusion to Jackson, this passage distinguishes between local instances of direct democratic politics and national narratives of a homogeneous imagined community united through representative, procedural government and its cultural forms. The tale that follows explores the possibility of a local collective working out power relations outside the legal, judicial, and executive maneuverings of the US nation. Disencumbered from national political norms, these local episodes—along with others in the southwestern humor tradition—yield an unexpected trove of alternative democratic positions.

Such insights have rarely been expected from a collection of writers who became the first to earn an enduring moniker primarily based on region, today variously called southern humorists or southwestern humorists.[2] The often interchangeable yet awkwardly imprecise designations for this regionalized genre are particularly telling as they pertain to the misfit status of these tales.[3] Although the tradition thrived in newly settled interior states and territories from Alabama and Tennessee to Louisiana and Arkansas (that is, the pre–Civil War Southwest), membership in this cadre included authors hailing from and writing about coastal states like Georgia and the Carolinas.[4] Individual sketches like those collected in Augustus Baldwin Longstreet's *Georgia Scenes* (1835) had been appearing for more than a decade in newspapers and books across the expanding nation when William T. Porter collected several and chose a title that included both regions: *The Big Bear of Arkansas, and Other Sketches, Illustrative of the Characters and Incidents in the South and South-West* (1845).[5] The tales and sketches of southwestern humor—later works of interest include those collected in Hooper's *Simon Suggs* and George Washington Harris's *Sut Lovingood* (1867)—were largely written about newly enfranchised common (yet really uncommon) men living on the peripheries of the nation from the later years of Jackson's presidency through the period of the Civil War. This style that Mark Twain would make famous on a national scale after the war has long been deemed an entertaining yet minor tradition.

The tradition presumably grew through a form of literary meritocracy—one resembling the process sketched out in Casanova's "world republic of letters"—in which many tales were written and some highly esteemed ones found their way from local sheets to national distributors.[6] Critical accounts repeatedly mark the same general trajectory, from unnamed locals to two regional venues—one traditionally "west" (the *St. Louis Reveille*) and the other traditionally "south" (the *New Orleans Picayune*)—and, for the supposedly true gems, to Porter's nationally circulating *Spirit of the Times*.[7] In addition to furnishing the conventional, nation-scaled rendering of the print circulation of this tradition, twentieth-century critics have employed national concerns to read the politics of these frontier sketches, typically in one of two ways. From one perspective, well-educated, Whig-leaning professionals crafted these humorous tales with the help of a narrative framing device—what Kenneth Lynn characterized in 1959 as a cordon sanitaire—to warn the rest of the country of the dangers of democratic excesses associated with the rise of the "common man" in Jacksonian democracy.[8] Some later critics have rejected Lynn's thesis, arguing instead that the tradition thrived on the tension between those plying the tools of modernity—that is, those of the professional classes establishing their version of order in the developing nation—and the folk garrulously celebrating the disappearing freedoms of the frontier.[9] While both general claims find some evidence in what turns out to be a rather heterogeneous tradition, both assume a standard national scale of reference as well as its telos, a national-regional dynamic that would become a rarely questioned norm in literary studies after the Civil War, thus producing the awkward critical misfit that I resituate in this chapter.

Unlike these approaches to this popular body of literature, this chapter approaches southwestern humor from an angle that starts with the local and suspends the telos of modernity as well as the nation, along with its preferred versions of orderly, well-managed literature as well as deliberative democracy. To be sure, some southwestern humor tales—particularly those that most emphatically employ the framed narrative to constrain vernacular expressions—supplemented the development of homogeneous (white, male, genteel) national identifications that often undergirded the cultural principles of liberal democracy.[10] Common man extraordinaire Davy Crockett stands as the most illustrative example of a figure setting the presumptive norms by which southwestern humor could be folded into a national narrative. Texts like those by Longstreet, Hooper, and Harris, alternatively reveal the varying degrees of the successful yet ultimately inadequate capacity of national models, institutions, and formal aesthetic norms to make sense of diverse communities negotiating power relations on their own terms. Instead, these messy and unrefined literary texts frequently portray localized sites in which politically conscious (un)common men and women both remain largely unregulated by the distant forms of national governance and engage in more immediate experiments with local democratic rule. While some might construe them as serving a more modern libertarian strand prioritizing individual freedom, these tales more often demonstrate investments in collective democratic living. They differ sharply from a version of "frontier democracy" that would drive the master political narratives from the era of Jackson through and beyond the era of Lincoln, and they resist compromise driven by the national push for coherence, order, and form through their type of vernacular aesthetics. Southwestern humor thus provides an insightful index of the tension between US nationalizing imperatives and the misfits that nevertheless inhabited its territory, voiced their collective ambitions, and presumed a less familiar but no less valuable version of democratic activity.

Unlike the Philadelphia novels that harken back to Revolutionary memory, the misfit texts of southwestern humor thrived in the present, even if advocates of progress preferred both then and later to see them as ephemeral and atavistic. While many inhabitants of the United States were caught up in the competing nationalisms taking up increasing amounts of space in both public print culture and more private exchanges, the figures in these tales seem far removed from and sometimes even hostile to the various nationalisms brewing between the 1830s and 1860s.[11] Unlike the national republic defined by constitutional management and procedural makeup, or even the critical protests of the Philadelphia novels, the version of democracy that these southwestern humor tales present is messy and unrefined, often taking place in a two-step operation I call *democratic play*. Using various literary strategies, the narrative establishes and often celebrates extraordinary local people largely detached from national political structures, which makes it possible for individuals to participate directly in collective decision making outside of any predetermined rules or hierarchies.[12] And unlike the national aesthetic norms that often operated to contain such democratic playfulness, these texts abjure any sense of authorial or editorial constraint. As the literary scholar James Justus has noted, although professionals like Longstreet, Hooper, and Harris "may have resented the raw terms of settling [in this region] ... their texts fail to show such resentment." On the contrary, the authors demonstrated such little control that they permitted their misfits "so many speaking opportunities that some [would] hardly shut up."[13]

Accordingly, this chapter starts by establishing context with the oft cited figure of Davy Crockett as the prototypical figure of southwestern humor and the complicated and often misunderstood local politics of the Southwest. From there I move to episodes from *Georgia Scenes*, *Simon Suggs*, and *Sut Lovingood*. The first text most forcefully aims to tame its subject matter by fitting it within a national framework. Longstreet's attempt reveals both anxiety and a fascination with the rabble's uncouth ways and their ascendance to fully authorized political (that is, voting) subjects, while also repeatedly revealing the fissures between a national model of deference and its implementation in local communities. To an even greater extent, Hooper's *Simon Suggs* and Harris's *Sut Lovingood* portray collectives in which the structures of nation—legal, political, and cultural—constrain the lives and political decision making of local inhabitants in only limited ways. Hooper's narrative, animated by elements of the carnivalesque and anti-official play, registers the most fully developed faith in alternative democracies operating on their own terms of democratic play. Conversely, Harris's bawdy tales reveal that exploding hierarchies and leveling the social ground yields a much uglier yet no less instructive form of democratic society.

Davy Crockett and Southwestern Politics in the National Aggregate

Besides Andrew Jackson, the most famous southwesterner to achieve national attention in the 1820s and 1830s was David Crockett. Riding the opportunities offered by an expanded electorate championing supposedly nonelite types like Jackson, Crockett was elected three times—albeit with two different party affiliations—to the US House of Representatives (1827–31, 1833–35) before joining the fight for Texan independence and suffering capture and execution at the Alamo in 1836. During his years on the national stage, he became the inspiration for James Kirke Paulding's popular drama *Lion of the West* (1831) and had his name appended to the title pages of five books that appeared between 1833 and 1836 (only one of which involved the historical Crockett).[14] Crockett's reputation took on mythic proportions when his name headed a variety of comedy-enriched and increasingly chauvinistic almanacs from 1835 to 1856.[15] Like other works of the southwestern humor tradition, early editions of *Davy Crockett's Almanack* carried a counterfeit southwestern imprint (Nashville, from 1835 to 1843); later ones bore the names of urban publishers in the east.[16] The tall tales of Paulding's play and the books provided much of the material that would reach an expanded audience in the *Almanack*. This combination of material has led many critics to cite the popularity of such works as being a key contributor to the development of southwestern humor and, in time, the success of Mark Twain.[17]

This version is understandable on the surface, given the *Almanack*'s combination of frontier humor with some occasional renderings in dialect. Take, for instance, the introductory writings of the fourth edition from 1838 under the catchphrase headline, "Go Ahead Reader": "I was born in a cane brake, cradled in a sap trough, and clouted with coon skins; without being choked by the weeds of education, which do not grow *spontinaciously* . . . I'm half-chicken hawk and steel-trap. So I will just let you know, reader, what I think about general matters and things in particular."[18] In what follows, the *Almanack* is filled with tales of both men and women fighting one another and/or wild beasts, with short aphorisms and toasts that fill out pages and with monthly astronomical and meteorological information interspersed. Few sketches in the 1838 *Almanack* keep up the rough idiomatic expression of "Go Ahead Reader." This careful framing formally folds the occasional and exceptional dialect ("spontinaciously") into a much broader narrative, one that ends up being explicitly nationalistic in the explanatory preface: "The Great Popularity of Col. Crockett throughout the United States, was evinced by the intense interest with which the accounts of his adventures and death were perused.... The succeeding almanacs... contain a great number of Wild Frolics and scrapes, together with adventurous exploits in the chase, both those in which he was engaged himself, and others that came within his knowledge." More of the same follows, and the preface concludes with an added touch of authenticity by stating that the "engravings are mostly taken from his drawings, which are very spirited. He drew on birch bark with a burnt stick."[19] Acknowledging Crockett's national reputation, bestowing an antique yet continuous presence (like what we saw in the material of Revolutionary memory in chapter 1), and ensuring more to come, this preface assures readers of its widespread appeal. But readers also see a heavy dose of national framing that incorporates and forecloses the expressive possibilities of such vernacular expressions.

In addition to having these formal qualities, the *Almanack* also engages an exceedingly abstract sense of national scope and geography (sometimes even stretching beyond national borders). In the same 1838 *Almanack*, stories are located in typical southwestern sites like Tennessee, Mississippi, and Arkansas, but tales are also set in Ohio, Michigan Territory (though by January 1838 it was a state), rural New England, and even one in England.[20] A powerfully individualistic and anticollective strain—one that fits the national brand of liberal democracy—is well captured in an oft copied passage that drops the idiomatic speech attributed to Crockett and enacts a western backwoods trope: "The Backwoodsman is a singular being, always moving west like a buffalo before the tide of civilization. He does not want a neighbor nearer than ten miles; and when he cannot cut down a tree that will fall within ten rods of his log house, he thinks it time to sell out his betterment and be off, to squat down in some distant place in the forest, build a log house, remain there just long enough to get a few acres under cultivation, and then pull up stakes and be off to some distant place."[21] The stark individualism, the antisocial qualities, the exploitation of land, and the restless mobility all merge into the conventional frontier type that lacks any vestige of humor in order to expose the harsh realities of western life. And yet, with all the multiregionalism of the *Almanack* and nonhumorous passages like these, critics have continued to conflate the Crockett material with southwestern types.[22] As passages like these demonstrate, though, *Davy Crockett's Almanack* is more about an abstract frontier within the nation that depends less on collective democratic values and more on individualistic exploits.

Best read as a representation of national literature, *Davy Crockett's Almanack* fits consistently within the framework of many more familiar axioms of the South in US national lore. One such characterization comes from the literary scholar Jennifer Rae Greeson, who has convincingly shown that a "concept of the South is essential to national identity in the United States of America." Expanding the temporal range of southern literature beyond its early twentieth-century heyday, Greeson identifies a "constant across US history" in the South's service as an "*internal other* for the nation, an intrinsic part of the national body that nonetheless is differentiated and held apart from the whole[,] . . . a symbiotic *ideological juxtaposition* in which each term is defined by reference to the other.[23] For Greeson, nowhere is this regional feature more apparent than in the imaginative literature produced between 1775 and 1900 and emerging from the metropolitan centers of the nation—New York, Boston, and even Philadelphia. The literary works of canonical figures like Charles Brockden Brown, Edgar Allan Poe, Herman Melville, and Walt Whitman provide ample evidence to back up her claim. Although Greeson does not address the *Davy Crockett* materials, many would be applicable within her framework.

Part of the reason for southwestern humor's misfit in both literary and political history of the South is a relatively unique and often forgotten moment in southern and national history. Like Greeson's claim about the constant position of the South as internal other, notions of "a solid South" have long existed throughout the nineteenth century (and beyond). In both the 1828 and 1832 presidential elections, for instance, Andrew Jackson virtually swept all ten southern states (save Maryland in his first victory, Kentucky and Maryland in his second), winning just shy of 100 percent of the vote in Georgia and Mississippi in 1832. But after the Panic of 1837, Jackson's party lost much of its grip on the region.[24] Consequently, national politics in the South from the late 1830s to the early 1850s saw a rare development. In the words of the historian Michael Perman, "For a brief moment of roughly fifteen years' duration, the South experienced competitive two-party politics. And then it vanished, never to appear again for well over a century."[25] It is in this period that the misfit of southwestern humor rose to semiprominence.

As much as national partisanship might invite a reconsideration of the role of southwestern humor as a cultural player in US literary history, a more localized look at southern political history generally, and at southwestern political history specifically, reveals an exceedingly disjointed social and political order that defies various historiographical attempts to fit all the disparities into a coherent master narrative. Aside from the issues of electoral politics, important discrepancies appear when one considers the physical topography that was very unfriendly to easy movement east to west across southwestern territories and states. Contemporary accounts like Timothy Flint's *A Condensed Geography of the Western States* (1828), Joseph Holt Ingraham's *The South-West* (1835), and Frederick Law Olmstead's *Journey in the Back Country* (1860) demonstrate the vast heterogeneity of southwestern peoples and politics, very much undermining later narratives proclaiming a "solid south."[26] This sense of semi-isolated and self-sustaining localities is echoed by more recent historians. William H. Freehling contends that even with settlement into the 1850s, different locales retained starkly different politics and concerns and ideologies, identifying a sharp contrast between national and imperial interests of coastal cities and the locally concerned values and actions of the more rural interior.[27] Moreover, as Thomas D. Clark and John D. W. Guice have noted, the pre-1830s Southwest was the locale of ongoing disputes on a macro scale between competing empires (United States, Spain, Britain, France) as well as on the micro scale within the most diverse socioeconomic region in the US territory.[28] These authors conclude with a caveat especially relevant to criticism of southwestern humor: frontier conditions in this region endured into the twentieth century. Possible factors? "Much of the [Southwest] lay for years buried in a virgin forest.... The river systems defied rapid internal commercial developments and railroad lines did not develop significantly until well after the Civil War. Consequently, to a large extent, the region now known as the Old Southwest was isolated ... and marked by localism until the mid-twentieth century."[29] Their argument, along with many other historical insights and cultural claims, invites a reassessment of the imaginative literature that emerged from these southwestern locales.

National Impositions and Democratic Play in *Georgia Scenes*

At the same time *Davy Crockett's Almanack* was developing its abstract caricature of a presumably atavistic culture that was nevertheless supporting the nation's individualistic democracy, Augustus Baldwin Longstreet carefully shaped his depiction of southwestern life into a form that, as critical history has told the story, appealed to the emerging tastes of bourgeois reading audiences in the late 1830s and early 1840s. His efforts garnered the attention of the New York City publisher Harper and Brothers, which brought out a second edition of *Georgia Scenes* in 1840. Longstreet's *Georgia Scenes* largely places its depiction of local cultural life within a narrative of national homogenization; however, despite its apparent endorsement of decorum and sociopolitical deference, the collection frequently reveals ways that the misfits exceed or escape the norms generated in concert with representative democracy and its favored civic institutions.

At first glance, the vernacular-soaked sketches seem apolitical, and primarily aimed at entertainment and perhaps the preservation of a particular time and place. Longstreet apparently thought so. In a letter composed shortly after the collection's initial publication in 1835, he wrote of his desire to fill "a chasm in history which has always been overlooked—the manners, customs, amusements, wit, dialect, as they appear in all grades of society . . . [for] who ever tells us of the comments and the wits and the ways of the common walks of life?"[30] In answer to his own question, Longstreet proffers *Georgia Scenes* as an attempt to rescue local culture from the historical dustbin. Throughout the scenes, however, Longstreet betrays his own discomfort with his subject matter, expressing regret in repeated authorial intrusions for disclosing scenes of violence, of uncouth manners and mannerisms, and of unrefined language. This conflict between heavy-handed didacticism and a professed desire to accurately represent the often-distasteful local folkways appears as early as the preface of the first edition. After celebrating his cast of characters, Longstreet concludes the preface with an apology to "those who have taken exceptions to the coarse, inelegant, and sometimes ungrammatical language, which the writer represents himself as occasionally using, *that it is language accommodated to the capacity of the person to whom he represents himself as speaking.*"[31] Longstreet no doubt knew that the linguistic offenses of his dialect-soaked aesthetics were the least of it, that readers would most likely take exception to the characters and their rude behavior.

Longstreet's apology thus suggests his attempts to play a mediating role. If he seeks pardon for the rawness of his characters, he also seems eager to intervene on behalf of a way of life and a population incapable of representing itself. The key term here—twice repeated in Longstreet's phrasing—is *represents*. Like other cultural and political representatives, elected or self-nominated, working within the constitutional framework, Longstreet, through his two narrators Lyman Hall and Abram Baldwin, wishes to represent a local community to the nation, to speak for local people in such a way that they can fit within a national culture.[32] Through the medium of print in transregional publications, Longstreet-as-representative softens the rough edges of his common characters as a demonstration of the degree to which his region can become a legitimate part of the national picture. Even if the author might esteem this version of the plain folk as virtuous yeomen of the republic, and thus as important symbols for the nation, he shows little confidence in their qualifications to speak for themselves or to act as fully authorized participants in the political realm.

Longstreet's strategies become clear in the opening scene of the collection, "Georgia Theatrics," in which the narrator Lyman Hall recalls a morning ride two decades earlier through the "Dark Corner" of Lincoln County. Hall's ride through the beautiful but morally compromised locale is disrupted by noises suggesting a vicious altercation. Determined to impose order, Hall hurries to the scene and arrives to find only a single person. Without any greeting, a flummoxed youth rebukes Hall: "You needn't kick before you're spurr'd. There a'nt nobody there, nor ha'nt been nother. I was jist seein' how I could 'a' *fout*" (*GS*, 11). Mistaking a theatrical performance for a brawl, Hall ends up humbled, made the butt of a joke. Hall frames his embarrassment, though, by reassuring readers that in the two decades since his ride, the Dark Corner has changed "from vice and folly to [a site of] virtue and holiness" (*GS*, 9). While Hall may not have succeeded in imposing decorum on the youthful performer in this scene, some agent has. Four scenes later, "The Fight" suggests what has wrought these changes. After describing the events of an otherwise good-natured fight between the two "best men" of the county, Hall delivers a closing monologue that echoes his earlier assurances: "Thanks to the Christian religion, to schools, colleges, and benevolent associations, such scenes of barbarism and cruelty as that which I have just been describing are now ... rare" (*GS*, 64). The narrative's reference to these types of disciplinary institutions points to what Christopher Castiglia has identified as an increasingly pervasive "discourse of institutionalism" that limited this era's democratic imaginary.[33] Playing a complementary role to the Constitution's containment of democracy, institutions such as churches, schools, and reform societies imposed social norms on local customs, providing a key supplement for national management and homogenization. Indeed, as discussed in greater detail in chapter 3, these institutions were hallmarks of what came to be known as the Universal Yankee Nation. Just as many in the Old Northwest would proclaim, Longstreet and his narrative find valuable allies in these benevolent institutions, regardless of what they meant to the prospects for democratic practice.

What should not go unremarked, however, is the youth's rebuttal in "Georgia Theatrics." As much as the narrative seems to impose homogenizing standards on its subjects, the local subjects and social practices the story represents often remain intransigent, if not oblivious to those standards. The characters in these and other sketches seem either ignorant of or resistant to the oversight of the intrusive narrator. Articulated in *their* distinct expressions that resist authorial control and institutional constraints, these stories employ a version of vernacular aesthetics that offers the ideal form in which democratic play might ensue. In "The Dance," the sophisticated narrator (this time, Baldwin) returns to the community of his youth and attends a dance at the home of a local magistrate. Early in the tale, Baldwin's articulate and condescending narration highlights the contrast between the local particularities and what he and his presumably national readership would take as proper norms for such an occasion. He details differences between the plain dresses of the "country girls" and those worn by the young women of "our republican *cities*." Further distinctions include the different manners of greeting—instead of "the custom of kissing," the folk employ "a hearty shake of the hand and smiling countenances"—and the lack of social rules: "Here were no formal introductions to be given, no drawing for places or partners, no parade of managers, no ceremonies. It was perfectly understood that all were invited to *dance*" (*GS*, 14–15). Baldwin thus accentuates the deviations from cosmopolitan social conventions to share an inside joke with his national readership. To some degree, he pokes fun at both, but his bias in favor of the sophisticates is clear. Oblivious to their social offenses, however, the local misfits merrily proceed with their dance.

Soon enough, Baldwin's narrative registers greater ambivalence toward both the high society he now claims as his own and the more rustic culture of his youth. No longer willing to just sit back and comment, he seeks common ground with the local community after discovering the presence of an old sweetheart, who happens to have married the squire. When he asks to be reacquainted with his former love, he assures his host, "Don't get jealous, squire, if she seems a little too glad to see me." To his overconfident guest, the squire responds, "No danger . . . she hadn't seen *me* then, or she never could have loved such a hard-favoured man as you" (*GS*, 16). Subsequently, his former sweetheart fails to recognize his name. Name-dropping and old dance moves also fail to spark her memory. Embarrassed, he retreats as the party continues on into the night. The scene closes with the last words of a letter in which the squire informs Baldwin, "Since you left here, [my wife] has been thinking about old times, and she says, to save her life, she can't recollect you" (*GS*, 22). When he arrives at the dance, Baldwin enters certain of his social and cultural superiority. He comes prepared to represent his old community and to explain the peculiarities of local culture to readers who, the narrative implies, share his urban refinement. Yet his perspective and his new social prejudice do not align with the associational life of this community, and he again becomes the butt of the joke. His old acquaintances show no interest in a representative who might translate their local customs into the national idiom, and theirs is the last word. This scene thus offers one of the clearest instances of vernacular aesthetics—the common voices that refuse to become abstractions within a broader national story.

While there is little in this tale to suggest political action, it does sketch the foundations of what I have called democratic play: a local collective less invested in a logic of representation implied in indirect, procedure-bound, representative democracy than in working out the contours of social interaction on their own terms. Even when the narrative would most like to manage or tame any excess, the tension between impositions consistent with national norms (Longstreet's prerogative) and alternative democratic collectives—neither resisting nor embracing, just functioning autonomously—remains unresolved. In "The Turn Out," for instance, Lyman Hall relates a 1790 visit to an old friend named Captain Griffin. As in earlier tales, Hall assures readers that elements of this visit—the captain's hospitality (*GS*, 73), the fertility of this locale (*GS*, 76)—have disappeared in the forty-plus years since. The story nevertheless lives on. The featured event of this visit involves Hall's and Griffin's observation of a schoolboy rebellion against a tyrannous schoolmaster. The students' demand for a weeklong vacation is politically encoded, punctuated by allusions to the American Revolution (a common convention at this point, as discussed in chapter 1). When the schoolmaster temporarily gains the upper hand in an otherwise well-balanced and good-natured fight, Captain Griffin cries out to the boys to remember General Washington, whose name instantly "cured their wounds and dried up their tears." On the surface, the evocation of the national father galvanizes the boys' rebellion, and they furiously renew their battle, gaining the assurance of a one-day holiday from their teacher. When the democratically inclined boys demand a week, they appear ready to win. As the representative heir of Washington, Captain Griffin imposes order and "after the common but often unjust custom of arbitrators, split[s] the difference." Hall waxes ambivalently between the assurance of constraint and the recognition of injustice in this type of arbitration, and also expresses dismay over the apparent weaknesses of his later contemporaries when he states that the teacher gave "some of [the boys] thumps which would have placed the *ruffle-shirted* little darlings of the present day under the discipline of paregoric and opodeldoc for a week" (*GS*, 81).

At the end of the day, the ancient nation asserts its authority, even as the boyish demos win their holiday. It would seem, though, that the old Revolutionary spirit has been lost within two generations. The disease-prone "*ruffle-shirted* little darlings" lack the collective democratic spirit necessary to fight for their interests.

As "The Turn Out" suggests a turning point in *Georgia Scenes*, that a depoliticized order is well on its way, the final scene, "The Shooting Match," initially follows suit as it superficially appears to resolve the tension between local determination and national standards in explicit political terms when Hall reasserts himself as virtual representative of an eclectic group of misfits. At the close of what has been a tale of social leveling—Hall finds common ground with a group of backwoods countrymen after finishing second in a shooting contest—Hall refuses his prize, raising suspicion about his intentions. He assures the crowd that he has no ulterior motive, that he is "not a candidate for anything." Yet, Hall's declaration effectively reminds both the crowd and his readers of the representative nature of managed democracy and the republican ideal that the best should rule. In response, one character seems to accede to that ideal when he declares, "If ever you come out for anything, Lyman, jist let the boys of Upper Hogthief know it, and they'll go for you to the hilt" (*GS*, 214). Such statements work on two levels. They fulfill Longstreet's stated objective in the preface that he would record the "comments of the wits and ways of the common walks of life" (*GS*, xlviii). They also reestablish national principles of political containment, in this instance ventriloquized through a commoner. They likewise reinstitute order on what the author presumes to be an excessively unruly scene. As the concluding scene, Longstreet's national imposition in effect gets the final word.

It is this idea of the "final word" that directs most readings of this tradition, or at least those that choose the nation as the conceptual point of departure. But imposing a conventional narrative structure on the entire collection of *Georgia Scenes* is as problematic as assuming that the frame successfully circumscribes and manages the excesses of these local cultures.[34] Reading these tales as misfits, however, resists such structuring devices and insists on the narrative resistance that these local communities present to a cultural and political elite—the flummoxed youth wittily rebuking Hall's unwarranted imposition, for example; the dance-goers ignoring the obligations of deference; the collective action of the schoolboys winning their holiday. Understanding *Georgia Scenes* as a misfit text also reveals how Longstreet's narrative mediates local and national, resisting the national ideological hegemony that literary critics often assume. Even as it seeks containment in the terms of the cordon sanitaire, the nation-oriented narrative becomes a suturing device that makes the seams between the nation and the local all the more visible.

As my readings of *Georgia Scenes* suggest, the plausibility of democratic play persists despite the author's attempted constraints. Whatever intent Longstreet had in seeking national oversight to tame backwoods eclecticism, the tales themselves project a more ambivalent relationship to the nation and its dominant narrative. Such readings thus counter Lloyd Pratt's broad claim about southwestern humor: "At no point does Southwestern Humor disguise its resolution to link its authors and its readers at the expense of the group that is the subject."[35] Even if some authors held this attitude, as Longstreet likely did, the subjects in the tales seem little concerned about being objects of derision. And while the majority of these sketches largely eschew formal politics, they do chart a path toward a way of life that is necessary for democratic politics. *Georgia Scenes* no doubt plowed the ground for later practitioners of the tradition. Johnson Jones Hooper and George Washington Harris would produce work that pushed Longstreet's innovations more prominently in the direction of both generative as well as reactionary democratic play.

Virtues of Shiftiness and Vices of Anarchy in *Simon Suggs* and *Sut Lovingood*

With the tumult produced by Indian removal, rampant land speculation, political corruption, and rapid immigration, largely unsettled Alabama offered a cultural ethos different from Longstreet's Georgia. Hooper's mid-twentieth-century biographer describes it this way: "And so it came to pass, for all his homespun jeans, his rawhide galluses and his bare feet a man was accepted for what he was, not what he had been, and no questions raised. It might have been frontier etiquette to ask a settler whence or even how he came to Alabama—but never *why*."[36] Amid this presumably egalitarian environment, Hooper harvested from the cultural scene around him one of the most memorable characters of the southwestern humor tradition.[37] But Hooper's narrative of the life of "Captain" Simon Suggs is not just the record of an odd character performing humorous antics in a peculiar place and time. It ups the ante on *Georgia Scenes* by inserting an unconventional figure into the running for political office, selling Simon's qualifications as a candidate for sheriff to the local voting public. In doing so, *Simon Suggs* satirizes the campaign biographies of the era.[38] But if Hooper intended to parody the form in order to demonstrate the absurdity of someone like Simon becoming an elected official, the narrative falls short. The narrative is at once tempered and ironized by a genteel narrator somewhat elevated above, though often sidelined by, the characters' vernacular exchanges, providing a formal, aesthetic design that complements Simon's oft repeated misfit aphorism, "It's good to be shifty in a new country" (SS, 12). In contrast to Longstreet's paternalistic wariness toward unmanaged cultural customs and democratic participation, *Simon Suggs* indulges more radical possibilities of democratic play at the expense of national social and political norms.

The narrative sets about the work of dismantling conventional social hierarchies and seeding the ground for democratic principles and ethics in the opening scene, when Simon gains his emancipation from Jedidiah, his despotic father. The episode works by deflating Jedidiah's overweening sense of self deriving from a presumption of a cosmopolitan urbanity, a consequence of his travels to the metropolitan city of Augusta. These travels have led Jedidiah to two conclusions: "The one was, that a man who had never been at Augusta, could not know any thing about that city, or any place, or any thing else; the other, that one who *had* been there must, of necessity, be not only well informed as to all things connected with the city itself, but perfectly *au fait* upon all subjects whatsoever" (SS, 23). The elevated language demonstrates a conceit that peppers the tale frequently. Simultaneously, the exaggerations expose the betrayal of more plainspoken vernacular, and it does so as if to signal the pending subversion of hierarchies and conventions. In this case, Jedidiah's self-aggrandizement exposes him to ridicule (from the reader) and undermines his patriarchal authority (in relation to Simon, who knows how to exploit Jedidiah's inflated ego). Jedidiah agrees to Simon's suggestion to negotiate the rules of a card game and corresponding wager: if Jedidiah wins, he punishes Simon and takes whatever money he is carrying; if Simon wins, he avoids his father's wrath and wins both his freedom and a horse. Under these mutually negotiated terms following the suspension of conventional hierarchies, Simon plays on his father's privileging of extralocal experience at the expense of local concerns, winning the game and his freedom.

This scheme does not, however, empower all equally. As in other episodes of southwestern humor, an African American character receives the violent retribution for the loss or subversion of traditional power relations. Simon's Black co-conspirator and playmate, Bill, interacts with Simon as an equal, frequently contending with him over the rules of their own games. But when Jedidiah catches the young men shirking their work, Bill receives a whipping, which affords Simon time to plot an escape from his father. As Shelia O'Brien notes, this incident, along with others like it, both reflected and invigorated a social order anchored to white supremacy.[39] Extending O'Brien's observation, we might see this reification of a social category's order as a kind of desire to reinscribe all social order, which includes the constitutionally managed variety. Simon may be able to overturn the level of social order that the story associates with cosmopolitan, if not national, pretensions, but his manifestation of local power is unable to escape the racial order, which acts as a placeholder for the larger social order. In *Simon Suggs*, not every character has full access to democratic play and thus to self-authorizing political action. Race and gender lines often determine the boundaries of democratic play, acting to stabilize—and thus determine the true limits of—social play.

Following his emancipation, Simon takes up a new pastime of tricking individuals who take it one step beyond his father's supposed cosmopolitanism and openly declare their investment in national norms. In one instance, Simon takes advantage of an unscrupulous banker who mistakes him for an elected state representative. While they are sharing a stagecoach ride to Tuscaloosa, the state capital, the banker takes Simon to be a man of authority and influence. "Your election," he assures Simon, in an idiom intended to showcase good breeding, "by the enlightened people of the important county you represent, is ample guaranty to *me*, that you are a gentleman of the nicest honor, and the most unimpeachable veracity" (SS, 49). As with Simon's father, the banker's pretentious elevated language rather than a more straightforward vernacular signals a misplaced faith in the superiority of supralocal identifications over locally defined and negotiated positions of power. While he never claims to be an elected official, Simon does nothing to dispel the banker's inference. In consequence, the banker offers him a "loan" to buy future votes in the legislature.

The scene does more than demonstrate Simon's ability to con; it also reveals the banker's interest in controlling the procedural tools of democratic governance. Presuming that Simon's representation occurs at a far remove from the interests and people he allegedly represents, the banker attempts to take advantage of the distance between government and population. Yet the joke is on the banker, along with anyone who assumes the abstractions of federal governance, and for the moment, wealth does not enhance a citizen's democratic participation (even though the attempt at a bribe suggests that actions like this do succeed). In the very next scene, Simon enters a barroom occupied by "men of fortune," rich and poor alike, with "a large proportion [being] members of the legislature" (SS, 55). Standing side by side with legislative representatives in the tavern, Simon enjoys the social equality that Timothy Gilfoyle identifies in barrooms of this era, which "endowed participants with feelings of liberty and independence while inducing a sense of equality."[40] The narrative thus collapses the distance between representative and represented in a space that fostered democratic ideals of liberty and equality, which signifies the first part of democratic play: marking the separation between local conditions and national norms. The tavern depicts a democratic space that is an alternative to the legislature, a space in which elected representatives do not stand in for a community. Instead, the second act of democratic play takes place: members of the community stand as equals, playfully negotiating the terms of self-rule.

To this point, *Simon Suggs* has emphasized the social elements of the place while demonstrating little explicit need for collective political action. The Indian uprising episode puts the challenges of alternative democratic societies to the test. As the quotation opening this chapter demonstrates, the text is well aware of the difference between local activities and national expectations. Such distinctions continue in the response of the local citizenry to the threat of Indian attack: "The yeomanry of the country—those to whom, as we are annually told, the nation looks with confidence in all her perils—packed up their carts and wagons and 'incontinently' departed for more peaceful regions" (SS, 83). The play on language connects with other moments of vernacular aesthetics. And unlike Longstreet's tales, which affirm the national symbol of the yeomanry while striving to manage any less-than-genteel behavior on their part, Hooper's narrative explicitly distinguishes the illusionary national symbol and its local instantiation.

Further distinctions between national and local scales appear more subtly when the narrative conveys the episode's temporal conditions. Theorists of the nation such as Benedict Anderson and Homi Bhabha have described how the nation is bound together by a simultaneous experience in empty homogeneous time.[41] Hooper's story, however, reveals that far from a sharing a national ethos, the local experiences hardly any sort of simultaneity—and thus little sense of imagined community—with other localities. Midway through this episode, the narrative distinguishes local time from any national standard: "It was at an early hour; in fact—speaking according to the chronometrical standard in use at Fort Suggs—not more than 'fust-drink time'" (SS, 97). Later, it conveys the drudgery of life in micro-space metonymic of the local: "Time at last began to hang heavily upon the hands of the inmates of Fort Suggs" (SS, 111). Both examples of a localized sense of time are unsynchronized with the progressive temporalities demonstrated in the opening scene's national allusions. Time is not an abstract measurement that can be translated across wide distances, thus tying together this locality with others and forming a nation; rather, time becomes a marker of certain kinds of activity or inactivity that can be materialized only through actual, experiencing lives negotiating their experiences on immediate terms.⁴²

Temporally disconnected from the nation, this locality becomes unmoored from hegemonic norms of national political procedure. Power structures are up for grabs, and Simon, who happens to be at Taylor's store "when the wagon, cart, and, pony loads of the 'badly-scared' mortality [begin] to arrive," stands ready to take advantage. Ignoring the curious and excessive use of commas, readers know that Simon knows something the others do not: "And he enjoyed these [frightened people] to the uttermost now, because he was well informed as to the state of feeling of the Indians, in all the country for ten miles around, and knew there was no danger" (SS, 85). How Simon knows this fact that escapes the rest of the community (and the federal government) is not disclosed, but his position as intermediary between the whites and the Creeks allows him to exploit the community's (and the nineteenth-century reader's) assumptions about Indians predicated on national views. Simon craftily assumes leadership over the eighty or so white refugees gathered at the store, after a majority agrees to make him captain. As an elected representative (not appointed, as in standard military practice), he declares martial law, renames Taylor's store Fort Suggs, and revels in his new power. In this way, the process seems to reiterate conventional national tropes. Instead of fostering the democratic play that had positioned him in leadership, Simon places himself above the constituents of his community and governs in a way that mimics national forms. His method of governance, in fact, veers toward despotism when he institutes martial law—plausibly, Hooper's jab at Andrew Jackson's methods in New Orleans in the War of 1812—and makes himself a representative of the executive and judiciary: captain, judge, and jury.

This ascendance to power proves short-lived, however, and the narrative quickly reveals Simon's inability to impose national standards on his local community. More importantly, it reveals how local community circumvents national impositions, regardless of the variety instituted. At the moment that Simon assumes his despotic role, the democratic play begins. Widow Haycock, who "desired to possess herself of a certain 'plug' of tobacco ... during the watches of the night," sneaks out of the fortifications and retrieves her supply (SS, 90). On her return, she makes some noise, setting off the pickets and causing Simon's incompetent army to fire under the presumption of an attack. In the face of the widow's unwitting dissidence, Simon maintains control by declaring a drumhead court-martial, an overreaction that parodies the very authority Simon would preserve. What ensues can best be described as a parody of due process. In preparation for the court-martial, Simon dresses himself in a costume that includes a rusty sword, a pincushion turned epaulette, and a handkerchief sash—a burlesque of formal martial uniform. In the trial itself, Simon's excessive and inaccurate use of legal jargon and constitutional language lampoons the elevated formality of national judicial standards, which, like Simon's martial costume, the rustic and cultural otherness of the local renders both ridiculous and ineffectual. In these ways, the narrative implies that mapping national forms of law enforcement on this local community through language that defies a conventional vernacular simply does not work. Simon nevertheless presses on, and he "condemns [the Widow] to be baggonetted to deth in one hour from this time, witness our hands and seals" (SS, 104). When the Widow begs for clemency, Simon responds, "I wish . . . thar *was* some way to save her. But ef I was to let her off with a *fine*, I might be layin' myself liable to be tried for my own life" (SS, 107). Along with his odd deferral to a mythic judicial authority that is nowhere to be found, Simon's malopropisms undercut his attempt to maintain power. Reading this from one direction would suggest that Simon and his ragtag community clearly need someone more competent to step in and assume leadership, something like Longstreet's institutions engineering progressive reform. On the other hand, Simon's failure to impose order betrays the narrative's implication of the absurdity of overlaying national management on a locality more amenable to alternative democratic practices.

In this and previous scenes, Simon's behavior recalls another literary tradition: the carnivalesque as theorized by Mikhail Bakhtin in *Rabelais and His World*. In Bakhtin's words, "Rabelais' images have a certain undestroyable nonofficial nature. No dogma, no authoritarianism, no narrow-minded seriousness can coexist with Rabelaisian images."[43] As the counter to official life, "carnival . . . marked the suspension of hierarchical rank, privileges, norms, and prohibitions . . . hostile to all that was immortalized and completed."[44] The breakdown of hierarchies in Rabelais's fiction evokes new types of interaction, spawns new kinds of communication, and creates an overall sense of newness in forms, words, and meanings.[45] Throughout the Indian uprising episode, Simon engages in antiofficial carnivalesque behavior. On the night of the widow's tobacco incident, for example, he and his lieutenant enjoy, "with a bottle of bald-face between them, . . . a social game of 'six cards, seven up'" (SS, 90). Amid this festive carnivalesque atmosphere, authoritarianism and conventional hierarchies prove unsustainable, and the participants can act democratically in common with one another.

In what initially appeared to be a new form of despotism, the antiofficial carnivalesque works to bring about justice endorsed by all participants: the widow is spared, and Simon's claim to ruling power is rechanneled back into the people. From this point, the narrative describes more good-natured carnivalesque gaming, including "*sorties* upon ox-wagons . . . dollar-pitching, and an endless series of games of 'old sledge'; as well as the occasional exhibition of chuck-a-luck table" (*SS*, 111). The formal language is now discarded in favor of a collectively employed vernacular, and the local collective enjoys a more egalitarian atmosphere. Shortly thereafter, the Indian uprising episode concludes with a playful engagement at a ball game between two villages of the allegedly threatening Creeks. The danger is exposed as a complete hoax, and both groups plan good-natured pranks against the other. Simon's absurdly comical behavior and the evocation of the carnivalesque project a new sense of social living that mocks national overdetermination, calling instead for an investment in the immediacy of local and dialogical engagement. Unlike Longstreet's attempted homogenization of local varieties, Hooper's play on the gap between the local and the national yokes a democratic way of life with actual democratic collective action. *Simon Suggs* thus unapologetically portrays a group of people self-determinedly—and successfully—engaging in ongoing negotiations of social living according to the localized dictates of democratic play.

IF *SIMON SUGGS* PLAYFULLY LEVELS the social ground and offers some scenes of alternative democratic action, *Sut Lovingood* demonstrates an even more radical horizon of possibility for the entire southwestern humor tradition. First introduced in 1854, Sut Lovingood made one appearance in Porter's *Spirit of the Times* before circulating in southern newspapers (with at least one significant exception, which I will address shortly). In 1867, Harris published a collection of twenty-four sketches with the New York–based Dick and Fitzgerald.[46] In nearly every episode, the educated narrator, George, foregoes the role of the conventional framer and turns the storytelling reins over to Sut's dialect-soaked tongue. What results is a combination of self-aggrandizement, self-deprecation, homespun philosophizing, and physical comedy. Like *Simon Suggs*, *Sut Lovingood* indulges in the subversion of traditional hierarchies, preparing the ground for democracy determined by local players and interests. Yet Sut's methods, which include numerous diatribes against representative figures of authority—elected politicians, law officers, church leaders—and frequent acts of violence, often seem little more than expressions of nihilism. Put another way, *Sut Lovingood*'s subversion tends more toward anarchy than toward a functioning democracy in the making. Although it is quite different from *Simon Suggs*'s positive representation of democratic play, *Sut Lovingood* marks a different point on the spectrum of this tradition's potential to imagine how local actions and social relations might operate through its incommensurable vernacular aesthetics and outside the normalizing tendencies of the national frame.

Like Simon's, Sut's defiance of arbitrary authority begins at home, where he recognizes from the very start that the hierarchical "law of the father" is fraught with nonsense, especially given his pedigree. In "Sut Lovingood's Dad Acting Horse," the family's plow horse has just died, and rather than buying or stealing a new one, Dad himself plays the role of horse. Excessively faithful to the role, Dad strips naked, chomps on a bridle, bites Sut, and kicks Mam. Mam's rejoinder—"Yu plays hoss better nur yu dus husban"—marks the extent to which this episode upends traditional notions of the familial order.[47] Subsequently, Dad stomps over a sassafras bush, upsets a hornet's nest, and runs through every possible obstacle before jumping off a cliff into a creek. Through it all, Sut looks on and issues many humorous taunts. Little has changed by the time of Dad's second appearance, in "Dad's Dog-School." In this episode, Sut's family joins in the attempted training of their young puppy, Sugar. To "make" the pup, Dad has Sut's sister Sall sew him up in a dead bull's hide and instructs Sut to sic the dog on him. Dad again plays his part wholeheartedly. When Sugar's teeth pierce Dad's cowhide costume, he breaks character, drawing a rebuke from Sut. Eventually, Sall intervenes with an axe to break Sugar's hold, taking a bit of flesh from the noses of both Dad and the pup. Having had enough, Mam ends the affair: "Hu ever hearn ove the likes bein dun by the daddy ove a famerly.... Now jis' quit, an' let that ar blasted roun-headed pup edecate hissef like yer uther childer dus" (*Sut*, 279–80). As in the earlier episode, Mam's slang underscores a prominent theme in both stories: no authority—particularly that based in patriarchy—is natural or unquestionable. Such an idea stands as precursor for alternative language and forms of democratic action.

The leveling of patriarchal authority figures becomes a trope that recurs throughout the Lovingood yarns, most often by means of Sut's distinctive strategy of describing these figures in animalistic terms.[48] Perhaps because of his marginalized status, Dad's bestial role serves as a playful (if painful) abdication of his representative position of patriarchal authority, creating space for others to participate in the exercise of family authority; conversely, because this tale is told in his unique and unironic vernacular, Sut could be offering his own radical refiguring of patriarchy. Either way, the event opens the door for often excluded others to participate in the exercise of family rule. Mam's equally unironic vernacular commentary serves as a jeering chorus exposing the foibles of Dad's schemes, demonstrating her appropriation of authority as an equal participant in the family's political dynamic. Sut's role in these tales is one of occasional player, close observer, and subsequent narrator. He does not become a substitute for his father, but rather sees past the patriarchal regime as well as other arbitrary forms of hierarchical marginalizing writ large on his community. He will go on to expose those who unjustly derive their power, merited or not (and most often not), from this regime.

By frequently employing animalistic metaphors, *Sut Lovingood* takes a different path than *Simon Suggs* in challenging national norms and the civic institutions that constrain alternative democratic possibilities. As one example, Sut undermines a religious authority when he targets Parson John Bullen, who is known for abusing both Sut and the rest of the community.[49] Sut times his retribution for the moment in a fire-and-brimstone sermon when Bullen introduces "hell-serpents" as his homiletic metaphor, which Sut renders material by releasing a sackful of lizards in the Parson's pants. Sut then uses a variety of animal metaphors associated with demonic possession to depict Bullen's histrionics, comparing him to an "ole sow" and describing how he "gin his back a good rattlin rub agin the pulpit, like a hog scratches hisself agin a stump" (*Sut*, 54). Eventually, Bullen strips away his clothing, and "he did the ... fussiest runnin I ever seed, tu be no faster nur hit wer, since dad tried tu outrun the ho'nets" (*Sut*, 57). As with Sut's father, the authority figure again becomes animal, at least metaphorically. With the explicit reference to Dad's experience of acting horse, Sut effectively binds the stories of these two authority figures together into a single narrative of subversion that works to level the social and political fields. When he uses this trope again in the exposure of the corrupt Sheriff Doltin (the representative law enforcer), calling him at various times an "ole sore-headed bar," "hoss," and a "high preshur snapin turkil" (*Sut*, 259, 260, 273), we know that no corrupt institution is above Sut's recourse.

By these unorthodox means, Sut's actions open his community to alternative structures of the political by reducing authority figures (who abuse their powers) to animals. And, as demonstrated, Harris's deep-seated commitment to irreducibly concrete and vernacular expressions makes for an often unreadable text. But here we might see the leveling go too far, making the ground too untenable for collective democratic action to happen. Because of his repeated claims to suffering from being a "durn'd fool," Sut's reliability is always under scrutiny. He might claim that the authority figures act corruptly with respect to the entire community, but his allegations can never be considered incontestable. More troubling, on subverting abusive authority, *Sut Lovingood* offers no alternative to the hierarchical relations it overturns. Sut's prefatory dedication—"Ef eny poor misfortinit devil hu's heart is onder a mill-stone, ... hu misfortin's foller fas' an' foller faster, ... ef sich a one kin fine a laugh, jis' one ... then I'll thank God that I *hes* made a book" (*Sut,* xi)—suggests the yarns are merely a compensatory pleasure or escape in the vein of *Davy Crockett's Almanack* rather than working for those exploited by the conventional structures of social and political authority, even under a nominally democratic one. Hoping his stories can bring amusement to those who suffer in a form of vernacular aesthetics, Sut seemingly longs for a world in which an alternative form of democracy could thrive outside the nation and the conventions and institutions it endorses. But to find evidence of such local politics at work requires a turn outside the texts themselves to consider how southwestern humor circulated within a literary marketplace.

Print Circulating Playful Democracies

Throughout this chapter, I have attempted to resituate the point of departure for reading this tradition, primarily in order to engage these stories in terms of their focus on local scenarios rather than assuming a nationalist frame, one that is certainly ever present but less determining than criticism historically suggests. Humorously subversive and valuably excessive, these tales imagine alternative democratic experiences in which variously realized instantiations of democratic play narrow the gap between individuals and their political agency. This chapter concludes with a brief consideration of the political work of these texts through their redistribution in print culture. In her account of national compression during this era, Trish Loughran largely depends on an archive consisting of antislavery texts, and no doubt these played a key role in the burgeoning sectionalism (or counternationalisms) leading to the Civil War.[50] The circulation of southwestern humor, however, conceivably had a different effect. Focusing on authors' biographies and a presumed urban readership has led to readings of this tradition's contributions to a homogeneous national male fraternity. Conversely, I have argued that the rough characters in these stories often exceed the policing action of genteel narrators, suggesting that local conditions may be as important for determining structures of power and decision making as national forms.

But what happens to the political imaginary when texts depicting such people as those represented in southwestern humor—people who live lives less determined by nationalist rhetoric and negotiate their own social living through their own vernacular in local forms of democratic play—circulate outside the national metropolitan centers in which our critical histories have tended to be oriented? Much has been made of the heavy hand of William T. Porter and his decades-long commitment to soliciting and supporting writers of this tradition. Having shifted his paper's focus away from horse racing after the Panic of 1837, Porter built up a cadre of contributors who filled his pages with their humorous tales. He provided to many of his favorites, Hooper among them, special assistance in the publication of their respective books.[51] When he published his own collection, he took care to proclaim the national stakes of his work in the collection's preface, citing the *Spirit of the Times* as the "nucleus of a new order of literary talent," meriting "signal honour on the rising literature of America."[52] Robert Gunn has rightly seen this preface—and particularly its "oxymoronic equation" of both originality and emulation—as "key to understanding national regionality as a style of representation in which regionality is premised on cultural processes of national incorporation. That is to say, national regionality depends not on the specificity of the local but on the evacuation of specificity from it, on the cultural standardization of regional variety and local type."[53] My highlighting of the democratic play in select episodes of southwestern humor challenges both Porter's contemporary and Gunn's critical attempts to perform and to circumscribe this sort of nationalistic work. Yet, other material supports a different narrative regarding the readiness of these local southwestern misfits to participate in the larger national game.

Further evidence challenging the process of national incorporation can be found in three prefaces appended to these stories as they were transformed from local newspaper articles into collected editions with a larger regional and national audience. They differ markedly from the nation-scaled prefaces of editions of the *Davy Crockett's Almanack* and Porter's anthologies. In *Georgia Scenes*, the preface casts doubt on the contents' broader contemporary interest: "The following sketches were written rather in the hope that chance would bring them to light when time would give them an interest, than in the belief that they would afford any interest to the readers of the present day" (*GS*, xxiii). Published a decade later, *Simon Suggs*'s preface expresses still more doubt about the story's appeal to a national audience: "If what was at first designed, chiefly, to amuse a community unpretending in its tastes, shall amuse the Great Public, the writer will, of course, be gratified" (*SS*, 6). The preface to *Sut Lovingood* reveals little interest in bookish and authoritative norms, even having Sut parody the tradition (as if to take yet another jab at arbitrary authority). When informed that he must have a preface, Sut responds: "Well, ef I must, I must; fur I s'pose the perducktion cud no more show hitsef in publick wifout hit, than a coffin-maker cud wif out black clothes, an' yet what's the use ove either ove em?" (*Sut*, ix). On the one hand, these might follow the convention of self-effacing prefaces. On the other, they express doubts that local humor and vernacular literary forms could achieve a more extended heterogeneous audience, and determining readerly expectations regarding the convention of a preface remains an enduring challenge. Whatever subtleties of irony on the intentional side, these authors' prefaces explicitly suggest that they did not believe the local communities they represented were, in turn, representable according to national norms. Or so some readers might have it.

As one way to disentangle this conundrum, take two instances of the culture of reprinting that dominated the pre–Civil War publishing scene.[54] On 11 and 18 April 1845, the (Concord) *New Hampshire Patriot* printed under the title of "Simon Suggs, the Shifty Man" two succeeding episodes, the ones involving Simon's emancipation from his father. In the 18 April edition, an editorial comment regarding "the following good 'un'" reminds readers that this is the second of two installments, and then offers a quick summary of the first episode: "It will be recollected that Simon, then a boy, was caught by his father—'a hard shell Baptist preacher,' in the act of playing 'old sledge' with a negro boy named Bill, for which the old man, with a handful of hickory sticks, threatened to take the bark of both of them, and marched them both off to 'the Mulberry,' the scene of all formal punishment."[55] As we have seen, this episode depicts Simon gaming his way out of trouble while Bill suffers a cruel beating. What attracted a nonmetropolitan New Hampshire reading public to such a tale? It does not seem, given the introductory frame, to intensify sectional difference, as the editors' designation of this "good 'un'" implies a sympathetic audience. The decision to print the second of these two episodes one week after the first assumes an interested readership and a taste for such sketches. A general curiosity for localized flavor in somewhat exotic settings might explain the interest. On the other hand, what might appeal to another local audience is the story's attention to the way power is negotiated outside the national apparatus, what I have characterized as varieties of democratic play.

If this cross-sectional camaraderie is understandable in the somewhat milder 1840s, then a later example proves even more intriguing. On 8 June 1861, another transregional reprinting occurred when the *Los Angeles Star* published an excerpt from a full story that had appeared months earlier in the *Nashville Union and American*.[56] Buried in the middle of the fourth page, the passage bears the title "Photograph of Lincoln—Read and Laugh, laugh and read—read it again and read it deeper" along with the signature "Sut Lovegood." Excerpted from a three-part story describing how Sut assisted Abraham Lincoln on his journey to Washington, D.C., for his inauguration, the passage features Sut's physical description of Lincoln:

> His mouf, His paw, and his footzes am the principil feeters, and his striking pint is the way them air legs ov hisn gets inter his body.... Ov all the darned skeery looking ole casses for a president ever I seed[,] he am decidedly the durndest.... I knocked a bullfrog once and druv a nail through his lips inter a post, tied 2 rocks to his hine toes and stuck a darnin needle inter his tail to let out the misture, and lef him thar tu dry. I seed him 2 weeks arterwurds, an when I seed ole Abe I thot hit were an orful retribution come unto me, and that hit were the same frog, only stretched a little longer.[57]

While unflattering portraits of Lincoln were common in the days surrounding his inauguration, in publications stretching across the nation, the *Los Angeles Star*'s decision to reprint Sut Lovegood's description—with his nearly impenetrable dialect and without the rest of the tale—seems odd. The reprint could simply reflect sympathy with a Confederate perspective. But the sketch's bestial transformation of the national patriarch might also speak to a broad, locally based desire to undermine the consolidation of national authority over the local and to create a space of democratic play in which individuals take part not simply in making decisions but also in determining the rules and the language by which those decisions are made.

Although it is difficult to reconstruct motives from the distant past, the two reprints offer alternative frameworks for understanding nineteenth-century scales of affiliation, and for thinking about the national in relation to the local at a time when such a discussion would certainly have redacted another set of scales—the controversy of national versus state sovereignty. As Lloyd Pratt has suggested, traditional assessments of the local as something irretrievably absorbed by national progress warrants revisiting.[58] Approaching these sketches from a local point of view and "reading democratically" offer new possibilities for understanding the negotiation of scales of affiliation and affection.[59] These reprints disclose little, if any, evidence of state, regional, or sectional identification; rather, they show cross-regional identifications between localities that do not readily fold into larger scales of region, nation, or section. In these instances, the idea of an imagined community of any extended dimension seems less likely than an interest in local autonomy and empowered participation in democratic life. If the Jacksonian era marked the expansion of more egalitarian democracy and rhetoric of popular sovereignty (for white, native-born males), it would seem that the readers of the Concord and Los Angeles newspapers found something in common with humorous tales that playfully deviated from national norms.

ULTIMATELY, THE PRODUCTION AND DISTRIBUTION of southwestern humor and its depictions of alternative forms of democratic living contest the often-undemocratic work of nationalizing imperatives. In the portrayal of an episode involving an Indian uprising, the circulating text of *Simon Suggs* details a group of people engaging in their present moment and negotiating the conflicts of Indian removal in terms of democratic play rather than terms determined by the constitutionally managed nation. Similar moments occur in *Georgia Scenes* and *Sut Lovingood*, in spite of the former's desire for nationally managed democracy and the latter's failure to fully realize functional alternatives. In each of these fictions, we see the persistence of locally determined democratic play.

Given their origins in the southern backcountry that has long served as the internal other for the nation (as Greeson has shown), along with their aesthetic messiness and formal unruliness, there seems little chance that such stories would establish new norms for political action. And yet, much of what they offer yields greater pleasure than the doom and gloom of the Philadelphia stories. Moreover, when they are juxtaposed to literary misfits of the Old Northwest—the region that saw itself as synonymous with the nation—we get an even more profound look at the ways that certain types saw national homogenization as a worrisome compromise with democratic ideals. Whereas the southern humorists playfully dramatized alternative democracies through their garrulous misfits, the authors of the Old Northwestern settlement narratives revealed them in more unexpected ways.

CHAPTER THREE

Northwestern Settlements, Popular Sovereignty, and Neighborly Democracy

Early in Caroline Kirkland's thinly veiled autobiographical narrative of settlement, *A New Home, Who'll Follow?* (1839), her pseudonymous narrator Mary Clavers complains of the greatest of challenges in carving out a new life in her newly settled rural Michigan village. Complaining at first of the "real vexations of an attempt to build on any but the smallest scale in a new country," she confesses the temptation to think "that every body is in league against you and your plans." But when she somehow "by extra personal exertion" eventually overcomes "some prodigious obstacle," individual satisfaction is compromised because she finds herself "in complete solitude, every soul having gone off to election or town meeting." She continues, "No matter at what distance these important affairs are transacted, so fair an excuse for a *ploy* can never pass unimproved; and the virtuous indignation which is called forth by any attempt at dissuading one of the sovereigns from exercising 'the noblest privilege of a freeman,' to forward your business and his own, is most amusingly provoking." To further illustrate her point, she details a time when she confronted a Mrs. Fenwick, whose family was "suffering from want of ordinary comforts." When she asks the young wife if she laments the sacrifices she must make for her husband to spend two days at an election, Mrs. Fenwick responds, "Yes, to be sure; but ought not a man to do his duty to his country?" Clavers condescendingly concludes, "This was unanswerable, of course. I hope it consoled poor Mrs. Fenwick, whose tattered gown would have been handsomely renewed by those two days' wages."[1]

In this early passage, readers encounter conflicts central to the narrative of a transplanted genteel woman adapting to village building in rural Michigan. It aptly demonstrates conflicting views of top priorities in this high-water era of participation in both politics and a developing market economy. For an otherwise genteel narrator who has often complained of boorish behavior and myopic acquisitiveness, praise—or at least, appreciation—might have been the likely response when encountering someone who has temporarily halted the low business of capital gains in order to participate in the high-minded responsibilities of elections and town meetings. In defense of the Fenwicks, one might appreciate the enthusiasm of someone bearing newly enhanced voting rights; Michigan was the most recently minted state in the Union, gaining admission in January 1837 and thus giving its residents a new form of empowerment and representation on an enlarged (national) stage. Instead, the passage reeks of elitist condescension about common folks and their wrongheaded privileging of shared political action instead of individual self-improvement. To the representative of the elite, democratic participation and self-development are not mutual but rather incompatible. Class distinctions stand front and center, with the narrator admonishing impoverished types for poor choices. And yet the quoted vernacular expressions—"the noblest privilege of a freeman" and "ought not a man to do his duty to his country?"— exhibit a clear grasp of the rights and responsibilities of US democratic citizenship. While Clavers suggests here that it is wiser to work and improve one's economic standing than to vote, popular opinion suggests otherwise.

Wrapped up in a much different tone and style, Clavers's opinions nevertheless demonstrate a frustration with her neighbors that bears resemblances to what we have seen in southwestern humor. To some this might be surprising, for the cultural reputation of the Northwest was far different from what we have seen to this point. Unlike inhabitants in the rural Southwest as well as urbanizing Philadelphia, Jacksonian-era citizens of the rapidly transforming Northwest were hardly presumed to be unfit for democracy. Instead, northwesterners garnered a reputation very much in line with what the 1780s Continental Congress had envisioned when organizing the Northwest Territory: they were seen as agents of private enterprise developing allegedly virgin land, sharing commercial ties with Atlantic and Mississippi Valley states, and forming publicly interested collectives built on liberal—that is, individualistic, contract-oriented—principles.[2] The rise to prominence of politicians like William Henry Harrison, Stephen Douglas, and Abraham Lincoln marked a new age of northwesterners' influence on the national stage.[3] Northwesterners proclaimed authentic connections to Revolutionary founders and embraced what Daniel Feller has dubbed the "Jacksonian Promise" of nationalization in the 1830s.[4] The frontier democracy emerging from this region—which decades later was rendered sacred in the writings of Frederick Jackson Turner—worked in concert with market capitalism to develop a regional identity that was virtually synonymous with the US nation.[5]

And yet, as the conflict captured in Kirkland's narrative demonstrates, parts of the Old Northwest share numerous misfit traits with the locales of the first two chapters, many of which involve the question of who is represented and empowered as democratic participants. The nation's expansion into the Old Northwest was hardly a story of natural, peaceful, commercially driven progress, but rather a harsh, piecemeal pursuit of imperial mastery, evidenced not only in national policies but also in the will of many people and their local practices.[6] As national policy, the Northwest Ordinance of 1787 lasted longer and held more constitutional authority than any other legislation from the otherwise weak federal government under the Articles of Confederation, providing guidance for territory and state making in the Northwest for nearly fifty years. But it was severely weakened as a governmental directive in the mid-1830s with Michigan's conditional statehood. Shortly after Wisconsin, the fifth and final state created from the Northwest Territory, was admitted in 1848—the same year that the United States acquired the western territories of the Mexico cession and the "Northwest" became the "Middle West"—state making had moved on from the designs of the Northwest Ordinance to principles under the guise of "popular sovereignty."[7]

The rhetorical shift from national oversight to popular sovereignty holds crucial importance for working through varieties of democratic thinking in US cultural history. In James Kloppenberg's taxonomy, popular sovereignty—the conviction that "the will of the people is the sole source of legitimate authority"—has always been foremost among the three key contested principles of democracy (the other two being autonomy and equality).[8] According to Edmund Morgan, *popular sovereignty* was originally a term employed to describe a tactic used by one group of empowered people (British parliamentarians) against another empowered figure (the monarch). While many everyday people in the early United States might have assumed that popular sovereignty meant the people had the power, the framers of the Constitution, Morgan asserts, wisely tamed such democratic impulses by empowering only their representatives.[9] Decades later, in the late 1840s and 1850s, popular sovereignty became the calling card of Northern Democrats looking to build national unity amidst the growing crisis of slavery's expansion west. Although historical accounts of popular sovereignty tend to focus on either the early national era or the last two decades before the Civil War, popular sovereignty had long been a contentious issue, particularly in states making up the Northwest.[10] Over more than a half century of settlement, the people of the Northwest—or at least the vocal few allegedly speaking in the name of the many—repeatedly insisted that migrants bore self-evident rights to self-government.[11] Mrs. Fenwick certainly thought her husband did, as she offers one sort of thinking on popular sovereignty—that their wills are the source of legitimate authority and could only be expressed by committing time and energy to democratic participation. Offering a different take, Mary Clavers criticizes those who would prioritize exercises of popular sovereignty when it compromised their standard of living. Such disparate demonstrations of thinking on the meanings of popular sovereignty illustrate what a contentious issue it was. And yet, few issues are more crucial for people seeking the real experience of living democratically.

Much as Turner did in his historical writings, many have assumed that the Northwest was homogeneous, that it championed familiar, liberal democratic values, and that *popular sovereignty* could serve as a catch-all term for the most prominent claims made by and on behalf of northwesterners and their political interests. Misfit texts from the Old Northwest, however, offer a provocative index of more contested takes on popular sovereignty and democratic practices. These texts demonstrate that unlike the disenfranchised urban dwellers of Philadelphia or the (un)common folk of the Southwest, many northwesterners saw themselves as very much fitting within the national schema. The texts likewise demonstrate that many were being treated as if their democratic inclinations did not really matter. To be sure, many literary works emerging from the region endeavored to create a version of democratic experience that looked much like that of East Coast precedents. And yet, diverging texts were published and garnered significant readerships, thus contributing to the democratic heterodoxy of the era. In the case of *A New Home*, Clavers's initial criticisms are fueled by the principles of self-oriented liberalism and its version of popular sovereignty determined by a national scale of reference. In time, though, Clavers changes, coming to see alternative democratic values beyond the liberal order and finishing in a very different place than where she began. She was not alone.

The heterogeneity of northwestern literature has largely been missed because, compared to other regions, there have been relatively few assessments of the early Northwest in terms of its literary culture either alone or as a constituent part of larger US literary histories before the Civil War.[12] To address this paucity of criticism and to mine some of its literary misfits for their alternative democratic theories, this chapter focuses first on the national stories of the Northwest through reassessments of its foundational document, the Northwest Ordinance, and the ways that representative literary texts—Cincinnati transplant Harriet Beecher's first published story, "A New England Sketch," specifically—contributed to the crafting of what later scholars have dubbed "democratic space" and its facade of popular sovereignty. Such democratic space featured a form of popular sovereignty that depended on a conventionally liberal script emphasizing the disciplinary work of self-control and transplanting communal institutions like schools and churches to guide that process. Although much of the region embraced these cultural principles and institutions that contemporaries characterized as the Universal Yankee Nation, we find misfits at play in the story of statehood in Michigan and its frustrated ventures in exercising local popular sovereignty. Key literary evidence appears in the evolving perspectives found in Kirkland's *A New Home, Who'll Follow?* Kirkland's early impressions, as already noted, match those of Stowe and constitutional framers who privileged self-improvement and property development. In time, though, her narrator moves outside her sequestered self-possession and class-based judgments into deeper engagement with the vernacular aesthetics of her community and the articulation of values that I call "neighborly democracy." As Nancy Rosenblum has pointed out, "neighboring" depends on an expansive and inescapable sense of spontaneous reciprocity, often falls well outside the procedural maneuvers of law and order and public policy, and thus becomes a key contributor to what she calls the "democracy of everyday life."[13] Unlike the version of popular sovereignty that took place in procedural debates in statehouses and in the US Congress—the type that made Michigan's push for statehood especially frustrating for those operating outside these venues—the neighborly democracy projected in *A New Home* refigures local political dynamics in a mutual and collective spirit that undergirds the shared interests of an initially stratified and disengaged population.

Over the next two decades, the Northwest would become the Midwest, and a new regional identity was solidified. In the words of the historians Andrew Cayton and Susan Gray, "By the 1850s, middle-class Midwesterners had flattened the complicated and contested history of the Great Lakes and Ohio Valley regions into a linear narrative of unimpeded progress."[14] With this development in mind, I turn to the work of another northwestern author, Metta Fuller Victor (1831–1885). Unlike the eastern native Kirkland, Victor had spent much of her younger years in the Northwest before moving to New York City and becoming an early contributor to the Beadle Dime Novels series in 1860. Victor drew on frontier Michigan experience for her first two dime novels, *Alice Wilde* and *The Backwoods Bride*, both published in 1860. Appearing within months of one another, these novels engage the two primary traditions of the region—*Alice Wilde* sharing political sympathies with Beecher's story and *The Backwoods Bride* following in the footsteps of Kirkland's *A New Home*. Juxtaposing these two novels not only demonstrates a lack of homogeneous politics in the earliest days of the developing dime novel tradition, but also complicates the flattened history of the Old Northwest and the varieties of democratic theories and practices on display there. To that end, I highlight the vernacular aesthetics in *The Backwoods Bride* and the ways it celebrates its own version of neighborly democracy.

Harriet Beecher, the Universal Yankee Nation, and Liberal Democratic Space

Harriet Beecher's first story, "A New England Sketch" (retitled "Uncle Lot" in later collections) was published after it won a literary prize contest put on by the Cincinnati-based *Western Monthly Magazine* in 1834.[15] The story makes the case for its setting in the first paragraph. Instead of reusing traditional but overdetermined European sites like Italy, Greece, France, or England, the narrator claims that New England is a "land of bright fires and strong hearts; the land of *deeds*, and not of words; the land of fruits, and not of flowers; the land often spoken against, yet always respected."[16] In compact form, the narrative right away establishes something Kathleen Neils Conzen has dubbed "regionality," identifying common traits of a nonjurisdictional place like a municipality or a nation-state with common and distinctive elements of identity.[17] Extending this trope, the narrative establishes the local village of Newbury, Connecticut, as highly insular, "for it was one of those out the way places where nobody ever came unless they came on purpose," and filled with residents "who make it a point to be born, bred, married, die, and be buried all in the selfsame spot." Newbury stands as a classic New England town, anchored by its institutions and conventions: "As to manners, morals, arts, and sciences, the people in Newbury . . . always stopped all work the minute the sun was down on Saturday night, always went to meeting on Sunday, had a schoolhouse with all the ordinary inconveniences, were in neighborly charity with each other, read their bibles, feared their God, and were content with such things as they had—the best philosophy, after all" ("NES," 170). With such a clear notion of this locale and its native culture, the narrative projects Newbury as an idealized and yet circumscribed place.

Choosing New England as the setting for her sketch seemed a logical choice for the twenty-three-year-old first-time published author, who had moved with her family from Litchfield, Connecticut, to Cincinnati two years earlier. Harriet Beecher was one of the many New England natives who had migrated to the Northwest in the 1830s, a migration pattern so remarkable that the region prominently came to be known as the "Yankee West." Her family's relocation to the Northwest makes them a secure fit within the profile of what Susan Gray has described as the pre–Civil War development of the "universal Yankee nation." In Gray's argument, transplants to the Old Northwest saw themselves—and were likewise seen—as "cultural imperialists" who were "were imposing New England values and institutions as the template of all American culture."[18] As a story set in New England and published in a western literary magazine, Beecher's first story very much performs this type of cultural imperializing work, undergirding the facade of popular sovereignty in line with national interests rather than demonstrating local people empowered collectively and democratically.

The primary way by which "A New England Sketch" accomplishes this feat appears in the ways that the sketch's outsider hero, James Benton, assimilates into this local community. Initial descriptions of James identify him as "one of those whole-hearted, energetic yankees" who "possessed a great share of that characteristic national trait . . . which signifies the ability to do everything without trying, and to know every thing without learning, and to make more use of one's ignorance than other people do with their knowledge." The narrative acknowledges that this "quality in James, . . . though found in the New England character, perhaps as often as any where else, is not ordinarily regarded as one of its distinguishing traits" ("NES," 170–71). Beecher's descriptions of different regional types newly joined together resembles those in James Lanman's *History of Michigan* (1839), which casts northwestern settlement as predominated by New Englanders and New Yorkers who were going through "a process of amalgamation. The sober, careful, and straightforward perseverance of the New England States is so mixed with the more daring entries of New-York, as to give vast impulse to the character of the people."[19] Lanman's characterization thus serves as a helpful gloss to the opening of Beecher's tale: James seems very much the New Yorker, and the local community in Newbury the New Englanders. In the story that follows, the New England side embraces James while also contorting him into a vision of itself.

The plot of the story—which achieves the oft desired aesthetic criteria of orderliness and unity—revolves around James establishing himself as the schoolmaster and a highly popular figure in town, developing an interest in the young Grace Griswold, encountering the thorny disposition of her father Tim, and discipling at the feet of her brother George, a minister whose sacrificial, pietistic guidance eventually leads to the happy wedding of all types into a prosperous community. Uncle Tim (also known as the eponymous Uncle Lot of later published versions) is a figure of contrasts, "a chesnut burr, abounding with briers without and with substantial goodness within" ("NES," 173). Always ready to do the right thing while also being endlessly recalcitrant and difficult, Uncle Tim is the ultimate individualist, expressed most clearly in his refusal to follow the town in its praise of James and instead "stoutly gainsaying every thing that was said in his favor" ("NES," 176). James slowly starts to win Uncle Tim over, not through manipulation but through earnest good-naturedness. At the same time, George preaches beautiful sermons and takes the well-intentioned James under his wing, all while he is slowly dying. With George's death and James's decision to go to college to become a minister, Tim finally reforms. The story closes, importantly, outside the isolated town of Newbury, with Tim visiting the now-married Grace and James, who has become a highly esteemed minister in his new town. The story's conclusion has thus been read as one of national prophesy, in the words of Marjorie Pryse; Beecher's "sketch records James's efforts at empathic relationship with the old man, in the process becoming a minister, marrying [Tim's] daughter, and becoming, in effect, both Uncle [Tim's] adopted son and Stowe's new American hero."[20]

Pryse's assessment that Beecher's story expands from describing an undistinguished provincial town to depicting a full-blown national hero is consistent with the ways that Yankee-ness came to fit so well with the story of US nationalism. It makes sense that Beecher would highlight the significance of schooling, whether in reference to James's occupation as schoolmaster or George and James's ecclesiastical training at college. The church's central role in town life and in individual conversation also stands out. While procedural politics are largely absent from the narrative, a clear sense of local self-determination prevails (or at least there is no state presence that might restrict it). Beecher thus highlights the three elements of Yankee values that Gray describes as the "triumvirate of church, school, and township government." These institutions served as anchors crucial for western migrants and settlements and explain why western Yankees perceived no clear threat from the unsettling elements of both the market and the relocations.[21] Writing for the *Western Monthly Messenger*, Beecher infuses these institutional anchors into her story. In doing so, she assured both the transplants in the Northwest and eastern readers that Ohio would be readily settled.

In this way, "A New England Sketch" was just the type of story that the Founders would have valued to support their policies to guide national growth and expansion in the trans-Appalachian West.[22] The Continental Congress had moved quickly in trial-and-error fashion to establish legal protocol for a region that was rapidly growing in population without clear oversight. Thomas Jefferson receives much of the credit for his role in this legislation, as he served on the committee in 1784 that proposed standards for both autonomous popular sovereignty within new territories and a corresponding system of land distribution, with uniformly laid-out grids that ignored topographical boundaries, to be filled with self-governing peoples in a progressively developing republic.[23] Among its many influences in US cultural history, Jefferson's plan has been taken up as precedent-setting in American literary historiography. Philip Fisher has noted how Jefferson's vision laid the groundwork for the literary invocation of "democratic space," due to its equality and logic of representativeness in sampling.[24] Hsuan Hsu has expanded on Fisher's assessment by noting that Jefferson's plans provided "a blueprint for democracy and a mechanism for colonial expansion, ... an abstract grid that places political, social, and terrestrial differences under erasure."[25] Well-known literary texts by such luminaries as Charles Brockden Brown, Herman Melville, and Walt Whitman have been shown to draw from a similar logic.[26] As noted above, Stowe's "A New England Sketch" likewise participates in this practice of eliding territorial difference and merging sampled national types while upholding formal conventions. Whether Newbury, Connecticut, or Cincinnati, Ohio, the places of New England and the Yankee West could be virtually the same, from a sociopolitical perspective—anchored by institutions and commerce and presumably democratic.

Stowe's story demonstrates the liberal sampling of "democratic space" made possible by Jefferson's plan. Moreover, it evidences the type of erasure that Hsu identified with the development of democratic space, particularly when it came to compromising the chances of three issues of popular sovereignty of a more neighborly design. First, Jefferson's original plan—like his draft of the Declaration of Independence—was revised by Congress before being codified—in this case, in the 1784 ordinance. Three years later, in its establishment of rules for territorial governance and state admission, the Ordinance of 1787 did not include Jefferson's lines ensuring self-governing ideals. The ordinance was enacted while delegates were meeting in Philadelphia to revise the Articles of Confederation, and the changes to it demonstrate strategies like those in play at the Constitutional Convention: the federal government removing power from local inhabitants and establishing stronger authority over popular interests and democratic opportunities across vast space.[27] Second, whereas Jefferson was convinced that westerners would want political equality and a version of popular sovereignty that meant they retained political power instead of turning it over to some distant representative, few legislators concurred. In the words of the historian Peter Onuf, the majority of congressmen assumed that "local autonomy and frontier democracy were not vital issues to potential settlers.... Settlement and economic development would come first."[28] Westerners' repeated exercises demanding popular sovereignty and democratic empowerment—sentiments captured in Mrs. Fenwick's opinions that opened the chapter—would prove Congress incorrect.[29] Third, and most importantly, theories of democratic space assumed that its precepts survived well into the nineteenth century.[30] The history of the Old Northwest, conversely, suggests a more awkward development of even more liberal, procedural versions of democracy across the region (and much less of the more localized, radical variety). By the 1830s, nearly three decades of statehood for Ohio and half as much for Indiana (1817) and Illinois (1818) created significant power differentials in the region, which were nowhere more evident than in Michigan's push for statehood. Joining the Union roughly two generations after Ohio, Michigan became the first state to receive conditional admission, which came in 1837 as part of the resolution of a boundary dispute. There was little experience in Michigan—whether historically or in Kirkland's contemporary representation in *A New Home*—to suggest democratic space filled with people exercising their wills in a legitimate and authoritative fashion.

Historically, conditional entry was hardly imaginable when Michigan first achieved official territorial status in 1805. During the War of 1812, the lightly settled parts of Michigan Territory—Detroit especially—suffered extensive destruction during the inland battles. Following the war, Michigan Territory struggled to attract settlers, despite the settlement-friendly work of the governor—and later, Jackson's secretary of war, the Democratic nominee for president in 1848, and a proponent of vocal popular sovereignty in the late 1840s—Lewis Cass. The completion of the Erie Canal in 1825 somewhat boosted immigration, but it took another decade before Michigan reached the sufficient population stipulated by Congress (60,000 inhabitants) to apply for formal admission into the Union. Just after achieving statehood, the Panic of 1837 and the depression that ensued slowed development once again. This sluggish history has led Malcolm Rohrbough to label Michigan an "enduring frontier."[31]

The more immediate push for statehood presents an even more complicated history, and one in which local and popular democratic aspirations were subsumed in national politics. The territorial legislature first petitioned Congress to begin the admissions process in 1832. Congress largely ignored the petition in 1833 and then denied it three times over in 1834. The major sticking point involved competing claims regarding the boundary line between Michigan and Ohio, a dispute that came to be known as the Toledo War.[32] Ohio was a state and had political representatives with voting power in

Congress; Michigan Territory was not, and had none.[33] After two more years of delays, territorial governor Stevens Mason began the process again. A state constitutional convention convened in the summer of 1835 and asserted territorial claims, including a claim on the port town of Toledo. Just before the convention adjourned in August, President Jackson sought to appease potential electors in Ohio, Indiana, and Illinois by firing Mason. But Michiganians countered Jackson's maneuver by electing Mason to be their first governor on ratification of the state constitution, which went into effect on 1 November 1835. Michigan ran itself as a state for nearly seven months before Jackson finally signed legislation that would admit Michigan as a state—on the condition that they accepted Ohio's boundary claim. Seeking "expediency" over "right," Mason wanted a piece of the 1836 federal surplus—the last in US history—and payout only went to states, not territories.[34] But the delegates elected to the First Convention of Assent in Ann Arbor rejected Congress's terms. Undaunted, Mason called for a second convention, and on 14 December 1836, the Second Convention of Assent approved Congress's terms for statehood.

With all the maneuvering, the idea of local popular sovereignty—that is, the idea that the inhabitants of Michigan were the legitimate source of authority—had become something of a joke. Michiganians not only suffered the steamrolling by Ohio, Congress, and Andrew Jackson in the venues of federal governance, but they also saw firsthand how an elected delegation that had initially refused to accept conditional admission got outmaneuvered by the political machinations of its own state leaders. While a $70,000 federal surplus payout might have soothed the wounded pride of some of the state leaders, everyday folks seemed to take these democratic compromises much harder. A local paper in Detroit inserted several tongue-in-cheek complaints against the perceived slights of federal steamrolling and less-than-democratic solutions. An 11 January 1837 report on a "Great Democratic Festival" reported a satirical set of toasts: "1st. *Democracy—equal rights to all.* . . . 2d. *The President of the United States.* . . . 3d. *Michigan.* . . . 6th *The Congress of 1836*. History in detailing its acts will point unceasingly to the sacrifice of the rights of Michigan upon the altar of political expediency."[35] After the news of the state's official admission to the Union arrived two weeks later, the editorials hit harder. On 11 February, one writer proposed a toast wrapped up in terms rather autocratic: "Hail, then—thrice hail happy STATE!—Well may it be said of thee, through much tribulation, hast thou entered the Union! The people have obtained their long-wished-for object. . . . May the acts of thy rulers be marked with virtue and true patriotism."[36] One month later, the grudge seemed more deeply set in, when the paper reported on 4 March that "today Martin Van Buren is inaugurated President of the twenty six states. His address we will publish—if not too long. We would make some remarks upon the subject— but the fact is . . . Van will have his own way, in spite of us."[37] Hard feelings no doubt extended well past the first few months, especially when the Panic of 1837 hit Michigan especially hard.

However one might understand the meanings of popular sovereignty on the national scale and alternatives of a more localized variety, these newspaper comments demonstrate a perception of injustice over the rejection of the popular will. One could, if one were to follow the moral of Stowe's story, take solace in the institutional anchors of the Universal Yankee Nation and trust that local self-governance would take care of itself in a healthy American polity. One could, like Mary Clavers rebuking the Fenwicks for privileging participation in an election over their family's financial matters, be satisfied with everyday folks being told to focus their attention on their own matters and develop property and community. But Clavers's story is part of a much more complex tale. Neither historians nor literary critics have read *A New Home* as being embedded in this complex history in which local popular sovereignty was repeatedly curtailed by national politics as well as individuated self-interest.[38] Unlike Stowe's short story, the narrative does not place trust in institutions and their values, and it reflects the faults of popular sovereignty in name but not in practice. In the process, *A New Home* projects a different sort of egalitarian project, built on the notions of neighborly democracy in the everyday.

Neighborly Democracy in *A New Home*

In the concluding chapter, Kirkland's narrator Mary Clavers remarks, "The growth of our little secluded village has been so gradual, its prosperity so moderate, and its attempts so unambitious, that during the whole three years which have flown since it knew 'the magic of a name,' not a single event has occurred which would have been deemed worthy of record by anyone but a midge-fancier like myself" (*ANH*, 187). If "three years" stretches back from the publication date in 1839 to the prestatehood year of 1836, apparently no one—the politically minded Fenwicks included—raised recordworthy complaints like those found in the editorials of the *Detroit Evening Spectator and Literary Gazette* concerning Michigan's conditional admission to the Union. Regardless, as a tool of sarcasm, the understatement that kicks off the forty-seventh chapter of Kirkland's narrative has by this point become a familiar figurative device. And despite her claims to the contrary, there seemed to be numerous recordworthy events—so many that Kirkland penned two more books before she exhausted the literary material drawn from her years in rural Michigan.[39] Perhaps as a way to clarify, Clavers notes that other towns have claimed positions as county seat, as sites of universities, prisons, and sawmills, or as cautionary victims of wildcat banking. It seems, then, that this no-count village has actually found a different form of unidentified success, or at least some sense of stability. In what has been a central tension of the novel—the narrator's genteel sensibilities awkwardly confronted by rougher types—the final resolution is a "conclusion wherein nothing is concluded" (*ANH*, 189). The central conflicts no doubt remain, but the lack of succinct closure nevertheless strikes a note far different from the scolding one that flavored Clavers's early rebuke of the Fenwicks' misplaced priorities. In its stead has risen an alternative appreciation for the ongoing everyday experience, one that has emerged over the course of a narrative that impressively narrows the gap between nominal (and often fictive) democracy and a living, breathing experience—for better and for worse—of a more neighborly variety.

A year after Beecher published "New England Sketch," Caroline Kirkland and her husband left their New York home to become principals of the Female Seminary in Detroit in 1835. They spent two years amid the frontline debates of Michigan's controversial struggle for statehood while trying their hand at land development and village founding in Livingston County just after Michigan was officially admitted as a state.[40] The family that grew in number to six stayed until 1843 in Pinckney—the town on which Kirkland's fictional Montacute is based—before returning to New York City after six tough years that most construe as a speculative failure. While their temporary relocation to Michigan might have proven an economic bust, it effectively launched one of the most successful careers in publishing by a woman in the mid-nineteenth century.[41] Knowing her impressive career, and taking a first pass at *A New Home*, one might think *A New Home* an unlikely compatriot with other misfits tracked in this book. The narrative of this pseudonymous "midge-finder" betrays an extremely well-educated, well-read author, who seasons her chapters with savory quotations that demonstrate an impressive familiarity with literary traditions.[42] It cites its own part in a well-known transatlantic literary tradition with a prefatory nod to Mary Russell Mitford, whose *Our Village* offered a model mixing both realism and humor.[43] *A New Home* was both a popular success, going through twelve editions by 1855, and well received by contemporary critics; anonymous reviewers at the *North American Review* and *The Knickerbocker* as well as Edgar Allan Poe thought it very good.[44]

As part humorist, part realist, and part literary savant, though, Kirkland penned a first text that challenges easy categorization, a fact ably demonstrated by the various genres ascribed to the book: satire, travel literature, and early realism.[45] Just as wide ranging are the assessments of the book's politics, which tend to privilege its feminist lens documenting the drudgeries of life in the west or to center its attempt to bring frontier citizens into the civilizing rubrics of liberalism and market capitalism.[46] As Sandra Zagarell has put it, *A New Home* "shows that ... [Kirkland] felt culturally and socially isolated on the frontier, where her neighbors were of a different educational and class background[,] and satirize[s] a range of habits, conventions, and states of mind of both the West to which she had come and the East she thought of as the locus of her readers."[47] Zagarell's synthesis draws on conventional markers of class and culture, East versus West, and the metropole/periphery of the imperial US nation. When read in this nation-scaled framework, Kirkland's narrative occupies the other side of the coin of two western writers whom Kirkland explicitly criticizes in the early moments of her narrative: James Hall and Charles Fenno Hoffman. Her narrative no doubt undercuts the highly romanticized conceptions of Hall's *Letters from the West* (1828) and Hoffman's *A Winter in the Far West* (1835), which popularized foundational myths of rugged individualism, an environment of abundance, and, in time, manifest destiny (a national issue I take up in chapter 4).

For many reasons, however, Kirkland's first narrative defies this easy fit into a national framework. Much as Michigan's conditional statehood makes the state a misfit in the regional and national history of the Old Northwest, Kirkland's narrative of village building in Michigan defies liberal conventions of US literary and cultural history. More than just social critique engaging the tension between eastern sensibilities and western roughness, Kirkland's narrative explores a unique variety of democratic experience that operates outside conventional social stratification. As Dana Nelson has argued, Kirkland's first novel presents "a specifically political lesson about how the daily equalitarian practices [she] encounters in frontier Michigan enhance [her] sense of community and belonging, and could, by extension, revitalize the larger practice of (white) US democracy."[48] Although there might have been lessons for the nation-at-large, Kirkland's narrative moves away from her own sense of assimilative community enhancement vis-à-vis democratic space and instead more poignantly reveals how cultural imperialism from afar has prompted alienation and communal disengagement, primarily because her neighbors very much prioritize democratic participation and an ethos built on reciprocity before individual material success. Moreover, because of Kirkland's early expressions of class prejudice, her narrative tended to naturalize class distinctions in rather illiberal and undemocratic fashion, in much the same way that other novels of this era did, as Joe Shapiro has pointed out.[49] After some initial adjustments, though, Kirkland's midge-finding narrative of nonevents—and, importantly, the language in which she embeds her discoveries—focuses less on her belonging and instead presents a localization of popular sovereignty through the guise of neighborly democracy.

This outcome takes some time to develop. The first pages, as criticism regularly suggests, depict an eastern tenderfoot struggling to navigate the natural and social terrain in the west. The opening also illustrates the tension between the business of liberal democratic space and the recalcitrant stuff that resists absorption into a national domain. Embarking with a claim that friends have sought a description of "the peculiar features of western life," Clavers declares her intentions to provide a "detailed account of our experiences . . . in a form not very different from that which they were originally recorded for our private delectation." Such a "veracious history of actual occurrences, an unvarnished transcript of real characters" would mostly likely be deemed "'graphic,' by at least a fair proportion of journalists of the day." The opening lines mark an antagonistic dynamic, with readers, author, and journalists on one side and the objects of Kirkland's study occupying another. Yet it differs from Beecher's invocation of regionality, dropping the defensive maneuvers and dodging its assimilationist work. Moreover, in the next paragraph of the first chapter, the narrative notes, much in the same vein of the conclusion, that "there are but meagre materials for anything which might be called a story" and that her "desultory sketches" will merely be "a meandering recital of common-place occurrences" (*ANH*, 3). The cause for this aesthetic challenge is "the habits of society which allow the maid and her mistress to do the honours in complete equality" (*ANH*, 4). Because of the general absence of deference and social stratification—except for that which Clavers brings with her from the East—the materials on hand do not lend themselves to conventional aesthetic forms that typically do the fictive work of naturalizing liberal democratic space.

The early chapters nevertheless portray Mary Clavers striving for compliance by means of conventional norms. This begins when Clavers papers over the Kirklands' two-year process of acquiring land and recruiting buyers by stating rather flippantly that her "husband purchased two hundred acres of wild land . . . and drew with a piece of chalk on the bar-room table at Danforth's the plan for the village" (*ANH*, 4). Scholars have mostly followed suit.[50] Such maneuvers—Kirkland's and later scholars'—have erased the material tensions of conquest and cultivation of western lands (an unfortunate tendency of those who champion nation-based democratic space). Clavers goes on to express great angst over her negative experiences with her paper-soled shoes in Michigan mudholes, her frustrations with western emigrant literature like "Hoffman's tours or Captain Hall's 'graphic' delineations" failing to prepare her for Michigan travel, and her disturbing night at an inn hosted by an eastern emigrant turned drunken master. She highlights the distinctions between cultures and norms with quotation marks and parenthetical explanations, such as her description of when she "first 'penetrated the interior' (to use an indigenous phrase)" (*ANH*, 6). But she also notes the politeness of one "as wild and rough a specimen of humanity as one would wish to encounter in a strange and lonely road" (*ANH*, 6–7). Such instances demonstrate a tendency at this early stage to emphasize rather than mitigate differences of class, language, and appearance, even as she notes the occasional kindnesses that this social and physical terrain has to offer.

The tension between criticism and appreciation continues, though, with condescending remarks largely taking the upper hand. On settling in Montacute, Clavers has courteous exchanges with neighbors, only to offer harsher comments afterward. When a Mrs. Danforth concludes her family's history with a pithy summation of their experiences in Michigan—"We had most awful hard times at first.... But that's all over now; and we've got four times as much land as we ever should have owned in York-State"—Clavers subsequently takes this individual instance of "self-gratulation" and grafts it into a representative story of the neighbors whose arrival preceded hers: "The possession of a large number of acres is esteemed a great good, though it makes little difference in the owner's mode of living. Comforts do not seem to abound in proportion to landed increase,... [and] that *home*-feeling, which is so large an ingredient in happiness elsewhere, [is] almost a nonentity in Michigan" (*ANH*, 22). Scholars have zeroed in on this statement, using it to support claims of Clavers's reduction of everything to the terms of normalizing domesticity and a bourgeois consumerist culture.[51] Such comments indeed demonstrate a devotion to core domestic, genteel, and liberal sensibilities of the East. In these first weeks, she finds that she can get on independently, for there are "ways of *wearing round* which give [her] the opportunity of living very much after [her] own fashion, without offending, very seriously, any body's prejudices" (*ANH*, 52). But she hardly seems satisfied with following her own ways, for in the next breath she implies no willingness to live and let live but rather to use "the silent influence of example [for] daily effecting much towards reformation in many particulars" (*ANH*, 53). This silent example could definitely be an ameliorating social practice connected to practices associated with liberal democratic space. It could also be, as Lori Merish has argued, one of the best tools enabling the slow but steady work of incorporating uncivilized westerners into the liberal economic order.[52] But although she is superficially nice and presumably harmless, her moral self-righteousness sows seeds of divisiveness.

In short time a distinction appears between the Mary Clavers who starts the narrative and the retrospective author who walks readers through her learning experience. The very next scene offers the most important pivot in Clavers's transformation from conventional liberal-minded cultural imperialist to articulator of more egalitarian neighborly democracy. In a chapter roughly divided into three parts, she first discloses news of the Clavers being swindled by a land speculator, an economic fraud that Annette Kolodny finds consistent with Mary Clavers's complaints about the literary deceptions found in emigrant writings.[53] Shortly thereafter, she reacts negatively to a neighbor visiting her house, assuming equality, and smoking a pipe. The chapter ends with the arrival of the refined Mr. Rivers, who seeks advice from distinguished people like the Clavers to determine if his son and daughter-in-law can find genteel society in rural Michigan. With this distinguished visitor Clavers commits the very wrong that she has frequently condemned: she misrepresents the scene. Realizing that she is "so much pleased with the idea of having a neighbor, whose habits in some respects accord with my own," she admits that she is "scarcely impartial" in her report on the town's prospects, focusing on the natural abundance and "determin[ing] sagely, that a life in the woods is worse than no life at all" (*ANH*, 57–58). The misrepresentation appears especially damning given her report on the land fraud and her disgust at the deference-lacking, pipe-smoking neighbor. But now that she has participated in her own version of a swindle, she revises her once elevated standards.

With the arrival of the younger Anna Rivers, Clavers puts a new disposition into practice. Seeing Mrs. Rivers's arrogance as the key to her struggle to adjust to western life, Clavers tries a new tactic, taking a maternalistic responsibility and stating, "In this newly formed-world, the earlier settler has a feeling of hostess-ship toward the new comer" (*ANH*, 64). This generous position largely depends on shared class sensibilities, but the contrast proves a helpful component in Clavers's own discoveries. She has little success adjusting her new neighbor's high-minded condition. But she has reformed her own habits, particularly when it comes to eliminating actions that gave "the impression that I felt *above* my neighbours." She proceeds to reflect on this: "However we may justify certain exclusive habits in populous places, they are strikingly and confessedly ridiculous in the wilderness. What can be more absurd than a feeling of proud distinction, where a stray spark of fire, a sudden illness, or a day's contre-temps, may throw you entirely upon the kindness of your humblest neighbor?" (ANH, 65). The illustrations that follow demonstrate new investments in a neighborly interconnectedness and indebtedness—ones free from the type of institutional anchors that Beecher had highlighted in "A New England Sketch"—and a more equalitarian approach to daily interactions. The education in neighborly democracy is brewing thanks to a new appreciation for amiability.

While explicit democratic vocabulary has largely been absent to this point, amid her transition Clavers begins couching more and more commentary in political terms. Although she is frustrated with the always presumptuous demands to share, she does find some sense of appreciation. When a six-year-old neighbor informs Clavers that her mother would like to borrow her sifter and take some sugar and tea "'cause you've got plenty," Clavers casts her thoughts in more equivocal terms: "It is so straight-forward and honest, none of your hypocritical civility and servile gratitude! Your true republican, when he finds that you possess any thing which would contribute to his convenience, walks in with, 'Are you going to use your horses *to-day*?' if horses happen to be the thing he needs" (ANH, 68). Her characterization of the "hypocritical civility and servile gratitude" that presumably flavored her interactions in the East implies a newly discovered appreciation for a social system freed from the negative baggage of class. But her use of the term *true republican* is the highest form of flattery and arguably contributes to some criticisms about Kirkland's disaffection for Jacksonian democracy (also evidenced in the quoted passage that opens this chapter).[54] That said, Clavers's commentary opens new space for alternative democratic culture that occurs not in conventional institutional forms like church or school but rather more immediately in neighborly conversation and exchange.

In addition to growing more amenable to the ethic of sharing, Clavers demonstrates a waning reliance on silent, exemplary correction. In a charming yet digressive anecdote about Philo Doubleday and his fastidious, henpecking wife Polly, readers see a home with little public-private distinction. Many neighbors come to see Philo Doubleday about public projects like roads or schools because he seems interested and perhaps responsible, but these visitors drive Polly crazy by dirtying her floor. As she passive-aggressively berates her husband, Philo responds by writing witty poetry on the wall. "This is his favorite mode of vengeance," Clavers states, "'poetical justice' he calls it" (ANH, 68). The pleasurable barbs that follow between husband and wife end up revealing that they are an extremely generous couple. Polly shares with Philo in taking the lead in communal exchanges around the village: "She will watch night after night with the sick, perform the last sad offices for the dead, or take to her home the little ones whose mother is removed forever from her place at the fireside" (ANH, 70–71). In this combination of both noninstitutionalized and dialogic exchanges—not in silent influence—the balance between individual autonomy and ethical reciprocity grows.

Much as silent influence cannot readily fold recalcitrant western types into an East Coast liberal culture, the vernacular aesthetics cannot be folded into some abstract national narrative. Spoken words matter here, as the Doubleday scene demonstrates.[55] Clavers follows this scene with a detailed rationale for her distinctive narrative style. She acknowledges that her "rambling gossiping style" of storytelling, "this going back to pick up dropped stitches, is not the orthodox way of telling one's story." In what seems a mid-narrative change of direction, Clavers rejects such a return and forges on, stating, "I feel conscious that the truly feminine sin of talking 'about it and about it,' the unconquerable partiality for wandering wordiness would cleave to me still; so I proceed in despair of improvement" (ANH, 82). While my arguments have rested on the notion of Clavers's transformational learning process, these words demonstrate that the learning process is not linear. She rejects what she dubs the typical "feminine sin" of going back and starting over, and instead forges new ground, rejecting the presumption of progress. Her formal decisions to move through her story without any clear sense of progress would thus work in tandem with a newly discovered appreciation for staying in the present. She does not need to reform these people according to a nationally ordained telos that Sacvan Bercovitch has identified as the central tenet of US national culture.[56] Instead, in her various descriptions, she depends on "periphrasis," or circumlocutionary speech, in order to present these alternative types (ANH, 115). Near the book's conclusion, she again acknowledges, "I believe I set out, a great many pages ago, to tell of the interesting changes, the progressive improvements in this model of a village of ours.... But I think I have discovered that the bent of my genius is altogether toward digression." She laments her inability to produce a coherent "History" and settles instead for "a collection of scattered materials of the use of the future compiler of Montacutian annals" (ANH, 177). Her self-admitted tendencies toward desultory sketches, periphrasis, digression—her failure to write a totalizing history like the one George Bancroft was making famous—formally undergird the alternative neighborly democracy that has been emerging with her new appreciation for these western ways.

To be sure, some of the conventional temporal dynamics of national progress and liberal reform remain throughout the narrative. After a lynch mob nearly hangs a troublesome ventriloquist, Clavers proudly asserts that "the most mobbish of our neighbors have flitted westward, seeking more congenial association" (*ANH*, 119). The passage expresses an appreciation that those with extralegal vigilante proclivities are moving further west. Also worth noting is that this singular instance of mob action in the entire narrative coincidentally comes with the presence of a ventriloquist, a figure who traffics in misrepresentation. While some might construe this as a failure to appreciate a joke or a performance, it also fits with the general condemnation of those like the emigrant guidebook writers and the wildcat bankers who compromise the potential reciprocity of neighborliness in Montacute. Mob action might be an affront to the law-and-order principles of liberal politics, but it can also be the clearest exercise of communal action that seeks to protect democratically the collective well-being.

The collective well-being rather than the ascendance of bourgeois norms becomes the yardstick by which Clavers comes to measure all varieties of politics in the Northwest. Complaints take special aim at types who fail to support the ethic of sharing in everyday experiences in favor of the individualistic freedom of the West. She criticizes a family called the Newlands, who "deny... themselves and their families every thing beyond the absolute necessity" and "instead of increasing their means by these penurious habits, they grow poorer every day" (*ANH*, 107). These are a burden on the community. Like her assessment of those with mobbing instincts, Clavers is thankful that "we have few such neighbours left," for "the wide west is rapidly drafting off those whom we shall regret as little as the Newlands" (*ANH*, 111). Such a reading could suggest a return of her old eastern gentility. While this lower-class type does offend her, she is also unimpressed with those on the other end of the spectrum of individualistic freedom. After sharing that a few settlers— English immigrants, specifically—keep away from the ethic of reciprocity and collective living free from deference and class stratification, Clavers contravenes conventional readings of the West both as a space of freedom and as one tethered together by shared commercial interests. The constraints here, as it turns out, are purely political: "The better classes of English settlers seem to have left their own country with high-wrought notions of the unbounded freedom to be enjoyed in this; and it is with feelings of angry surprise that they learn... that this very universal freedom abridges their own liberty to do as they please[,] ... that the absolute democracy which prevails in country places, imposes as heavy restraints upon one's free-will" (*ANH*, 139–40).

In this light, Michigan falls well short of providing a place for freedom of opportunity and self-possession. Although they are freed from the constraints of class stratification, the responsibilities in the everyday maneuverings, which Clavers dubs "absolute democracy," anger English migrants who expected "unbounded freedom." Shortly after this moment, Clavers provides a multichapter digression about the Hastings, a couple caught up in the romance of unbounded freedom in the pastoral setting. While she sympathizes with this genteel couple, she does not celebrate their isolation.[57] Her loyalties have clearly shifted.

Meandering through desultory sketches, Clavers delivers a guarded yet newly born appreciation for the equalitarian spirit that carries itself in the quotidian aspects of life. In her representations of a community in which neighbors assist one another in raising houses, fight fires together, help one another navigate illness, and borrow from one another, she portrays the give-and-take of a neighborly democratic ethos. To be sure, she is unimpressed with the weakness of religious practice, and she is even more sarcastic about the establishment of the Female Beneficent Society, with its gossipmongering and backhanded politics. But newfound delights come in the everyday politics of shared living rather than domestic home development. In this light, Clavers's opening preface makes more sense. There, she declares that "an unimpeachable transcript of reality" could have been her "traveller's privilege." But she has chosen the enhancements that any author could employ. Her decision to feature "glosses, and colourings, and lights, if not shadows" results not from the prerogatives of authorship, but rather from her responsibilities as a neighbor, for she knows that to publicize unvarnished tales and "throw them in the teeth of one's every-day associates might diminish one's popularity rather inconveniently" (*ANH*, 1). There had been plenty of that with the frustrated attempts at popular sovereignty in the run-up to Michigan statehood. While Beecher's story worked to paper over such discord, Kirkland's late-1830s narrative appears amid the tumultuous years of conditional statehood and meets these conflicts head-on, delivering an enticing alternative democratic variety.

Metta Victor and Her Misfit Dime Novels

Michigan residents' experiences of popular disempowerment and the tendencies in Kirkland's village toward more neighborly democracy take on new resonance when considered in relation to the general narrative regarding the consolidation of what would become midwestern regional identity over the next two decades. As noted, with Michigan statehood, the formal powers of the Northwest Ordinance were virtually extinguished. But it did not lose its cultural influence. In Peter Onuf's words, "Apotheosis and negation alike contributed to the translation of the Ordinance into a 'higher law,' disconnected from the mundane political world."[58] Pointing to their economic success as living testimony to foundational principles, northwesterners frequently cited their successful marriage of private enterprise and free institutions—abstract principles drawn from the Northwest Ordinance and transplanted by the Universal Yankee Nation—as regionally distinctive yet truly American. As such, the ordinance continued to foster a national program of liberalism undergirded by the communal institutions and material networks of commercial activity. Outside this master narrative, a general tension between liberal democracy and its alternatives persisted, specifically in the case of a lesser-known northwestern-turned-eastern author, Metta Fuller Victor (1831–1885).

Whereas Kirkland moved from east to west and back east again, Victor's early years were much more peripatetic. She was born in Western Pennsylvania before a series of relocations: to Wooster, Ohio, as a child; to New York City in her late teen years; back west to Ypsilanti, Michigan; and then to Sandusky, Ohio, in her twenties. In Sandusky she married Orville Victor before moving in 1856 back to New York City, where she remained for the rest of her life. Both Victors would go to work for the Beadles. Metta Fuller Victor drew on her frontier Michigan experience for her first two contributions to the publisher's Dime Novel series: *Alice Wilde* and *The Backwoods Bride*, both in 1860. Of the first dozen dime novels published in that year, Victor's two romances stand out from the sensational and historical tales of Indian captivity and sea adventures. But these two novels, published a mere three months apart, present two very different varieties of democratic politics. *Alice Wilde* seems deeply invested in the national program of cultivating liberal democratic space through a combination of abstraction and reliance on institutional anchors in lieu of explicitly political activity. *The Backwoods Bride*, on the other hand, foregrounds questions of democratic politics in relation to issues of public opinion, majority rule, and property rights. Read together, these two dime novels reflect a tension similar to that which animates Kirkland's *A New Home*: the prescriptive national management of democratic space versus the more local, egalitarian process of more neighborly democracy.

Victor's early oeuvre as a whole demonstrates a variety of forms of political engagement. Although lesser known in the present, she published prolifically across five decades of the nineteenth century. Prior to the first two novels in the Beadle Dime Novels series, Victor wrote in many different genres and media and under several different pen names, starting at a very young age.[59] Her first story, "The Silver Lute," was published when she was thirteen, and her first book, *Last Days of Tul: A Romance of the Lost Cities of the Yucatan* (1847), appeared when she was fifteen. Following these, she penned a collection of poetry, two temperance novels, a collection of mystical and fantastic short stories, and *Mormon Wives: A Narrative of Facts Stranger than Fiction*. *Mormon Wives* is dripping with sentimental conventions of the day that condemn the social practices of the upstart religious minority, but its preface features substantial engagement with the Kansas-Nebraska Act, the issues related to Utah statehood, and the politics of what she unflatteringly dubs "squatter sovereignty."[60] As this brief bibliography suggests, Victor at times penned more belletristic texts that shared few explicit ideas on contemporary issues, and at other times demonstrated a significant interest in the politics and political philosophies of the day.

The appellation "dime novelist" might lead one to readily assume Victor's adherence to a rather formulaic variety of writing that projected a consistent and clear politics. Such cheap literature allegedly forged chauvinistic masculinity, flattened class politics in urban locales, and ordained US exceptionalism and imperial expansion. But recent critical assessments of dime novels from Michael Denning, Bill Brown, and Shelly Streeby have demonstrated that despite the critical leanings of early collectors and their framing of a tradition around what Denning characterized as "the pioneer spirit of America," dime novels were an exceedingly heterogeneous genre of writing.[61] As the description of her early books demonstrates, Victor likewise produced a heterogeneous body of work, much of which could arguably be labeled precisely in line with the broader assumptions about dime novels and their nationalizing cultural work. As Catherine Ross Nickerson has shown, Victor's "career as a writer of dime novels is a startling mixture of commercialism and reform politics; she was clearly a writer who knew how to work the literary marketplace, but she seems also to have been genuinely impassioned by the questions of temperance, slavery, and Mormon plural marriage."[62] One of her most famous postbellum dime novels, *The Dead Letter: An American Romance* (1866), engages national questions of reunion, largely through work that Nickerson describes as "hygienic and disciplinary" according "genteel ideas of rightness."[63] *The Dead Letter*, recognized as the first detective novel in US literary history, has cast a lengthy shadow in occasional studies of Victor as well as studies of the politics and scope of the Beadle series.

Returning to two of Victor's rarely considered novels that appeared as the Beadle series was first released does not just raise questions about Victor's fit within US literary history. It also promises an unexpected disclosure of different types of political thinking on display in a mass cultural form on the eve of a national election that would spur secession and civil war. As noted, the two novels offer two very different meditations on democracy. *Alice Wilde: The Raftman's Daughter* was the fourth Beadle Dime Novel, appearing on 1 August 1860. It locates itself in highly generic terms, in no specific time or place apart from somewhere in the Northwest, with most events occurring upriver from a generalized Center City at a time when a sawmill operator was thinking he might upgrade to steam technology. In contrast, *The Backwoods Bride: A Romance of Squatter Life*, published on 1 November 1860, anchors its locale to Michigan on the first page of the narrative; although it remains vague on the date, later clues suggest a time just after statehood, when one of the central characters is voted into Congress. Whereas *Alice Wilde* focuses on the natural purity of a young woman born in an untamed wilderness, *The Backwoods Bride* addresses rather emphatically the issues of squatters, majority opinion, and the limitations of law enforcement. In the former, readers encounter frequent laments over the absence of much-needed institutions that would help people progress to more enhanced exercises of disciplined self-control, but they also receive assurances that the recalcitrant landscape and population would no doubt succumb in due time under the dictates of liberal democratic space. In the latter, readers experience a different type of intractable Northwest and a different sort of popular conflict, largely wrapped up in questions of majority opinion and rule, rightful ownership of property, and a more agonistic form of neighborly democracy.

Alice Wilde features the eponymous Alice Wilde and her father, the raftsman David Wilde. These two live with their Black house servants, the comically loquacious Pallas and her husband Saturn, in some remote area upriver from the up-and-coming Center City. David Wilde is a successful timber cutter and sawmill operator, a key cog in the supply wheel for the growing city. Among the many men who work for David is Ben Perkins, who has a deep love for the teenage Alice. When David brings a business associate, Philip Moore, upriver on his raft to see the operations firsthand, David seems hardly aware of Philip's developing interest in his attractive daughter. But Ben Perkins sees, and he tries several different tactics to discourage the East Coast transplant Philip. In time, Philip suffers a beating, and everyone presumes it was Ben. During Philip's convalescence, there is a huge wildfire, and Philip proposes to Alice. Before they can marry, though, he must return to Center City; before he can return, winter comes and the river ices over. When the Wildes go to Center City after a worry-filled, isolated winter, they meet Philip's business partner and learn that he has returned east, presumably to marry an old love. Distraught, Alice asks her father to allow her to go to school, and David grants her wish. When Alice performs several months later in a talent show, Philip, newly returned, professes his undying love once again. Ben has lost his mind at this point and threatens to destroy their happiness. He kidnaps Alice on her wedding day, but a tornado intervenes and gives Alice time to escape, and eventually she gets back to Philip and her father after Ben is fatally wounded. The young couple live happily ever after with their father.

The thriller follows a tightly woven plot, folding its characters and storyline into a conventional national narrative of progress and assimilation. It demonstrates a successful eastern migrant, David Wilde, trying to build his prosperity in relative isolation and to keep his daughter perpetually in his care. The eastern gentleman, Philip, enters David's controlled environment and disrupts the Edenic scene, not by attracting the innocent young beauty—a development that would not really upset the otherwise oblivious David—but by setting off the uneducated Ben Perkins, spurring him into committing a series of crimes: attacking Phillip, stealing his mail, and eventually, kidnapping Alice. In the background of this love triangle, the cultural setting lies somewhere between Beecher's Danbury and Kirkland's Montacute. As the site of a rural business providing raw materials for the rapidly growing Center City, there is little evidence of village building in David Wilde's locale. More specifically, there are no institutions of church or school or local self-government present here. But that does not mean they are not highly desired. Early on, the Black house servant Pallas comments in dialect—a style that suggests tourism and performance rather than authentic voices—after receiving a new dress, "'Ef we only had a camp-meetin' to go to now,' she said, . . . 'It's four year, come next' mon', since we went to dat meetin' down de riber."[64] Later, the narrative describes Ben Perkins as a heathen without "education which would teach him self-control and the noble principle of self-government."[65] The rapidly growing Center City does boast a school, which Alice eventually attends. And the narrative contrasts life in Center City rather sharply with the crass materialism from the glimpses of scenes from the East, for which Phillip has departed. Altogether, *Alice Wilde* presents a conventional romance with the occasional sensational flourish, all with the trappings of taming the West. The cultural backdrop very much suggests a land ripe for democratic space, purified of eastern corruption and idyllically waiting for institutions to take their grip and ensure good liberal self-governance. It is "A New England Sketch" with a little more sensation, and a far cry from the neighborly democracy of Mary Clavers's Montacute.

The Backwoods Bride shares the same general storyline of an eastern gentleman falling for a young northwestern girl and some previously arrived locals trying to obstruct his plans, yet it integrates a much more explicitly politicized background with some very stark discord. Unlike the initial judgments of Kirkland's Mary Clavers and the animosity they generate, the class tensions in this novel are much higher. In the foreground, the dashing Harry Gardiner arrives at a camp meeting after having purchased land from the government. He faces considerable opposition from squatters, even though he offers to either buy them out or let them rent the land. The squatters raise considerable opposition, led by a decently educated eastern transplant named Enos Carter, a widower who arrived in Michigan with his sister Debby and daughter Susan a year earlier. Finding no compromise, Harry is challenged by the squatters multiple times over, first through the legal apparatus and later with lynch mobs. During this process, he and Susan fall in love. As Harry repeatedly tries to secure his land as well as his prospective bride, often through disguise and duplicity, the squatters continue to team up against him, and Susan frequently aids his narrow escapes. In time, though, Harry is kidnapped and presumed dead, and the Carter family moves on to become hosts of a rural inn. When they host some rough men who turn out to be counterfeiters, Susan learns that Harry is still alive, and she foils the counterfeiters' schemes. After one more kidnapping, this time of Susan, her father discovers a convalescing Harry, and together they hunt down and kill the gangsters. The reunited couple now enjoys a much more neighborly environment and witnesses three more marriages in this village, just before Harry is elected to Congress by the squatters and moves permanently with Susan to Washington City.

The complex and less carefully woven plot clearly holds much more sensationalism and subterfuge than *Alice Wilde*. Its specificity of setting (Michigan) and its explicit take on a variety of political issues demonstrate an even more profound engagement with questions like popular sovereignty on a local rather than a national scale. Pronounced questions about property rights, law enforcement, and majority rule recur throughout the narrative. From the moment Harry arrives in the middle of a three-day camp meeting, the question of legitimate claims to western lands fuels the dramatic tension. The narrative largely champions Harry's right by repeatedly praising his honor and his graciousness, but it also issues sympathetic apologies for the squatters' position. The third-person omniscient narration differs markedly from Kirkland's narrower perspective, offering justifications for the various claims that the different constituencies represent.

As matters grow more political, readers come to learn that the unnamed Michigan county has a clear justice system in place, with a jail and a court trial that seems to uphold law and order in the face of potential lynch-mob justice. Beyond those institutions, though, the narrative sees a more affective set of political relations that arise in response to the courage Harry Gardiner demonstrates in the face of "the wild cries, the shaking fists, and mustered oaths" of the crowd: "His bearing won the admiration of every one who had not some personal motive in disliking him, [for there] were landholders and rich men scattered through the county, who had had great trouble with the squatters, and these, of course, sympathized with him." But the sides are determined not just by the easily drawn lines of class; Harry also wins support from "the worst of men [who] always set a high value upon physical courage," which means that "Harry had also a large body of friends among the dregs of the collected crowd."[66] At this early stage, affinities of public opinion—a key index of popular sovereignty—do not follow obvious lines, but rather something more intimate, in the vein of neighborly esteem. When the jury tenders a verdict of not guilty, Harry is immediately seized by the lynch mob, only to be rescued by his newly won friends. Whereas the passive-aggressive neighborly conflict of *A New Home* is clearly absent from this conflict-ridden town, in *The Backwoods Bride* readers see more openly antagonistic conflict between neighbors.

As the property disputes between Harry and the squatters die down for a bit, the narrative presents a more egalitarian moment in a time of celebration, one that resembles the episode in "The Dance" of Longstreet's *Georgia Scenes*. With the scheduling of a ball to which all are invited, the narrative lavishes significant praise on the inclusive spirit of the "regular western break-down." Everyone is invited, reflecting the strong sense of community: "Every human being within twenty miles is a neighbor and a friend. Everybody borrows and lends—take care of each other in sickness, and help each other when hard-pressed" (*BB*, 45). While Harry Gardiner and the landowners might have other ideas about the neighborliness of this town, the depiction of the ball suggests a baseline condition built on mutuality. The interconnectedness on display contributes to the ethic of reciprocity that is crucial for the chances of neighborly democracy. Unfortunately for these prospects, the ball ends up providing cover for a disguised Harry to dance with Susan Carter, only to be discovered by rivals who make plans to try to lynch him again. Harry escapes a second time, thanks to Susan's intervention, and the good times of this neighborly exchange come to an end.

While many readers might presume that the squatters are in the wrong, the narrative sympathizes with them several times over. One source of frustration for the squatters is consistent with the issues of misrepresentation that had plagued the chances for neighborly democracy in Kirkland's *A New Home*. Harry endears himself to very few when he assumes his disguise to dance with Susan. An even greater complaint against misrepresentation appears in the much longer scene concerning the counterfeiters at the Carters' inn. When Susan alerts a sheriff in the next town to the presence of the counterfeiting gang, she helps him raise twenty-five men to form a posse and capture the gang. That counterfeiting stirs up such a commotion in this rural Michigan town seems fitting, given the ubiquity of counterfeiting around the country—and especially in the Northwest—in the 1830s and 1840s. As Stephen Mihm has noted, counterfeiting was a notoriously common practice prior to the Civil War. In no other venture did the nation's government exert less power over the various states and localities than in the regulation of counterfeit notes and coins. And yet, counterfeiting, Mihm contends, played a primary role in growing the national economy at exponential rates.[67] The irony in *The Backwoods Bride* is that counterfeiting stirs up a desire for law and order, and, one might assume, a desire for stronger national controls to foreclose such criminal acts of misrepresentation. Tellingly, though, when the sheriff explains to Susan that he might have a tough time imprisoning the gang, she presents a surprising prospect: "Give them the benefit of lynch-law at once" (*BB*, 92). Susan's recommendation proves unnecessary. When the posse successfully captures the majority of the men, who are tried, convicted, and serve out their time in the penitentiary, a "general feeling of joy pervaded all that part of the State, to think so many of the rascals who stole their property and flooded the county with counterfeit coin, had at length met their deserts" (*BB*, 93). Whereas the heroine had been an advocate of lynch-mob justice to settle a personal score, the people are largely grateful that the system is fair—and democratic—once again. The narrative offers no suggestion that this whole sordid affair reflects an old practice that is slowly going away in the name of progress or that some national oversight has made corrections. The satisfaction comes in local people bringing about their own collective justice.

When Harry and Susan are reunited and their conflict with the squatters is over thanks to the combined efforts against the counterfeiters, the narrative could seemingly conclude with a couple of weddings of some of the minor characters. Whether or not it was to add a few more pages to fit the dime novel's conventional length of 128 pages—another sign of vernacular aesthetics that antedated prescriptive formulae—the narrative stretches out one more chapter with an extended tale that suggests yet another exercise of neighborly democracy: the nomination of Harry to Congress. Backed by several quoted voices, the villagers "made up their minds to run [Harry] as an independent candidate, and to work with all their might and main for his election, irrespective of party or party interest." To this point, there has been no explicit mention of political partisanship in town, so the choice of running Harry as an independent is unexpected. The narrative, though, expresses a more measured reaction: "It was a curious instance of the unreliability of popular opinion—this almost religious enthusiasm of the masses in favor of the young man whom, one year before, they had threatened with the [icy] pond, the tar-barrel, and the rope" (*BB*, 124). And yet, the scene that follows suggests something even more curious. On the day of the election, Aunt Debby arrives at the polling place and offers a free dinner to everyone who votes for Harry, and the "double motive of a good man and a good dinner was too much for the wavering; and the regular candidates, seeing their own hopes burst... concluded to cast their own votes in favor of their rival" (*BB*, 125). Harry and Susan move to Washington, and "having once got into the stream of politics, could not get to shore again, and [have] been wafted on from honor to honor" (*BB*, 127). Although Harry had initially moved to the Northwest for the presumable freedom from obligations in the East, he is now stuck with the responsibilities of government.

Harry's election to Congress offers a curious ending to a novel that has been so deeply invested in questions of a more conflict-filled exercise of popular sovereignty according to the practices of neighborly democracy. Property rights, public opinions, and collective action have all taken center stage in this local space. Although the tension between property owners and squatters dominated the legal and extralegal issues in the early stages of the novel, by novel's end the antagonists find united cause against an even greater threat in the figure of the counterfeiters. Together, they employ their collective will to address the more egregious wrong and then sort out lesser clashes by more collegial means.

IN THESE NORTHWESTERN MISFITS, readers encounter a popular sovereignty that is exercised in ways quite different from in the national scene, where the concept was called on to determine the legal status of slavery in newly born states. Instead, the challenges of establishing the will of all the people as the legitimate source of authority seem paramount. Particular conflicts stand out, and not everyone gets their way, but the general population ultimately sorts out their collective remedy with a strengthened neighborly ethic of reciprocity. The remedy's source in *The Backwoods Bride* is quite different from that seen in "A New England Sketch" and *Alice Wilde*—narratives that tethered hopes for social good to Yankee institutions like schools and churches that would deliver progressive change. *A New Home* and *The Backwoods Bride* disrupt the orderly narratives of this prominent national discourse.

Of course, these misfits did not operate in isolation. As we will see in chapter 4, which addresses issues from the Far West, select California gold rush novels were at the same time disrupting the tidy version of an intertwined national discourse—manifest destiny. While I separate consideration of these two national discourses of popular sovereignty and manifest destiny in these chapters, each one reinforced the other. Their imbrication had significant consequences for the health and viability of the people who stood in the path of the nation's march toward progress. Although institutional reform and public safety might protect some, alternative democratic imaginings seemed to be the greatest need for all.

CHAPTER FOUR

Interbellum California, Manifest Destiny, and Contingent Democracy

When Richard Henry Dana Jr. spent several months in 1835 trolling up and down the Alta California coast on the merchant ship *Pilgrim*, he was not impressed with the culture he encountered. Nor did he find much of anything resembling the challenges and opportunities of neighborliness on display in the Northwest. Midway through listing a variety of grievances couched in his coming-of-age reminiscence *Two Year before the Mast* (1840), he posits a specific complaint against the political culture of the northernmost Mexican state, which seemed democratic in name only: "The government of the country is an arbitrary democracy; having no common law, and no judiciary. Their only laws are made and unmade at the caprice of the legislature, and are as variable as the legislature itself." His judgment likely arises from a heavy dose of racial prejudice, which frequently appears in his other comments about Alta Californians. Yet, in this assessment he cites a different reason for the nation's failure to convene an ideal democratic republic, one that presumes logistical problems rather than apathetic or untrained people. Mexican citizens "pass through the form of sending representatives to congress at Mexico," Dana writes, "but as it takes several months to go and return, and there is very little communication between the capital and this distant province, a member usually stays there, as permanent member, knowing very well that there will be revolutions at home before he can write and receive an answer."[1] Here Dana apparently rejects Madison's optimism about large democracies in Federalist 10 and recycles centuries-old skepticism of the chances of representative governments establishing order and control over peoples spread out over vast spaces. Although he is critical of the Mexican government, Dana's reflections presciently forecast challenges the US nation would face within the next decade.

Given his immediate experience of sitting day after day on a San Diego beach, waiting expectantly for a ship to take him back to his safe haven of Boston, and enduring a pronounced sense of isolation, Dana's reflections on the challenges of negotiating and establishing control over such a vast and isolated territory are understandable. When Dana first boarded the *Pilgrim* in the late summer of 1834, his immediate social circle in Cambridge was very much caught up in the hustle and bustle of nationalization (emblematized by the celebrations of the Revolutionary shoemaker George Robert Twelves Hewes, as discussed in chapter one). When he arrived in California, Dana gained firsthand knowledge of the difficulties with a transcontinental nation (Mexico) exercising jurisdictional control over the territorial spaces within its purview. Whereas the networks of railroads and canals as well as a developing print culture were beginning to create material linkages between different regions in parts of the eastern United States, peripheral California suffered for multiple decades without even a readily transferrable connection to a national center within a month's journey.[2] What was left was a disorderly social and political order, at least in Dana's estimation.

Because of the impracticability of a networked polity guided by a capital center, Mexican and US settlers along the California coast had long practiced forms of self-rule in Alta California. During the period of governance under the Estados Unidos Mexicanos (1824–35) and the República Centralista (1835–46), a system of alcalde governance had become common practice.[3] This version of localized law and order typically appeared to be more aristocratic and militaristic than democratic due to its convergence of judicial and executive powers in the hands of a single individual. During the interregnum years (1846–50), however, the alcalde system became less hierarchical, integrated more civilian control, and developed into a functional system of hybridized self-rule practiced by native Californios (landowning citizens of Spanish descent) and migrants from the eastern United States and Mexico. As the California historian Kevin Starr notes, early texts from this era—including Alfred Robinson's *Life in California Before the Conquest* and Walter Colton's *Three Years in California*, both published in 1850—romanticized this fusion of US and Mexican cultures, both social and political.[4] Traveling on behalf of Horace Greeley's *New York Tribune*, Bayard Taylor further contributed to this reputation of democratic self-rule, starting in the mining camps, working his way to the state constitutional convention held in the spring of 1849, and delivering his reports in the 1850 publication of *Eldorado*.[5] In these narratives, California's presumed transformation from isolated polity to well-oiled, state-run democratic machine marks one of the fastest and most impressive implementations of constitutional democracy in world history.

Reports of such extraordinary developments in this distant land were no doubt buttressed by—and further contributed to—the popular 1840s logic of manifest destiny. Manifest destiny was born in New York periodicals, employed by zealous politicians, and fostered by eastern print culture.[6] It provided the ideological justification for western expansion, a nation-building enterprise that millions of US inhabitants never saw firsthand. In its third appearance in print, the term *manifest destiny* added a new democratic tag to earlier iterations that had focused solely on the needs of growing populations to inhabit available space: "And that claim is by the right of our manifest destiny to overspread and to possess the whole of the continent which Providence has given us for the development of the great experiment of liberty and federated self-government entrusted to us."[7] This national habit, which applied to the governmental purchase and semicontrolled inhabitation of virtually any territory west of the Appalachians since the nation's founding, now had a name with its 1840s arrival in print, along with a liberal democratic purpose.

As critics have made clear in the last several decades, this moment marked a new conception of national expansion in the lead-up to and the wrap-up of the US-Mexican War: it was no longer assumed to be a natural process of human evolution, and the term *manifest destiny* euphemized a more aggressive and militaristic strategy of imperial conquest.[8] Nineteenth-century literary scholars and cultural historians have likewise unmasked the rhetorical and aesthetic qualities of national expansion and imperialism under the rubric of manifest destiny. They have shown how it has served as a darling of master narratives of US history, a shame-diminishing feature of national forgetting that distanced later generations of Americans who have assumed the praiseworthiness of pioneering figures who braved the wilderness in the settlement of an otherwise empty territory.[9] Easterners and nationalists might have been able to make assumptions about democratic proclivities and a commercially oriented settlement of western territories and states under the rubric of democratic space. And they might have also conveniently overlooked and forgotten the nondemocratic imperial conquest of Indigenous peoples and lands.[10] But the question remains as to how well their stories actually aligned with stories about life and democracy in western spaces.[11]

In the stories and myths that emerged about and from the population-booming days of the California gold rush, readers find great variety. Eastern-based perspectives like Dana's and Taylor's and the anonymous writers of *The Democratic Review* have garnered the majority of attention. Triumphalist consensus-making efforts in later accounts built on these assessments while ironing out the ambivalence, especially when it came to histories of literary production in the early days of California statehood. For instance, in a 1950 speech assessing the literary output of California following the Treaty of Guadalupe Hidalgo in 1848, Dixon Wecter claimed that "the civilization of California sprang up full-grown, self-assured, more than a shade sophisticated. . . . Footloose men from all states and most nations flocked to the diggings. The intelligent, highly cultivated jostled elbows with the rough and ready. The unlucky often laid aside pick and pan to try their hand at trade, politics, journalism, literature."[12] Accounts like these subsumed the multivalent and multilateral collisions of peoples and cultures as fortune-hungry migrants from other parts of North and South America, Europe, and Asia poured into newly acquired territory that a mix of Amerindian, Mexican, and Californio populations had long claimed as home.[13] In spite of recent correctives to histories like Wecter's, California social history between the US-Mexican War and the US Civil War has primarily been narrated under the guise of manifest destiny and the gold rush and from the dominant register of the individualistic white prospector and his hypermasculine adventures—monumentalized in fictive accounts of the rough-and-tumble era by Bret Harte. If literature gets credit for promoting a whitewashed account of gold rush–era sociopolitical life, as Susan Lee Johnson has made plain, then to what degree does it matter that Bret Harte did not start writing about California until the 1860s?[14] While much of literary production in the first decade of California statehood largely fell into the category of firsthand accounts of California life produced for eastern, urban audiences, the 1850s scene was more contested than critical histories have typically attested.[15]

The tendency to map US national prescriptions onto the newly acquired territory of interbellum California (1848–61)—whether in the historical moment or in later critical ventures—has greatly distorted histories of the aspirations and practical ventures of local politics in California. To be sure, plenty of people imagined the imposition of US national practices to be a suitable strategy for assimilating the thirty-first state into the Union, especially those who, like Dana and Taylor, had experienced the consolidation of white- and male-dominated, liberal constitutionalism in the eastern states. Later historians, from Hubert Howe Bancroft and Frederick Jackson Turner to Henry Nash Smith and Leslie Fiedler, would readily identify the most prominent of the frontier states as a crucially constitutive element in the national imaginary. Much of the literary production in California during this decade-plus—largely firsthand accounts with relatively few ventures into the realm of imaginative fiction—contributed to the national narrative.[16] But the two misfit texts I take up in this chapter, John Rollin Ridge's *The Adventures of Joaquín Murieta* (1854) and Louise Clappe's epistles that were later collected as *The Shirley's Letters* (1854–55), resist easy folding into this national narrative and speak back in fascinating ways. The vernacular aesthetics of these stories demonstrate the frustration of attempted overlays of national jurisdiction—particularly in the prosecutions of law and justice—on the vast space of territorially isolated

California. These stories are largely ones of formal failure, demonstrating that the only thing that appears manifest is not destiny but rather ongoing contingency.[17]

Accordingly, this chapter opens with historical and literary context provided by Taylor's account and Bret Harte's famous short stories and the consensus-making aesthetics that worked in concert with the master narrative of manifest destiny, the nation, and its version of individualistic liberal democracy. From these more orderly stories, I delve into the aesthetic maelstrom that is Ridge's first edition of *Joaquín Murieta*. Ridge drew on a smattering of sensational newspaper stories published in 1852 and 1853 and produced his own episodic account in one continuous yet highly disjointed and messy narrative plunge. Ridge's novel delivers an ambivalent portrayal of his once noble protagonist, blaming his banditry on the injustices of those who would exclude him from opportunity in California. Importantly, the novel pushes back against progressive, assimilationist impulses and defies critical attempts to merge it with the national narrative. I then discuss Clappe's "letters," published in twenty-three installments in a short-lived, San Francisco–based literary periodical called *The Pioneer*. On the surface, these portraits of life in the mining camps seemingly echo the early moments in Kirkland's *A New Home* (that is, the musings of a genteel woman writing for an eastern audience). More poignantly, though, the letters depict the failures of the camp as the product of a botched imposition of national prescriptions. I argue that in a contingent time of great optimism, oppression, and failure for so many, Clappe's and Ridge's fictive imaginings reject romanticized tropes of California settlements and work through the political impasses of their immediate time and place, and in the process, reimagine new forms of law and justice and the need for a more empowering form of localized democracy that better addresses the exigencies of their moment.

Manifest Destiny, Bret Harte, and the West in the National Imaginary

Bayard Taylor's *Eldorado* leaves no doubt that this newly conquered land served as the unquestionable emblem of manifest destiny and triumphalist liberal democracy. He offers few if any qualifications for this now-hybrid population of long time residents and recently arrived prospectors, regardless of locale and evidence of cultural sophistication. Regarding the region of the mines, Taylor lauds the workings of impromptu self-governance: "From the beginning, a state of things little short of anarchy might have been reasonably awaited" due to the heterogeneity of the constituents. "Instead of this," Taylor opines, "a disposition to maintain order and secure the rights of all was shown throughout the mining districts."[18] Taylor identifies a similarly inclusive democratic spirit in the organization of the state. As the US Congress spent the spring of 1849 embroiled in debates over the expansion of slavery into new territories, they left decisions about California's provisional governance unconsidered when the session adjourned. The California territorial governor, Benet Riley, called for a state constitutional convention, toured the state to drum up interest in elections for delegates, and organized the convention to start on 1 September 1849 in Monterey. It was made up of a representative "proportion of native Californian members to the American" populations and unencumbered by commitments to national parties in the east, and Taylor claims "a perfect harmony of feeling existed between the citizens of both races."[19] The state constitution that was drawn up over that month featured some democratic mechanisms like the foregrounding of a declaration of rights (including women's right to property), a prohibition on slavery, and the election of judges; less inclusive elements like bans on nonwhite citizens' rights to vote and to testify in court made the final cut as well.[20] Taylor's final assessment is reminiscent of George Bancroft's rendition of harmonious founding: "The members of the Convention may have made some blunders in the course of their deliberations; there may be some objectionable clauses in the Constitution they have framed. But where was there ever such harmony evolved out of so wonderful, so dangerous, so magnificent a chaos? . . . [In the end] we have another splendid example of the ease and security with which people can be educated to govern themselves."[21] Papering over any discord, Taylor's idyllic portrait fits squarely within popular expansionist rhetoric of the era. It also testifies to the desire for and execution of democratic self-rule.

The perfect literary partner to Taylor's idealized account of state building in California is Bret Harte. While he did not migrate to California and start writing about it until the 1860s, Harte nevertheless casts a long shadow over early California gold rush literature. In many ways, his most heralded writings worked in close conjunction with what Joseph Urgo has identified as Harte's effective "[expansion of] the definition of the United States by linking an imagination of California to it."[22] His first published story, "The Legend of Monte Diablo" (1863), demonstrates a loyalty to the logic of manifest destiny with an added dose of Whiggish progressive history. Published in *The Atlantic*, the story harkens back fourscore years before the gold rush and features a confrontation between a hardworking Jesuit priest and the Devil disguised as an elderly hidalgo, divulging the romantic yet inevitable march of progress and the teleology of nation building by means of swaggering men and their extraordinary measures. Subsequent tales work more subtly in service of nation and empire while also at times offering promising representations of collective democratic potential. In stories like "The Outcasts of Poker Flat" and "Tennessee's Partner," Harte draws on sentimental tropes of honest miners and wily outcasts finding common bonds, even in the face of abject failure or death. Such stories have led critics away from readings concerned with procedural politics to focus instead on more traditional concerns like the quality of his art and his apparent cultivation of bourgeois reading audiences.[23] Commenting on the author's ability to manipulate rhetoric and effect, Harold Kolb has argued that Harte's "energies are devoted to manipulating his characters for effects, not to realizing them as human beings." Consequently, such stories resemble those told by "the outside narrators in the frame tales of early Southwestern Humorists."[24] While such frames were not always successful in containing the misfits in those tales, as I argued in chapter 2, Harte's stories tend toward the Davy Crockett tradition and those of its ilk, focusing on individuals, employing a canned version of the vernacular, and leaving real politics to the managerial classes.[25]

One of Harte's most famous stories, "The Luck of Roaring Camp" (1868), nevertheless stands out for its imagining and articulating a local society coming together and making collective decisions in an all-inclusive spirit resembling a neighborly democracy even more robust than that on display in Caroline Kirkland's village. "Roaring Camp" is a prominent story that has received its share of critical attention, and many have understood it as a West Coast salvation parable: a Christlike figure, Tommy Luck, is born in a rough-and-tumble camp to a single disenfranchised mother and is claimed by no father, and he appears to redeem the ragtag encampment before nature cruelly intervenes.[26] Alternatively, Axel Nissen has appreciated the depiction of men crafting an alternative to "bourgeois domestic establishments" that challenges "the essentialism of Victorian domesticity's gender roles and ideals."[27] While such interpretations are valid, I highlight the ways that this distinctive polity follows much the same script that we saw in Hooper's *Adventures of Captain Simon Suggs*, stopping short of letting such characters appear as a viable, sustainable democratic collective.

In their initial demonstrations of collective self-rule, the men refrain from marking the birth of Tommy Luck by detonating a barrel full of gunpowder and allow a quieter salute with a handful of revolver shots. They contribute gifts as a sort of trust for the newborn orphan, even though their gifts are humorously inappropriate. The men proceed with a "formal meeting of the camp to discuss what should be done with the infant. A resolution to adopt it was unanimous and enthusiastic." A more dialogic and dissent-filled democratic undertaking ensues in "an animated discussion in regard to the manner and feasibility of providing for its wants." Given the circumstances, the group's style of debate arouses a new form, which the narrative describes thus: "It was remarkable that the argument partook of none of those fierce personalities with which discussions were usually conducted at Roaring Camp."[28] Instead of sending the child to a neighboring camp that included women or bringing in a female nurse, the men assume all responsibilities for raising the infant. In this early experiment with collective decision making to address immediate needs, the group numbering a hundred or so men expresses more confidence in its own operations than in those determined outside of the group.

After they achieve some success with this strategy, outside threats induce a new sort of exclusionary practice that marks the limits of this alternative, more radical democracy. Steps are taken to ward off immigration, yet external influences persist, this time in the form of a proposition to build a hotel to bring in "one or two decent families to reside there for the sake of 'The Luck' [Tommy]." While the group is tempted by the normalcy of order and civility, democratic discourse remains, albeit in more fractious, partisan forms. In the face of the majority in favor of building the hotel (financed by the camp's good economic fortune), a "few still held out. But the resolve could not be carried into effect for three months, and the minority meekly yielded" ("Luck," 25). Unlike the earlier instances of collective decision making, this event takes on a more difficult prospect, as the majority wins without consensus. Whether achieved through evolving fractious partisan politics or the tyranny of the majority, institutionalized propriety seems increasingly inevitable. Before any more decisions can be made, natural forces intervene. In the middle of the night, the North Fork River washes over its banks and floods the camp, "washing away the pride, the hope, the joy, the Luck, of Roaring Camp" ("Luck," 25). A rescue boat from a neighboring camp—the outside connection that the camp had previously eschewed as much as it could—returns a dripping wet and dying Kentuck (the likely father of the Luck), holding the dead child in his arms ("Luck," 26). The possibilities of ongoing democracy of this variety cannot resist the outside pressures of persistent social and political forces, and perhaps even natural forces.

For those who think that the individualistic ideologies driving life in the California gold rush would inhibit the formation of collective enterprises, Harte's story imagines a group of individuals coming together and addressing their particular conditions via a form of collective decision making that bears all the markers of an inclusive, people-empowered democracy. By the end of the story, the refined aesthetics and tone of inevitability make it clear that this experiment will not last, and that more familiar, nationally prescribed ones will soon arrive. External forces and national prescriptions knock on the borders of this jurisdiction, and the short story genre demands the aesthetic reckoning of order and form.[29] While it is an entertaining read, Harte's story—based in the historical conditions of the gold rush yet written more than a decade afterward—sidesteps the historical tensions of competing multiracial, multiethnic cultures and their corresponding power plays.[30] As Susan Lee Johnson puts it, Harte's stories "represent a narrowing of the field of moral conflict, in which relations of power among various human communities, as opposed to those among individuals, rarely surface."[31] Thus they become complicit in silencing the differences of the gold rush, a practice consistent with the terms of manifest destiny and the most revered stories of the liberal tradition. To find the democratic alternatives of more nondestined contingency, we must look to the misfits.

The "Topsy-Turvy, Hurly-Burly Mass of Events" in *Joaquín Murieta*

In the opening paragraph of one of the messiest novels of the nineteenth century, *The Life and Adventures of Joaquín Murieta, the Celebrated California Bandit*, the narrator declares: "I sit down to write something concerning the life and character of *Joaquín Murieta*, a man as remarkable in the annals of crime as any of the renowned robbers of the Old and New World, who have preceded him; and I do this ... to contribute to those materials of which the early history of California shall one day be composed."[32] With a brief nod to a transhemispheric genealogy, the narrative narrows the focus to a specific place and time as the setting for its highly particular history, declaring that "the character of this truly wonderful man was nothing more than a natural production of the social and moral condition of the country in which he lived." In the next paragraph, the tight focus broadens. Admitting that there were, in fact, two actual Joaquíns who bore at least five different surnames between them, the narrative jumps to expanding scales of transnational affiliation by disclosing that "Joaquín Murieta was a Mexican, born in the province of Sonora to respectable parents and educated in the schools of Mexico" (*JM*, 8). The shiftiness of scales is not an especially radical move in literary discourse, but it could be construed as a substantive error since the narrative had just insisted on local specificity in the preceding paragraph. Further conceptual problems crop up with the implication that this impressive character—this "truly wonderful man"—is a type no longer fostered by California in the narrative present. If there was a destiny, it is now complete (yet hardly manifest). As the first two paragraphs demonstrate, though, the narrative's capacity to keep a tight rein on any sense of aesthetic framework, much less this trope of inevitable manifest destiny, seems dubious. With the jurisdictional changes in 1848 and then the population boom of the gold rush years, maintaining control, or even just telling coherent stories in the moment, proved elusive.

Making sense of these contentious times in the rapidly evolving sociopolitical climate was no doubt challenging in their historical moment, and Ridge's representation of the events involving the figure of Joaquín Murieta did little to clear up the complicated history of the outlaw who had become famous in newspaper reports of the day. In many ways, Ridge's novel fails to do what most readers have come to expect from literature—instead of turning chaos into cosmos, or creating order out of the disorder of everyday life, it delivers a rather chaotic narrative that only exacerbates confusion in the young state. Put another way, *The Adventures of Joaquín Murieta* provides one of the more perplexing experiences of meaning-making ventures in all of nineteenth-century US literature. As a novel, it struggles to establish any sense of organic unity. In fact, it embodies the very criteria that Tocqueville had expected from a democratic culture: formal qualities are disregarded, it is stylistically messy and incoherent, and it was likely sped to press rather than carefully measured and deliberately thought through. Indeed, the roughly paced narrative, the awkwardly shifting narrative perspectives, the many instances of convoluted syntax and grammar, and the lack of chapter divisions all make for a difficult read. As a result, Ridge's 1854 narrative defies critical conventions and sensibilities built on the principles of the liberal tradition. I argue that Ridge's literary misfit demonstrates the failure of US national prescriptions, particularly in the form of liberal-oriented law and order, to take hold of the vast and unruly local space of California.

While Ridge experienced limited success as an author and eventually died in obscurity, the tale he captured enjoyed a prodigious afterlife.[33] Ridge has the distinction of bringing together conflicting reports and publishing the first full account of the bandit's life, but it was quickly appropriated and took on mythical proportions as it was recast in forms serving a variety of interests. In 1858, Charles E. B. Howe published *A Dramatic Play Entitled Joaquín Murieta de Castillo, the Celebrated California Bandit*. No records of a staged performance exist, but the melodrama largely follows an *Othello*-like plot in which a noble Joaquín is seduced by the evil Padre Jurata.³⁴ A second and even more popular narrative appeared in 1859 published by the *California Police Gazette*, plagiarizing most of Ridge's 1854 edition yet removing any ambivalence in Joaquín's character for a more sensational and biased account of the notorious outlaw. In short time, this version became the primary historical record, in spite of Ridge's published complaints. A "third" edition appeared in 1871, four years after Ridge's death, with John R. Ridge listed as author, under the imprint of Frederick MacCrellish. As the story lived on, untethered from Ridge's first text, it took on several new lives in the twentieth century, including] an anticolonial text reproduced in a variety of media throughout the Western Hemisphere.³⁵ In these, Joaquín Murieta is at times a dangerous criminal in need of extermination, at other times a subversive hero fighting for equal justice; the wide range of depictions are, I contend, logical outcomes of the ambiguities and formal inconsistencies in Ridge's original narrative.

In the last few decades, scholars have offered insights into this complicated text, stirring up debate over the author's plausible intentions, the text's contributions to the construction of racial and nationalist identifications in 1850s California, and insights into transnationally and imperially constituted structures of feeling.³⁶ The vast majority of these have relied on familiar critical conventions that I am challenging in this book. John Carlos Rowe, for instance, has argued that *Joaquín Murieta* displays Ridge's advocacy of a romantic individualism in line with prominent liberal ideologies of the mid-nineteenth-century era. Starting with assumptions about Ridge's biography—that he shared his Cherokee father's assimilationist impulse—Rowe argues that Ridge employs material from the imperial conquest of California "to develop his position on the assimilation of 'foreigners' into the United States as part of a rational legal and cultural process guided by the prevailing myth of 'American individualism' and its economic complement, free-enterprise capitalism."³⁷ The series of affronts against Murieta that drive him to his murderous rampage do not strike at his native identity as Mexican; rather, Rowe identifies violations of privacy, property, and civil rights that affront "his *American* identity."³⁸ To some degree, Rowe has a point. Joaquín did initially seek a life in California with hopes of securing individual rights and economic gain. But his quest was compromised by others seeking precisely the same. The imposition of a rights-based legal economy from the more settled eastern United States might seem desirable for the purposes of establishing order according to the rule of law, and perhaps this is what the historical person John Rollin Ridge wanted. And yet, Rowe's critical move assumes a national frame of reference. Alternatively, Molly Crumpton Winter has argued, "Murieta and his band of outlaws strike randomly and without warning, shaking up communities as well as new foundations of a state that was trying to overlay white hegemony on a previously and currently pluralistic territory."[39] Indeed, Ridge's novel suggests that the imposition of a less than democratic totalizing regime, especially one that ignores local particularities, inevitably leads to violent outcomes. Inferentially, this misfit text then calls for a version of democratic action that the nation promises will be made manifest but as yet has failed to deliver.

The first half of the novel details Joaquín's arrival in Alta California, his initial pursuit of individual gains through a variety of means, and attacks against him by figures who "bore the name of Americans but failed to support the honor and dignity of that title" (*JM*, 9). In short time, these "Americans" enact lynch-mob justice, raping Joaquín's wife, whipping him, and hanging his half brother. Joaquín undergoes a dramatic change in character, which is rendered in a swath of mixed, awkward metaphors: "His soul swelled beyond its former boundaries, and the barriers of honor, rocked into atoms by the strong passion which shook his heart like an earthquake, crumbled around him. Then it was that he declared to a friend that he would live henceforth for revenge" (*JM*, 12–13). From there, the narrative unfolds in a series of rapidly shifting episodes that portray Joaquín and his seemingly ubiquitous banditti terrorizing the countryside from the spring of 1852 through May 1853. Joaquín's men, sometimes working in concert, at other times individually, enjoy success and failure as they steal horses, rob a variety of California inhabitants, and, when it suits their fancy, indiscriminately kill whomever they please. The narrative travels quickly over the California landscape, roaming as far north as Mount Shasta and as far south as Los Angeles, all without chapter breaks. As quickly and incoherently as the narrative moves across space and through time, Joaquín faces incredible odds, succeeding and failing in arbitrary turns. In perhaps his most impressive moment, Joaquín, inexplicably alone, fights off fifty Americans and escapes unscathed by quasi-supernatural means (*JM*, 55–58). Later, he is captured by a group of Tejon Indians. After whipping and disrobing their prisoners, the Tejon eventually release Joaquín and his comrades, who then wander the countryside naked and hungry until they are fortuitously rescued by an ally (*JM*, 35–38).

These details offer just a small sampling of the random adventures captured in the always awkward aesthetics of the text. And to this point, the characters have operated without a stated plan. That changes when Joaquín declares that he will "arm and equip fifteen hundred or two thousand men and . . . kill the

Americans by 'wholesale,' burn their ranchos, and run off their property at one single swoop" to avenge both himself and his country, before retiring to Mexico (*JM*, 75). Wreaking havoc all over the state for quite some time, Joaquín and his inner circle are eventually captured and killed by Captain Harry Love and his state-authorized posse. Before his capture, though, the text seems to arrive at some coherence by foregrounding legal and political issues in three key moments: a courtroom scene, the emergence of multiple vigilance committees, and citizens petitioning the legislature. In nation-scaled, liberal democratic readings like Rowe's, these developing scenes could be construed as increasingly effective executions of law and order. Alternatively, reading these scenes without assuming a national scale of reference and through their vernacular aesthetics, I contend that these moments of competing legal codes demonstrate limited faith in the execution of national procedural politics and imply the need for alternatives that better address the political needs of this locality.

Just after Joaquín's declaration, a courtroom scene marks the introduction of the first real presence of formal law and order. The narrative shifts from its typical concrete, name-dropping, declarative voice to a vague, abstract, atmospheric one. It sets a vague scene with a "large crowd gathering in and around a cloth-building in a little mining town, which looked like a half-venture towards civilization in the midst of that wild and savage region." Inside the building is a "dark-skinned man ... with a huge log chain around one of his legs," and by his side "a huge, old fellow with blue eyes, sandy hair, and a severe look, ... the Justice of the Peace in the district" (*JM*, 91–92). The narrative digresses to indicate complications of scale, pointing out that this "office [of Justice of the Peace] ... possessed a jurisdiction as extensive as many of the county courts of other and older states of the Union" (*JM*, 92). Despite the incongruities of national norms and the vast California space, the enlightened figure of the law stands between a dark prisoner named Vulvia and a lynch mob hovering outside, championing color-blind legal ideals of due process and habeas corpus. The details of the case seem highly circumstantial, but if Vulvia did not commit this particular murder, the narrative assures readers that he has committed plenty of others. The rule of law appears to be delivering justice to the dark-skinned criminal. But then "a young man superbly dressed ... with gentlemanly dignity" enters, identifies himself as Samuel Harrington, and declares that he has come to retrieve his hired man (*JM*, 94). After presenting five or six letters addressed to him and written by hand, Harrington's "identity" is confirmed; the Justice immediately releases the prisoner with apologies for any inconvenience. When the two men head out of town, the narrative finally lets readers in on the hoax, disclosing that they both have a "hearty laugh" over Joaquín's con artistry (*JM*, 95). The now released Vulvia asks Joaquín how he has come upon the letters, to which Joaquín flippantly replies, "Oh, easy enough. I killed a fellow on my way down here the other day and found them in his pockets—and d—d little besides, too!" (*JM*, 96).

Besides the uneasy humor in this scene, what stands out is the narrative's portrayal of a half-completed institution of US law and the ways that people are sometimes recognized, more often disguised, and most disturbingly, disposed of under this compromised legal systems.[40] In this case, Vulvia has been wrongly accused. Nationally ordained law initially intervenes against his unjust racial profiling and lynch-mob justice, upholding progressive ideals of US democratic rule of law. Yet these positives are undercut by the failures of identification and a whole host of circumstantial evidence, and only the chance arrival of a man who claims to be Samuel Harrington prevents another man from being convicted of a crime he did not commit. Neither Vulvia nor Joaquín are correctly identified, suggesting that national legal standards have adapted poorly to the embodied experiences of this local scene. The narrative implies instead that a different sort of ordering system is needed in this place. Law and order are not a bad idea, but the system must take closer account of actual individuals and actions in local proceedings.

Shortly thereafter, the narrative teases out the consequences of national prescriptions failing to take hold, first with the portrayal of a notable individual and later with the description of a collective body (neither of which turns out well). When a slew of crimes breaks out in Calaveras County, "among the boldest, most firm, and energetic whom the crisis brought forth was Capt. Charles Ellas" (*JM*, 110). In its description of this new figure of the law, the narrative characterizes Ellas as a "chivalrous son of the South" whose "bosom [bore] the marks of severe and dangerous hard-to-hand [sic] conflicts." The narrative deems Ellas a plausible participant in these scenes, for "at a juncture so important as the period of which I speak, a man like Ellas was most naturally looked to as a leader and intrusted with a large amount of discretionary power, so necessary to be used in perilous times when the slow forms of law, with their snail-like processes, are altogether ... inefficient" (*JM*, 111). The man bearing the marks of an archaic legal code on his very body *seems* the right man to render justice when US-ordained law has failed to do so. Ellas's subsequent actions, however, only meet violence with more violence. The narrative follows Ellas in pursuit of Joaquín for quite some time. Like the judge in the courtroom scene that preceded these episodes, he encounters Joaquín (multiple times) but fails to recognize him as the object of his pursuit. Ellas kills his share of supposed criminals, but the narrative grows even hazier and more disorderly at this point. The alternative legal code Ellas represents is just as flawed as the one in the courtroom scene.

Without explanation, Ellas fades out of the picture. The narrative shifts from an individual solution to a collective one—one with vestiges of democratic-oriented action: the formation of a vigilance committee. Tellingly, the narrative delivers this news in the passive voice: "It was resolved that *everybody* should turn out in search of the villain Joaquín. . . . Thus was the whole country alive with armed parties" (*JM*, 135). Readers could construe this development as a community coming together to take collective action to rectify an adverse situation, a hallmark of local democratic decision making. Given the notoriety of the Vigilance Committee of San Francisco in 1851—addressed in my discussion of *The Shirley Letters*—this form of popular action bears the marks of what critics have dubbed "mobocracy." Chaos ensues: "Arrests were continually being made; popular tribunals established in the woods; Judge Lynch installed upon the bench; criminals arraigned, tried, and executed upon the limb of a tree." Here readers see one of those moments when local democratic action becomes just what the skeptics have projected. Racial profiling and increasing violence come after the judge in the courtroom scene has failed and after a southern transplant (Ellas) has tried to implement his archaic code of honor by taking whatever action he wants based on his own discretion. At this point, even the narrative seems perplexed, casting this frustration as an aesthetic challenge of representation: all the "pursuits, flights, skirmishes, and a topsy-turvy, hurly-burly mass of events . . . set narration at defiance" (*JM*, 135–36).

After the narrative confesses its own inability to create order out of disarray, procedural state governance finally steps in. Democratically petitioning the government, citizens allegedly lobby their representatives for redress, and the state responds. Once again, though, the political move is rendered in the passive voice: "A petition, numerously signed, was presented to the [State] Legislature, praying that body to authorize Captain Harry Love to organize a company of Mounted Rangers to capture, drive out of the country, or exterminate the desperate bands of highwaymen, who placed in continual jeopardy both life and property." The narrative that has lacked specificity in most of details goes on to add this explicit historical note: "A bill to this effect was passed and signed by the Governor on the 17th of May, 1853, and a company was organized by Harry Love on the 28th of the same month" (*JM*, 145). Readers witness collective democratic action on a scale larger than that in play with the formation of local vigilance committees, in the form of procedural petitioning that spurs the legislature to address a problem for the common interest. But readers also encounter adaptation of national norms. The key here is the suspension of the constitutional rights to trial by jury and habeas corpus when the state authorizes "extermination" as a legal option. One could say that finally, we see national law being amended to address local needs.

This legislative action works. Love succeeds where the courtroom, Ellas, and the vigilance committees have not. After numerous chases, he eventually gets his man. For progressive, nation-oriented readings, this conclusion serves as a neat and tidy sign of procedural representative governance eventually winning out. Love follows proper procedures, the rule of law and a new sense of order are established, and California residents can return to their everyday lives pursuing economic opportunity. But this reading glosses over details that could easily be lost in the messiness of the narrative presenting these concluding events. Like Ellas and countless others before him, Love does not recognize Joaquín when he first confronts him. During their standoff, Love, with pistol pulled, questions seven men who tell convoluted stories. When Joaquín sees an old acquaintance among Love's men, Byrnes, he assumes he will finally be recognized and makes a break for it, nearly escaping before being shot and killed. But the narrative insists on misrecognition: "The Rangers returned to the point from which they had started. As yet, all were ignorant of the true character of the party which they had attacked." Apparently, Byrnes has not seen Joaquín, but on "going up to the dead bodies, one was immediately recognized by Byrnes as that of Joaquín Murieta" (*JM*, 155). Again, the passive voice, the awkward syntax, and the lack of naming tellingly double down on the uncertainty, almost as if the narrative doubts the Rangers' success.

In short time, these doubts grow. Love and his Rangers must produce the body, for "it was important to prove, to the satisfaction of the public, that the famous and bloody bandit was actually killed, else the fact would be eternally doubted.... [So Love] caused the head of the renowned Murieta to be cut off and ... to [be] preserve[d]" (*JM*, 155–56). The narrative goes on to describe the strange travels of the preserved head at exhibitions around the state. When the legislature subsequently pays Captain Love the promised reward of $1,000 on delivery of head, and then decides to pay him $5,000 nearly ten months later, the narrative once again struggles to make sense of the historical record. It eventually resolves itself with a trite moral in the closing paragraphs—"there is nothing so dangerous in its consequences as *injustice to individuals*" (*JM*, 158)—yet this retreat into a dose of classical liberalism seems off base and fails to clarify the matter. Jesse Alemán has read the conclusion as demonstrating that any sort of attempts at assimilation of racialized bodies to

134 *Chapter Four*

a variety of Americanisms ultimately ends, as it does in *Joaquín Murieta*, in dismemberment.[41] The novel thus gives the lie to assessments like Bayard Taylor's that California is effectively implementing political justice for all peoples within the multiracial, multiethnic population of California. Linked up with the other failed ventures in establishing law and order—from the early courtroom scene to the movements of Ellas and various vigilance committees—the conclusion demonstrates that the implementation of orderly, procedural governance under the guise of liberal democratic norms does not stand on firm ground in 1850s California.

But the impact of Joaquín Murieta does not end with the narrative's conclusion. Later publications like the dramatic script and the *California Police Gazette* version present little to none of Ridge's ambivalence about the titular character and instead endorse white supremacist rule in California. Ridge's supposed return to the story in his subsequent edition, moreover, demonstrates the relentless march of the nation, even for those who might critique its dictates. Set next to the "first edition," the "third edition" attempts to refine the rough edges of the first. For instance, one change comes in the form of chapter divisions headed by prefatory summaries. Additional backstory providing reasons for Joaquín's emigration, a lengthier justification for the organization of Harry Love's posse, newly added affidavits that confirm the head in the jar belongs to Joaquín Murieta—these revisions and enlargements in many ways clean up the ambiguities and ambivalences of the first edition. Their greater significance stems from the fact that the third edition is the version of events that Hubert Howe Bancroft and Theodore Hittell, grandfathers of California history, both took as faithful history.[42] Taking note of the revisions, then, seems crucial to understanding how a misfit like the 1854 *Adventures of Joaquín Murieta* can be tamed and folded into national narrative.

Some changes are seemingly minor and occur at sentence level. For instance, regarding Joaquín's character in relation to the state, in the final sentence of the opening paragraph of the first edition, "his individual history *is a part of* the most valuable history of the State," becomes in the third edition, "his individual record becomes a part of the most valuable, *because it is* a part of the earliest history of the State."[43] The former privileges Joaquín's story as a product of local circumstances, acknowledging the social construction and systemic nature of both individual and collective experience. Conversely, the latter cites value in more progressive fashion, declaring Joaquín's individual story to be important because it is presumably cordoned off as history in secure control of the present. It is a small but telling change, one that revises the hierarchy of importance and brings the 1854 misfit into better alignment with the national history of order and form.

In addition to changes at the sentence level, the 1871 edition includes additional features that provide normative rationale. The 1854 version had straightforwardly highlighted his respectable birth and education, that the war had wreaked havoc on his country, and that with "his heart's treasure—a beautiful Sonorian girl" he would pursue his "fortunes among the American people, of whom he had formed the most favorable opinion" (*JM*, 8–9). Short on speculation and delivered with a positive tone, the original narrative establishes a clear context for the noble yet conflicted figure seeking new community. The later edition spends more time establishing the character of Joaquín in Mexico, but in much less attractive terms, particularly in the new backstory to his partnership the beautiful Sonorian girl, now given the name Rosita. Joaquín seems more of a playboy in this version, for he has "nothing to do but ride his father's horses and give a general superintendence to the herding of stock upon the rancho," and so he becomes a frequent visitor to Rosita's father's home, especially while the father is absent. In due time, their father comes home from a trip and discovers the young lovers "in a position, as Byron has it in the most diabolical of his works, 'loving, natural, and Greek.'"[44] The disgraced couple disembark together in search of new fortune. The narrative's expansion depicts Joaquín as seducer and frames his emigration to California less as a desire to find a more productive community and more as a product of his own private, individual self-preservation. The noble figure of the first edition seems much less so in the third.

A second amplification occurs with the details leading up to the organization of Harry Love's posse and the legitimation of its activities. In the first edition, the circumstances are rendered in the brief quotation already shared. The 1871 edition adds a catalogue of these "tributes levied upon citizens[:] . . . the constant arming of private companies for the protection of the lives and property of citizens . . . drain[ing] the pockets of private individuals. . . . Women and children . . . suffering from constant fear, . . . removed to more thickly populated localities, with great trouble and at heavy expense. American owners of ranches . . . impoverished. . . . The condition of things, in short, became intolerable."[45] Unlike the first edition's generalization of "tributes," the third edition's extended list of offenses represents a preponderance of evidence that more convincingly justifies the juridical choices of legislative action. As one last exclamation point on this more effective rule of law, the third edition trumps the first edition's "thorough identification of the head of

Joaquín" by adding copies of two sworn affidavits, one from a priest and the other from one of Joaquín's fellow Sonorians.

The changes in the 1871 edition ultimately make for a better story. But it is also a revisionist history, indicative of the progressivist tendencies in US cultural, political, and literary historiography. In effect, the changes are not very different from the publisher's preface appended to the 1854 edition, citing the author's Native American heritage in the racist discourse of the noble savage. Whereas that preface failed to rein in the excesses of the work's vernacular aesthetics and the alternative democracies that were conjured with it, the later text appeared to be more sanitized and thus more congruent to the national project—a text akin to Taylor's and Harte's productions. Perhaps the 1871 edition serves only as a representation of a destiny that is finally becoming manifest, albeit more than two decades after the fact, and only after the Civil War has recalibrated national scales of reference. This historical development only underscores the contingency of the 1854 moment and its need for a democracy that addresses the powers of the people.

One might anticipate that there would be more sophisticated writers in California, besides the author of the 1854 *Joaquín Murieta*, making progressively better sense of California within a national framework. Bayard Taylor told one variety of events in California's earliest moments and met his publishing deadlines, and Bret Harte told versions more than a decade later. And while these nation-oriented narratives loom large, the stories from another semifamous contemporary of Ridge suggest a more complicated situation calling for something more fitting than constitutionally managed liberal democracy.

The Shirley Letters, Vigilance, and Contingency

Louise Amelia Knapp Smith Clappe arrived in California with her husband in 1850. She recorded and embellished many of her experiences in twenty-three letters addressed to her sister Molly detailing life in gold-mining camps in 1851 and 1852. In the eighth letter (dated 20 October 1851, published in September 1854), she delivers several condescending remarks about her new neighbors in a mining camp before settling on one in particular: "Among other oddities, there is a person here who is a rabid admirer of Lippard. I have heard him gravely affirm that Lippard was the greatest author the world ever saw."[46] To what degree Shirley finds this literary infatuation to be offensive is unclear, but her characterization of this man as cultural oddity continues: "He *studies* Lippard just as the other folks do Shakespeare, and yet the man has read and *admires* the majestic prose of Chilton, and is quite familiar with the best English classics!" (*Shirley*, 56–57). Having made her refined literary sensibilities clear, she proceeds to pair this unfavorable depiction of a Lippard fanatic with an equally condescending portrait of the "Squire," an oafish man claiming to be a justice of the peace. For the first time in her eight letters, she directly engages the politics—theoretically and practically—of the ragtag community. She explains that the "Squire" lacks popular support from the community, who prefer "to have the fun of ruling themselves" and complain that "he was not elected by the voice of the people, but that his personal friends nominated and voted for him." After an unflattering depiction of his appearance, she meditates on the inherent nature of leadership. She concludes that "although the 'Squire' is sufficiently intelligent and the kindest-hearted creature in the world, he does *not* possess the peculiar tact, talent, gift . . . to keep in order such a strangely amalgamated community." She wishes him all the best, "for justice in the hands of a mob, however respectable, is at best a fearful thing" (*Shirley*, 57–59). Clearly, the best are not ruling here—in literary appreciation or law enforcement—and Shirley fears the repercussions.

The Lippard fanatic and the pathetic Squire make for an unusual pairing of critical commentaries in Shirley's otherwise jovial letter. They also offer an insightful juxtaposition in the broader context of the series of letters. As these examples demonstrate, other than their overlapping years and locations of publication, few narratives could have less in common than Ridge's *Adventures of Joaquín Murieta* and the letters written by Louise Clappe, which were published serially in San Francisco's first and short-lived literary periodical *The Pioneer* and then collected in the twentieth century under the title *The Shirley's Letters*. (Rumor has it, though, that they share at least one more intersection.)[47] Although Ridge's style lacks the belles lettres attributes on display in many of Shirley's epistles, the two works do have more in common. Whereas *Joaquín Murieta* demonstrates the misfit of California in the national political space via a sensationalistic and violence-filled narrative, Shirley's "Letters" offer a much different literary approach to representing the failure of nation-oriented liberal democratic norms to take hold on the ground. As a result, Clappe's letters issue another California-specific rebuke of the predominating nationalist logic of manifest destiny.

Long appreciated as one of the rare works of the California gold rush era told from a woman's perspective, Clappe's letters have been a treasure for later scholars. In the late nineteenth century, the California native turned Harvard philosopher Josiah Royce declared the letters a "marvelously skillful and undoubtedly truthful account."[48] A century later, Sandra Lockhart expanded on this take: "While many women diarists and letter writers of the Gold Rush focus on their personal griefs and hardships, Shirley compassionately observes and records the plight of the miners and their women and children."[49] Framing Clappe's most notable text in the larger context of the times, Marlene Smith-Baranzini, editor of a 1998 reissue, concludes her introduction with a critical take that expands beyond California borders and into US literary history: "The Shirley letters fit thoroughly within a tradition of national literature in which such compelling voices of the nineteenth century as Richard Henry Dana, Ralph W[aldo] Emerson, and Harriet Beecher Stowe capture and articulate their response to an essential moment in American life.... Today, she remains California's foremost gold-rush raconteur, continuing to enchant readers."[50] Such are the typical takes on this literary figure, which belatedly fit her within a national frame of reference and affirm a notion that her destiny as nationally significant author, like that of her nation and its version of democracy, has been made manifest as well.

In their historical moment, the literary productions of Louise Clappe contain a more complicated and disjointed history than these critical assessments suggest. The complications start with the published home of all twenty-three letters, *The Pioneer; or California Monthly Magazine*. The magazine ran for two years, in 1854 and 1855, and its founding editor F. C. Ewer had grand visions of a relatively conventional literary periodical with national ambitions, combining articles on politics and science along with literary materials like new or recycled poetry, stories, sketches, and book reviews. In its opening issue, *The Pioneer* announced its ambitions to produce "a medium through which our domestic talent may manifest itself," so long as "the work is conducted with due regard to dignity, and its energies are sincerely directed towards sustaining an elevated standard of taste."[51] Their stated plan was to fulfill "a similar want in California, to that which in New York is so fully supplied by the pages of the Knickerbocker."[52] Recognizing that literary tastes and fashions have relocated from faraway places, claiming a desire to promote local authors, endeavoring to serve California as *The Knickerbocker* does New York— *The Pioneer* would do it all.

In its two years of publication, this original plan was amended numerous times, from switching printers and making changes to the design layout and typography to significantly altering its political messaging from unmitigated national boosterism (as in C. E. Havens's "America as it was to America as it will be") to a more conservative assessment of the legal precedent of states' rights (as in B. S. Brooks's "State Rights").[53] From a cultural perspective, by the middle issues of the first year, the magazine turned away from its male-oriented focus to appeal to a more distinctly feminine taste. The August 1854 issue, for instance, contains the article "What California Wants," a manifesto about the need for more female migrants, along with Shirley's Letter Sixth, which shifts from commentary on her travels and early experiences with funerals and surgeries to a more domesticated description of her log cabin.[54] This toggling between championing national ambitions while privileging local authors, printing proexpansionist nationalist policies while promoting unabashedly local needs, aptly demonstrates the ever-shifting nature and aims of this two-year periodical, which was consistent with the complications of making sense of this vast, disconnected space of California and its incorporation into the United States.[55]

The one constant of Ewer's journal of misfit pieces and sensibilities was a new letter from Shirley each month, headed with either the title "California in 1851" or "California in 1852." Because they were printed in every issue of the *Pioneer*'s two-year run from 1854 to 1855, scholars have long claimed that they were always intended for publication, a conjecture that lends itself to further presumptions that the letters stand as a unified text.[56] Much of these presumptions benefit from the fact that the letters would be pulled together, more than a half century after their initial periodical publication, in two collections: the first an illustrated version printed in 1922 by the private press of Thomas C. Russell, and the second in 1933 by Grabhorn Press. These two books did much of the work of uniting these otherwise disparate letters into a coherent whole. The most recent edition of *The Shirley Letters*, edited and introduced by Smith-Baranzini and published in 1998 by Heyday Press, carries this tradition forward, further erasing any past discontinuities.

As literary scholars have shown, however, totalizing accounts of serialized publications can lead to oversights. For one, serials have been shown to promote less obvious individualism and greater concerns with collectives, a tendency that works against the liberal tradition and opens possibilities for alternative democracies.[57] Moreover, as my discussion of *The Quaker City* and the southwestern humorists demonstrated, critical maneuvers that lump serialized texts into books at later dates obscure the record of democratic ideas for those living in their contingent moment. Clappe's project had more regular distribution to the public than Lippard's or the humorists' did, but the letters nevertheless reveal a changing trajectory.[58] Because critics have assumed that her letters were influential to near contemporaries like Mark Twain and Bret Harte—no matter how unlikely it is that these two writers came across every issue of the literary periodical a decade later and thus read all of her letters in order—few have speculated on the letters' various meanings for readers in 1854 and 1855.[59] *The Adventures of Joaquín Murieta* presented one version of developing politics in California in this particular moment, in all its messiness. Eschewing the sensationalist myth-making qualities of that text, Shirley's letters offer even more reason to assess their alternative representations of democratic norms.

In Shirley's narratives, as in *The Adventures of Joaquín Murieta*, readers encounter a text that superficially suggests something of a manifest destiny, but more often reveals the cracks and fissures and a more enduring sense of ongoing contingency in social and political life. In the opening lines of Dame Shirley's accounts, the narrative provides a strong sense of just how unconventional this account will be. The account of her travels from San Francisco to the North Fork of the Feather River in "Letter First" (dated 13 September 1851, published in two parts, in January and February 1854) is a combination of expectations defied and ambivalence exacerbated. Unlike the account of Mary Clavers in rural Michigan, the narrative expresses no disgust with the environment nor with its resident humanity. With limited concern for their own well-being, Shirley and her husband repeatedly get lost. Once among other migrants, they confound their predecessors with news of their adventures—sidestepping dangerous Indians and grizzly bears, eating any food that is provided, and riding mules over the roughest of terrains. The narrative records the collective response from those who preceded them: "Here they informed us that 'we had escaped a great marcy'—as old Jim used to say.... But seriously, dear M[olly], my heart thrills with gratitude to the Father, for his tender care of us during the journey, which, view it as lightly as we may, was certainly attended with *some* danger."[60] Quoting the language of earlier arrivers and pairing their cordoned-off vernacular with a genteel nod to divine intervention, Shirley offers a sense of destiny ensured, with providential care guiding these decorous yet ignorant travelers through the epic wilds of California. Before the letter's conclusion, though, cracks in this story appear when she acknowledges a different stroke of luck. Writing of her perilous descent on a mule into the canyon of Rich Bar, she admits that "my courage was the result of the know nothing, fear nothing principle; for I was certainly ignorant, until I had passed them, of the dangers of the passage" (*Shirley*, 15). Her nod to the retrospective knowledge betrays the undermining element of the whole venture: only after traversing all these incidents can she paint it all in a fresh light fueled by destiny-laden rhetoric.

Further discrepancies appear with new letters. "Letter Third" presents Shirley's take on the early history of the aptly named mining community of Rich Bar. She explains that a group of men set out from Marysville to pursue a report of of gold, and the search came up empty until they randomly stumbled on the uninhabited valley. During a one-night camp, before heading back out, two men happened to turn over a large rock and discovered a "sizable piece of gold," which led to the rest of the party sticking around long enough to stake off the territory to the extent that the law permits. By the end of the month, the camp had grown into a settlement of 500 men. The narrator seems less than impressed with this happenstance: "Such is the wonderful alacrity with which a mining town is built" (*Shirley*, 26). Whatever triumph that might be, by the very next paragraph, fortune turns the other way: "Shall I tell you the fate of two of the most successful of these gold hunters? . . . Elated with their good fortune, seized with a mania for Monte, in less than a year these unfortunates—so lately respectable and intelligent—became a pair of drunken gamblers" (*Shirley*, 27). Economic determinism aside, the passage notes that fortunes here are fickle and destiny is far from ensured. The march of national progress lacks a secure foothold; it is ever subject to the turn of the cards and the desires and dissipations of individuals.

Such capriciousness in the dictates of fortune in some ways set the camps up for collective democratic activity, but these experiments end up demonstrating that the more orderly, liberal variety—Shirley's preference—seems ill suited for this locale. While the first letter suggests that the natural surroundings might have proven recalcitrant for the semiknowledgeable traveler (as they had with Kirkland's Mary Clavers), life in the new settlement is filled with even greater complications. The episodes with the Lippard lover and the justice of the peace demonstrate some of the first oddities. In the next epistle, dated nine days later, on 29 October 1851, but published one month later, in October 1854, readers see a curious instance of law and politics in Rich Bar. The letter features the trial of Little John, a man accused of the theft of $400 in gold dust. Shirley assumes Little John's guilt and demonstrates limited faith in the congenial form of justice that ensues. What the narrative shows, though, is a rendition of due process and collective action—in its own ad hoc kind of way. Assuming a lynch mob is forming, Shirley proceeds to reveal that the camp is holding a vote to determine whether a trial can be held in the neighboring camp. There, the members elect a president and jury, and two attorneys are appointed. After a short prosecution and a colorful defense, the jury finds Little John guilty and orders a sentence of whipping. The story is one of legal and juridical irregularities, for sure, and Shirley renders it all in rather condescending language. But it also reveals the capacity of these people to adapt collectively, to seek justice, and to keep the peace.

This peace-keeping trend does not hold. The collective and democratic prosecutions of justice start to suffer, and so does the formal and aesthetic quality of the letters. An odd epistle of miscellaneous incidents, Letter Tenth (dated 25 November 1851, published November 1854) depicts Shirley's own discovery of gold, a tree nearly falling on her cabin, a complaint against women's rights activists known as "Bloomers," and a strange anecdote of a captured pheasant. As the linearity of the overall narrative suddenly hits a rough stretch, scholars who presume that these letters were always planned for publication should take pause at this peculiarly unstructured moment. One might argue, as Josiah Royce did, that "artistic defects [are] inevitable in a disconnected series of private letters," or as JoAnn Levy has, that "exuberance for her experience overwhelmed Mrs. Clappe's penchant for the stilted and literary phrase."[61] Such critical apologies for these aesthetic flaws make sense, given the ways that Shirley's letters in many ways contribute to a hallmark of a capitalist-anchored US liberal democracy—a bourgeois celebration of cross-class ethicality—as Brian Roberts has identified.[62] This commitment to a sense of narrative progress, though, belies the content that has been and will be represented.

Development toward more orderly politics and prosecutions of justice seems to have been significantly arrested, and Shirley's appraisals do little to establish a coherent response as she levies judgments that are increasingly inconsistent. Her comments raise important questions about legitimate democratic action in local places. Specifically, she draws a strong distinction between what has taken place in her own camp and the actions of the more widely known Vigilance Committee of San Francisco in 1851. Her appreciation for the latter is unquestioned. In Shirley's account, she claims that, unlike the collective in her own camp, with its questionable undertakings, the San Francisco "Vigilance Committee had become absolutely necessary for the protection of society. It was composed of the best and wisest men of the city. They used their powers with a moderation unexampled in history." In praise of their restraint, she asserts that "they laid [their powers] down with a calm and quiet readiness which was absolutely sublime, when they found that legal justice had again resumed [its] course." She especially appreciates the ways that the committee members "took ample time for a thorough investigation of all the circumstances relating to the criminals who fell into their hands; and in *no* case have they hung a man who had not been proved beyond the shadow of a doubt, to have committed at least *one* robbery in which life had been endangered, if not absolutely taken" (*Shirley*, 81). As these comments make clear, Shirley is especially interested in collective democratic action that employs careful deliberation and the consistently protects life and property. Adhering to such liberal conventions typically earned high praise, even in the case of prolonged extralegal practice, as with the San Francisco Vigilance Committee.

From an historical perspective, Shirley's approbation of this most famous of nineteenth-century vigilance committees and her preference for its style versus that on display in her own camp presents some provocative quandaries. San Francisco saw not one but two substantial instances of vigilante justice: the aforementioned committee of 1851, and another after the composition and publication of Shirley's letters in 1856. Shirley's characterizations are consistent with many historical assessments that have lauded the reserved and deliberate workings of both committees. Basing their assessments on interviews with prominent leaders of both committees, the historians Hubert Howe Bancroft and Theodore Hittell, like Shirley, lauded the civic-inspired, deliberative patriotism of self-selected men leading the two committees.[63] Josiah Royce rendered a similar judgment in his work of California history and moral philosophy.[64] All justified the two committees' actions while acknowledging what William C. Culberson has diagnosed as the sources of vigilantism in the United States: "When civil government was not sufficiently organized or able to control or punish violators of public peace, community leaders of the Old West often took matters into their own hands, and met violence with violence."[65] As the case of *Joaquín Murieta* demonstrates, and as Shirley's letters show, there appeared to be limited social order regulating political differences, and vigilance committees abounded.

More recent assessments of the two vigilance committees in San Francisco, however, have raised doubts about these famous historical assessments paying such high tribute. According to the historians Robert M. Senkewicz and Nancy J. Taniguchi, the committees were populated by men who had a profound sense of self-interest, and they have found very little evidence of selfless, civic-minded, democratic patriotism.[66] Given these revelations, it seems likely that at least some segment of public opinion would have raised an eyebrow at Shirley's extended compliments for their work. Regardless, Shirley's letters that appeared periodically in 1854 and 1855—especially this one, which explicitly references the 1851 San Francisco Vigilance Committee, and others that note repeated formations of more local varieties, sometimes in jest and other times in full seriousness—no doubt contributed to the ways that readers thought about democracy. In Shirley's depiction, the retrospective account of the San Francisco Vigilance Committee erases any antagonisms and does work similar to that of George Bancroft's history of Revolutionary figures and Harriet Beecher's literary construction of democratic space. Writing in a more present-tense mode, Shirley more skeptically depicts the workings of ragtag vigilance committees as seemingly arbitrary exercises of justice, according to her liberal sensibilities.

But if her take on the local committees registers complaints about arbitrary actions and questionable justice, her opinions about various issues merit charges of arbitrariness. In the very next episode, Shirley details a case involving two men who abandoned a third to die of exposure. The two men are held over for trial, but with no evidence to convict, they are eventually released and sent on their way. Even though the semblance of legal apparatus appears, the callousness of these men—in Shirley's mind, criminal conduct—is especially heinous. She writes, "Although they have been acquitted, many shake their heads doubtfully at the whole transaction.... The desertion of a dying friend under such circumstances... is in truth almost as bad as actual murder" (*Shirley*, 83). Her complaints are understandable, but also curious. She admits that there is no evidence to convict, which would seemingly adhere to the principles of liberal jurisprudence. Yet she disputes the decision. Her arbitrariness largely matches the apparent capriciousness of law and order more generally. The narrative nevertheless offers evidence that democratic actions are proceeding in Rich Bar, even if they are not happening according to the whims of the genteel narrator and her normative sensibilities.

In the next letters, Shirley's representations of the local ethos once again appear to be quite subjective. With disapproving consternation, she shares the details of the majority of men in town celebrating Christmas in a weeks-long drunken revelry, and in the process developing a mock vigilance committee much in line with the southwestern humor tradition (for instance, Simon Suggs's mock trial) to deal with those less inclined to imbibe. In another, readers encounter a compelling depiction of "equitable justice" after five men decamp without paying their creditors: "A meeting of the miners was convened, and 'Yank'... was appointed, with another person, to go in search of the culprits and bring them back to Indian Bar." The pursuit proves successful, and Yank returns the culprits to the camp. "The self-constituted court, after a fair trial, obliged the five men to settle all liabilities before they again left the river" (*Shirley*, 93). Other than the prefatory comment about equitable justice, Shirley shares no judgment. She later details the "Frenchmen on the river celebrat[ing] the revolution of February 1848" and records their speech: "We could not help laughing at their watchwords. They ran in this wise; 'Shorge Washingtone, James K. Polk, Napoleon Bonaparte! Liberté, Egalité, Fraternité! Andrew Jackson, President Fillmore, and Lafayette!' I give them to you, word for word, as I took them down at the time" (*Shirley*, 93). Despite her sarcastic tone, readers nevertheless encounter a functioning democratic polity that addresses wrongdoing, that allows for celebrations made of mash-ups. To be sure, pure political philosophies are absent in a demos like this, but a hodgepodge of democratically inclined thinking nevertheless merges with democratic action. Shirley does not recognize it as such, but like the pre-Revolutionary protesters or the vernacular expressions of southwestern humorists or Mary Clavers's neighbors in Michigan, their viability remains.

Readers of subsequent letters, however—at least the few who in 1855 were tracking the linear narrative across episodic letters published a month apart—would soon discover that the prospects of national standards reforming the populations of Rich Bar seemed especially bleak. The breakdown of functional collective rule begins, coincidentally, with the depiction of a Fourth of July celebration. While the residents of the camp are proud of the symbolic value of Independence Day, postcelebration incidents demonstrate the poor fit between the nation's ideals and the people on the ground. In the first sign of troubled connections between local and national, "the Committee of Arrangements had not been able to procure a copy of the Declaration of Independence" (*Shirley*, 127). After a couple of speeches and the reading of a rather egalitarian poem, Shirley's faith is renewed. When a subsequent dinner includes two recent arrivals with all the fashions from the East, along with a bona fide captain from the US-Mexican War, the promise of manifest destiny once again appears to be on the table. Before the dinner concludes, though, the pride-swelling patriotic celebration dissipates into a fistfight in the barroom. On Shirley's walk home, her entourage encounters "noisy shouts of 'Down with the Spaniards,' 'The great American People forever,' and other similar cries" (*Shirley*, 130). The violence and the chauvinistic behavior prompt a lengthy meditation on the prejudice and inequality on display. While national ideals might spark patriotic revelry on this day of celebration, the community needs something more to ensure life, liberty, and happiness for all.

Shirley's next letter details the beginning of the end for the camp. The occasional injustice and the more congenial time of mock vigilance committees and uneven executions of justice now seem long gone. Ethnic tensions on the rise, violence growing, a new vigilance committee forming—Shirley expresses disappointments with these disorderly developments. In the final four letters that cover the last few months in the mines, Shirley grows numb to the violence and increasingly recalcitrant with specific details. Another murder simply "has given us something to gossip about" (*Shirley*, 144). When the vigilance committee arrests but eventually acquits a clearly innocent man, she resignedly declares, "Oh, public opinion in the Mines, thou art in truth a *cruel* thing, but at the same time, thank God, most *fickle!*" (*Shirley*, 145). Later detailing a return to the longer settled American Valley to attend a nominating convention for the coming election—her husband is a delegate—she shares some sense of hope that state-ordained law and order stand ready to arrive. But Shirley forecloses the possibility of development and manifest destiny, admitting that this excursion offers few signs of progressive civilization. Enduring illness and abject accommodations, Shirley shares far more details of her private sufferings, and the few mentions of the convention convey little enthusiasm. The convention "came off," but the most memorable elements were the prominence of "horse-racing, and gambling, in all their detestable varieties, [which] were the order of the day" (*Shirley*, 159–60). When the couple eventually returns home they find that the mines of Rich Bar and Indian Bar have all been abandoned, and the time for departure back to San Francisco has come.

BOOM AND BUST ARE A CLEAR PART OF GOLD RUSH LORE, but the latter stages of Shirley's letters—and Ridge's novelistic experiment *Joaquín Murieta*—have really been all bust. National order is long delayed, and its arrival seems unlikely, aborted by the rise of a violence-prone mobocracy brought on by the incompatibility of national norms in the vast space of California. As the most forward-looking locale in the newly established continental nation, early California in many ways was seen as the future of the United States and the most cherished emblem of progress and manifest destiny. The imaginative literary texts of John Rollin Ridge and Louise Clappe tell a very different story. Whatever the intentions of the respective authors, these stories disrupt the presumed continental manifestation of national, democratic principles.

Back in "the States" (to borrow Shirley's oft used phrase), other conflicts that spoiled fellow feeling were brewing across the nation, with battles over the destiny of the nation focused primarily on the issue of slavery. For many, slavery was *the* national ailment. For others, it was a symptom of an even deeper problem: the failures of democracy in the United States to live up to its loftiest ideals. As we see in chapter 5, for two notable free Black authors in the metropolitan center of the nation (New York City), this disenchantment led to some of the most imaginative and most radical takes on democracy—more radical because they were more modest and more basic than what was attempted in California.

CHAPTER FIVE

Black New York, Antiracist Dignity, and Basic Democracy

To me, one of the most striking and confounding closing passages in nineteenth-century US literature appears in *Life of William Grimes, the Runaway Slave* (1825). Expressing hopes that his book will cure his impoverishment and help him chart a plan for his future, he raises the proposition of one additional money-making venture that addresses concerns beyond his own individual prospects. Grimes declares, "If it were not for the stripes on my back which were made while I was a slave. I would in my will leave my skin as a legacy to the government, desiring that it might be taken off and made into parchment, and then bind the constitution of glorious, happy and free America. Let the skin of an American slave bind the charter of American liberty!"[1] On the surface, Grimes's qualified proposal highlights a nation-oriented prescription to provide remedy to his personal ills. Yet the tangled grammar and syntax complicate this interpretation. The conditional phrasing and subjunctive voice eventually give way to the transitive and exclamatory, but not before the former two sentences raise the issue of material bodies and their role in delivering the promises of the American Revolution. Sustainable life in the present, in common, is a priority. Neighborly petition is considered and yet discarded. Contingency is the entrenched condition. A radical reform of the nation's constitutional charter—ideally and materially—is necessary.

Grimes's closing lines highlight the need for reform across the nation, and within the African American literary tradition (as well as plenty of others in the pre–Civil War decades), he was hardly alone. Mid-nineteenth-century African American literary history has typically been embedded within a national scale of reference. Fugitive slave narratives provided faithful first-person renderings of experiences of the enslaved; Black-authored abolitionist essays and sermons argued for the immediate or gradual conclusion of chattel slavery; novels published in the 1850s sought a new genre and venue to enunciate antislavery sentiments; the Black press established all the materials needed for an imagined national community—and all rightly assumed that slavery was a national problem and established their respective scales of reference accordingly. Even the voices that spurned the idea that Black people and white people could coexist in the United States—Martin Delany in *Blake*

(1859), for instance, or late 1850s proponents of emigration to Haiti, like Henry Highland Garnet—sought nationalist options to establish a framework for alternatives.[2] With the Liberty Party developing a platform aimed at the "denationalization of slavery" in the early 1840s and the Compromise of 1850 creating an even more widespread notion that slavery was a national rather than a sectional institution, there seems little room for African American literary production to have operated on any scale other than a national one, with its predominating norms.[3]

Although such ideas have dominated narratives of African American cultural history, numerous scholars, including Frances Smith Foster, Xiomara Santamarina, and Eric Gardner, have clearly demonstrated that this is a reductive gloss of an exceedingly heterogeneous and polycentric tradition.[4] Constrained to the default of a (white) liberal hermeneutic tradition, the conventional tools of literary criticism attuned to white, Eurocentric cultures have often proved wanting. Fortunately, recent cultural and literary histories have significantly altered the scope of pre–Civil War African American studies and importantly prompted new conceptions of nineteenth-century American literature in general.[5] At the intersection of literary studies and the study of US democracy, Ivy Wilson, Lloyd Pratt, and Derrick Spires have convincingly argued that numerous nineteenth-century African American writers presented some of the most radical of political philosophies through their imaginative writings.[6] Among these, Spires's book focuses on the everyday forms of democratic experiences in relation to a not-yet constitutionally defined version of citizenship, regardless of whether the writers or their subjects were recognized and treated as such. Importantly, Spires's conception maps out alternative sites besides state-sanctioned citizenship and lays the foundation for cultural texts as political performances, much as I have been claiming these misfit texts implicitly do in their storytelling aims.

If the literary misfits of Philadelphia and the Southwest were the productions and representations of white men experiencing most, if not all, the rights and privileges that would come to be enumerated in the Reconstruction Amendments as the grounding of national citizenship, then they could be assumed to be inherently conservative rather than progressive. On the contrary, the politics they share with writers from the Northwest and California demonstrate consistent attraction to more egalitarian democratic ideas and show that rights and privileges were not prerequisites for imagining alternative democracies. As the previous chapters demonstrate, scholars can miss these common threads when we fit such texts within the default of a liberal-oriented framework built on ideologies projected by a patriarchal, white supremacist, manifest destiny-driven nation with deeply embedded imperial ambitions. Similarly, when we look at African American writers operating in what had become the cultural and capitalistic center of the nation and contributing to nonwhite, nonmainstream venues within the print public sphere, national prescriptions and liberal sensibilities can occlude radical political imaginings of this period, especially those articulated by thinkers who developed significant doubts about the chances for disenfranchised people under the federal and state constitutions. Much of the critical tradition in African American studies has rightly focused on the diasporic and transnational aspects of its history. But there also existed localized responses to this particular moment when nationalisms of both assimilationist and exceptionalist trajectories seemed misframed and off target.

In this final case study, I offer a reading of two African American episodic texts in 1850s New York City: James McCune Smith's *Heads of the Colored People* series (1852–54) and William J. Wilson's series *The Afric-American Picture Gallery* (1859). These texts provocatively engage, I contend, a political construct that Josiah Ober has dubbed "basic democracy." This alternative political form untethers democracy from more conventional signs of liberalism, including self-possession, property rights, rationalist contract-based societies, and parts earning more meaning than wholes.[7] Instead, basic democracy signifies a commitment to collective political action grounded in the principle implicitly underlying William Grimes's concluding appeal—civic dignity. In Ober's words, "Like liberty and equality, dignity is necessary for collective self-governance and must be preserved by democratic rules."[8] To what degree these literary texts could influence rules makers to ensure the preservation of dignity is unclear; nevertheless, the sketches promote the conferral of dignity on those who have been denied it, and thus articulate the need for new norms in politics, culture, and society. Aided by Ober's theories, I offer an assessment complementary to Martha Jones's legal study *Birthright Citizens* (2018) and her keen insights into the legal battles that free African Americans in Baltimore waged in pursuit of both rights and citizenship, which had yet to be clearly defined across the nation as a whole. Acknowledging a lack of clear connection between rights and citizenship before the Reconstruction Amendments—essentially, a question of which served as a prerequisite to the other—Jones contends that "Black Americans' efforts were aimed at securing rights that evidenced their citizenship. Still, when rights were denied, free Black people inverted the argument: citizenship was said to be a gateway to rights."[9] For many well-known African American texts in this game-changing decade—Frederick Douglass's in particular—rights were crucial.

Conversely, this chapter highlights Black writers who imagined a local politics grounded in civic dignity that would counter the rights-based proclivities of the constitutional nation and its procedural tenets.[10] Doing so enabled them to craft narratives that imagined the empowerment of all persons—whether autonomous rights-bearing subjects or not—conferred with dignity and capable of engaging in collective self-rule.

Displacing the national framework and the liberal conventions within which African American literature has often been fitted, I first address the only fictional work by the most prolific African American writer of the century, Frederick Douglass. In "The Heroic Slave," Douglass establishes democratic empowerment within a conventional aesthetic framework anchored in notions of historical assimilation, individualistic self-possession, and formal order, similar to what we have seen in Harriet Beecher's first short story and Bret Harte's western tales. While Douglass's perspectives and theories certainly shifted during his pre–Civil War public career, his less well-known interlocutors developed more experimental writings, largely in an irreducible and unrefined vernacular, that deviated from liberal and nationalist orientations. Through the often discordant and provocative writings of Smith and Wilson, I show an evolving disenchantment with nationalist orientations of order and an insistence on civic dignity rather than liberal self-possession. Their works present a range of semiautonomous misfit figures who push back against the more common respectability politics of the era. Their texts weave in and out of formal coherence. They likewise meditate on the ways that, as much as self-reliance and self-making were heralded in the era, democratic politics required a more basic starting point than a paternalistic bootstraps narrative, as well as "a dynamic, self-reinforcing equilibrium" to ensure that all would be both willing and able to participate.[11]

Frederick Douglass's Liberal Aesthetic

The vast written production of (and on) Frederick Douglass defies generalization. Having drawn a wealth of scholarly attention, the most famous of nineteenth-century African Americans has been portrayed in so many different ways, and the often incompatible appropriations of later generations also are legion. In the words of David Blight, "In one lifetime of antislavery, literary, and political activism, Douglass was many things, and this set of apparent paradoxes make his story so attractive." Most pertinent to this study, Blight characterizes Douglass as "a radical thinker and a proponent of classic nineteenth-century political liberalism;...he strongly believed in self-reliance and demanded an activist-interventionist government at all levels to free slaves, defeat the Confederacy, and protect black citizens against terror and discrimination."[12] Douglass's combination of radical activism with his devotion to a less than radical variety of political liberalism has indeed cast a long shadow.

In his one experiment with imaginative literature, Douglass fashioned a provocative representation of an historical event—the 1841 slave insurrection aboard the *Creole*, led by the memorably named Madison Washington—in an inventively narrated novella. Douglass's motivation to experiment with fiction logically arose after the enormous success of Stowe's *Uncle Tom's Cabin*. In his role as editor, Douglass had responded with some ambivalence to the bestseller, printing numerous reviews of the serialization and later the book in *Frederick Douglass' Paper*. As Robert Levine has shown, Douglass acknowledged the criticism of the more problematic representations in Stowe's novel, but he also carefully shaped the terms of its reception for his readers and championed the net value of her fictive enterprise.[13] Given this appreciation of Stowe's fiction, it makes sense that Douglass would adapt his journalistic skills to the task of politically active imaginative writing.[14] In this way, he might take the good and reform the bad and deliver a compelling narrative that could embrace more perspectives and move more people to an antislavery position.

Drawing on material from his own lectures that had experimented with different emphases in the somewhat murky historical record of the *Creole*, "The Heroic Slave" appeared as early as December 1852, in Julia Griffith's money-raising anthology *Autographs for Freedom*, and subsequently in a serialized version in March 1853 in his own paper. It did not have the same impact as Stowe's sentimental bestseller, but because of its author's fame, it was widely read. Over the last several decades, Douglass's one work of fiction has drawn significant critical interest. Like Stowe's novel, it has received various levels of praise—for its aesthetic achievement, for its brand of antislavery politics, for its imaginings of ways out of suppositions about Black inferiority.[15] Assumed in most of these assessments is the grand scope of Douglass's address. As with many Black-authored texts of the pre–Civil War period, the presumption largely involves a national or transnational/diasporic scale.[16] Though he was interested in the diasporic nature of Black nationalism and the possibilities provided by the oceanscape of the Atlantic, Douglass needed some form of fixed jurisdiction in which his appeals to natural law could play out—presumably the US nation.[17] Douglass's anchoring to the spatial scale of a fixed jurisdiction as well as the temporal frame of US history no doubt served practical needs. Regarding its cultural politics, Douglass's novella defaulted to the nation's distinctively individualistic and liberal order.

Undergirding this national scale of reference and substantive liberalism are the formal, aesthetic qualities of the story. Douglass's one work of fiction is a carefully crafted one, with four balanced chapters, dialogue between eloquent speakers, intentional moves of characters on- and offstage when violence takes place, and precise names and metaphors throughout—all of which combine to form a well-crafted literary achievement built on a measured approach. Douglass claims in his opening that the narrative will only offer "glimpses of this great character[,] . . . a few transient incidents [that] afford but partial satisfaction[,] . . . [a figure largely] enveloped in darkness."[18] But the craftedness and order of the novella suggest something more in line with constitutional prescriptions of the US nation.[19] As the foremost African American writer and thinker of the pre–Civil War era, Douglass has always loomed large.[20] His expedient default to the terms of liberal democracy and its concomitant aesthetic framing in this one work of fiction—even if his other writings suggest alternatives—established a strong political current against which other Black New York writers of imaginative leanings would have to strive.

From its opening, "The Heroic Slave" makes many claims on the legacy of the American Revolution. By the third sentence of an opening gambit that hails Virginia for its unequaled production of significant figures in US lore, the narrative declares, "History has not been sparing in recording their names, or in blazoning their deeds." Formal, progressive history—the type that George Bancroft championed—looms large here, authenticating the experiences of representative types. This framing leads to Virginia being cast in "enviable distinction among her sister States." But a notable Virginian of extraordinary merit has been left out, leading the narrator to declare, "There stands the fact, that a man who loved liberty as did Patrick Henry,—who deserved it as much as Thomas Jefferson,—and who fought for it with a valor as high . . . as he who led all the armies of the American colonies through the great war for freedom and independence, lives now only in the chattel record of his native State" (*HS*, 4). Clearly the narrative aspires to recover an unofficial hero and render him an equal among the sacred actors. The choices to highlight Henry, to use em dashes to set off Jefferson, and to go without naming George Washington are deliberate and rhetorically effective.[21] This new figure will be fit into the pantheon of heroes of the American Revolution who were particularly bold in speech and in fighting action.

Douglass's opening appeal to Revolutionary figures has drawn significant attention from critics.[22] As discussed in chapter 1, on Philadelphia, claiming ownership of the Revolution's legacy had become a regular practice in these days of nationalization. To claim a place in the legacy, then, would have seemed a valuable component in Douglass's integrationist scheme. As John Ernest has noted, though, "In all forms and forums of historical writing, African Americans necessarily had to contend with and against the developing tradition of white American historical thought."[23] In this fictionalized account of history, Douglass's opening gambit bypasses this and places the yet-to-be-named hero of a more recent era in the company of a group from two generations prior. The maneuver demonstrates the same general inclination that prominent white historians—along with Philadelphians and northwesterners—were employing to develop clear roots to the Revolutionary moment. If Douglass, as Ernest, Pratt, and Russ Castronovo have argued, produced historiography that avoided white historians' tendency to rely on vague and abstract language, especially when seeking direct connections to Revolutionary legacy, then this opening moment of "The Heroic Slave" seems like a moment when he very much employs the general tendencies of writers promoting the liberal tradition and takes a different course as he shifts from nonfictive journalism to imaginative writing.[24] Regarding historical precedent, "The Heroic Slave" plays the more traditional nationalist game even as it subverts the tradition by inserting a new Black hero into official history.

As the narrative goes on to situate its protagonist in historical, progressive time, it likewise develops methods of representation that further demonstrate Douglass's adherence to the liberal tradition of literary expression. As numerous critics have noted, Douglass faced a tough bind when developing strategies for representing this particular historical event. Whether building on the fugitive slave narrative tradition and developing voices of self-authenticating Black people, or overrelying on the individualistic and the masculine to the detriment of a more revolutionary brand of politics, Douglass deferred to principles of self-possession and transactional relationships.[25] The heroic figure of Madison Washington, the white men like Listwell and Tom Grant, even the unnamed men populating a decaying tavern in Virginia—they all reflect what John Stauffer has identified as Douglass's conviction about aesthetics serving as the key operative to resolving the paradox of representation of a man once understood as enslaved and later as free. According to Stauffer, Douglass believed in a "true art" of "accurate and 'authentic' representation of blacks, rather than caricatures such as blackface minstrelsy." From this, he understood freedom as "a matter of aesthetics in both a representational and rhetorical sense: the slave acquired subjectivity by being represented; and the reader would, Douglass hoped, be transformed by his representation."[26] Such convictions would bear out most tellingly in his one work of fiction, and they do so through conventional norms of individualism.

Douglass's orderly aesthetics and emphasis on individualistic self-possession through eloquent speech produce an heroic story, but they also place limitations on the potential alternative democracy that would default to the collective; they likewise raise the principle of dignity, only to push it way down the list of priorities and thus eschew its significance as a foundation for collective democratic opportunities. Following the prefatory opening in which the narrative situates this tale in the historical record, the scene is populated by two figures: Washington and Listwell. As Listwell first overhears and then looks on, Washington questions his rationale for staying put, asking whether he lacks the courage to escape. On recognizing his innate courage in recent actions to save a drowning man and to beat back a raging bull, Washington climactically answers his own question: "Could a coward do that? *No,—no,—*I wrong myself,—I am no coward. *Liberty* I will have, or die in the attempt to gain it" (*HS*, 6). As the narrative moves on, it begins to generalize many of Washington's comments in its only moment of denouncing the institution of slavery, which broadens his sense of injustice: "Scathing denunciations of the cruelty and injustice of slavery; heart-touching narrations of his own personal suffering, intermingled with prayers to God of the oppressed for help and deliverance." But this brief thought is soon overrun by a litany of individuated and interiorized self-focus as these prayers are immediately "followed by presentations of the dangers and difficulties of escape, and formed the burden of his eloquent utterances; but his high resolution clung to him,—for he ended each speech by an emphatic declaration of his purpose to be free" (*HS*, 7–8). Individual liberty stands as the first demand, to some degree in the service of his own dignity.

The conceit of the scene depends on the impact on the other figure in the scene, the Northwesterner riding through rural Virginia who happens on Washington's soliloquy. Listwell has been noted as Douglass's ideal listener, who hears the story of an enslaved man in the right way and resolves to be abolitionist.[27] The narrative describes the as yet unnamed figure as one who paternalistically has "long desired to sound the mysterious depths of thoughts and feelings of the slave" (*HS*, 7). The narrative displays the interiority and the sacred selfhood of both actors. Yet Listwell is hardly sounding depths, which would suggest an intentional search or an endeavor of discovery. Instead, he is riding through the woods, passively comes upon Madison's soliloquy, and eavesdrops. Never does he confront Madison. Instead, the "speech of Madison rung through the chambers of his soul, and vibrated his entire frame" (*HS*, 8–9). Absent here is any treatment of Madison with a form of noninfantilizing dignity. The scene appears dialogic, but there is no actual exchange. Although dialogue becomes central to the next three chapters of the text, readers see no interracial dialogue at this early stage—just two individuals declaring related but separate resolutions. These grand speeches do the work of inscribing the wrongs and the need for political change, but they do not necessarily build the foundation for that political change to come via collective, democratic activities. The next two chapters, the first featuring an escaped Madison in Ohio and the second back in Virginia after Madison has been captured while trying to free his wife, make some amends in the direction of collective action as Madison accepts the help of Listwell on two occasions: first to get him across the Canadian border and later, after his capture when returning for his wife, with the files that will aid his eventual escape. Such moves imply the need for interracial cooperation.

Yet this collaborative work seems a secondary concern compared to the climactic focus on Washington's inimitable heroism aboard the *Creole*. In the final chapter, the first mate of the *Creole* (Grant) admits to a dubious companion at the tavern, "The leader of the mutiny was as well fitted to lead in a dangerous enterprise as any one white man in ten thousand.... It was a mystery to us *where* he got his knowledge of language" (*HS*, 47). Unlike Douglass's 1845 *Narrative of the Life of Frederick Douglass*, which famously credited his acquisition of literacy to both his own cleverness and the graciousness of Lucretia Auld and several unnamed Baltimore boys, "The Heroic Slave" imagines Washington's command of language as a preternatural gift. Later, after the mutiny and the squall, Grant admits, "I felt myself in the presence of a superior man; one who, had he been a white man, I would have followed willingly and gladly in any honorable enterprise. Our difference of color was the only ground for difference of action" (*HS*, 50). Grant's admission is matched by the actions of the other enslaved men, who, in the narrative's closing sentence, "marched, amidst the deafening cheers of a multitude of sympathizing spectators, under the triumphant leadership of their heroic chief and deliverer, MADISON WASHINGTON" (*HS*, 51).[28]

At the end of the day, Douglass's paternalism and devotion to heroic male individualism shine through. They eschew the notion of a more collective democracy, and there is limited space for dignity beyond that which the central character seeks for himself. Apart from Listwell and Grant, the other characters—the nonwhite ones especially—have mostly been shadows. The story indeed authenticates the central figure and makes the case for his eligibility as a fully vested, rights-bearing figure. The price is the sacrifice of the protagonist and the dignity of other disenfranchised peoples. Whether this was truly worth it for the good of the collective is not addressed. With the writings of other Black New Yorkers, dignity would become a more central issue, one that was crucial for the stakes of developing a localized ethos that could lay a firmer foundation for collective democratic empowerment for all, especially those who had long been lacking it.

The Dignified *Heads of the Colored People*

After James McCune Smith published the sixth installment of the *Heads of the Colored People* series in *Frederick Douglass' Paper*, Douglass penned a "Letter from the Editor" that expressed discontent over Smith's choices of representative subjects in the series. In the letter dated 15 May 1853, Douglass writes of a recent trip to New York and records his own observations of "the character and occupation of the colored people who reside" there. He notes that popular opinions have developed from seeing types "in rags and idleness, or dressed up in the gaudy trappings of waiters and flunkeys, dancing attendants behind their chairs at table, in hotels or steamboats, or forming a part of their grand equipages (the ebony to set off ivory), rolling down the life-thronged Broadway."[29] As a counter, Douglass offers alternative impressions with a few descriptions drawn from the institutionalized settings—"in their places of business, at their churches, and in their literary and benevolent societies"—in order "to get any just idea of their character or condition." In praise of the Congregational Methodist Church, Douglass testifies "to the order, neatness, and intelligence" on display. He likewise encountered "six establishments belonging to and under management of colored men, bearing all the marks of material prosperity." These, Douglass claims, are better representations of free Black people in New York, figures who bear all the ideal traits of manhood (his examples are all men), intellectual and material property, and inconspicuous forms of self-possession. The concluding sentence states, "Why will not my able New York correspondent bring some of the real 'heads of the colored people' before our readers?"[30] Lacking ambiguity, Douglass's criticisms fall well within the discourses of liberal individualism (as in "The Heroic Slave") and institutionalized Yankee culture.

Smith's experimental sketches to this point had likely started well enough for Douglass's standards, albeit just barely. "The Black News-Vender" (25 March 1852), "The Boot-Black" (15 April 1852), and "The Washerwoman" (17 June 1852) did not depict property-owning men demonstrating the marks of intellectual and self-possessing virtues, but the eponymous characters were all hardworking and presumably self-sufficient. The next three—"The Sexton" (16 July 1852), "The Steward" (24 December 1852), and "The Editor" (18 February 1853)—offered less flattering portrayals: one man stole from other Black people, another smuggled property into and out of the country, and the third, though a newspaperman, did not know how to read or write. These three, it would seem, were likely the sketches that garnered Douglass's disapproval. That Douglass's letter appeared three months after "The Editor" makes one wonder what sort of new contribution had arrived on Douglass's desk from his New York correspondent. In any case, Smith's portraits from that point forward carried a more promising trend of representations, steering away from any unflattering portraits to one that celebrated the mechanical arts in "The Inventor" (9 September 1853), one that theorized racial relations of the day in "The Whitewasher" (30 September 1853), and two final entries titled "The Schoolmaster" (3 November 1854 and 17 November 1854), neither of which followed the conventions of earlier sketches and instead offered various complaints against current politics and occasions of intellectual deceit.

Whatever the dustup between the erstwhile colleagues-in-arms (having met on the abolitionist circuit in the 1840s, Smith would pen the introduction to Douglass's 1855 *My Bondage and My Freedom*), these provocative sketches demonstrate an important distinction in political projects within the imaginative literature penned by these two brilliant leaders.[31] James McCune Smith was born enslaved in New York City in 1813 and declared free on New York's Emancipation Day in 1827. After training at the distinguished African Free School in Brooklyn, he went on the University of Glasgow in the 1830s, earning his BA, MA, and MD. On his return the United States, he established himself as a scholar activist throughout the 1840s and experimented with literary endeavors in the 1850s.[32] Like Douglass, Smith broke with Garrisonian abolitionism and its extranational and nonviolent tactics, and his investment in the formation of the Radical Abolitionist Party in 1855 and its backing of Gerrit Smith for president suggests that he maintained a sincere interest in national politics. These ventures yielded little to no electoral success, and his criticism of the newly born Republican Party in the latter part of years of the decade suggests a substantial disenchantment with the prospects of national change. It is doubtful that he was ever fully convinced that national procedural politics could produce his desired reforms.

Throughout the tempestuous 1850s, with his commitments to and frustrations with national politics, Smith continued to write prolifically. As the New York correspondent to *Frederick Douglass' Paper*, his column was signed with the name "Communipaw," a curious choice in relation to other periodical pseudonyms, but one that signified his subversive convictions.[33] His writings ranged widely through science, history, and politics, and the periodical essay offered the ideal format for him to let his experimental mind wonder widely. With the *Heads of the Colored People* series, though, Smith delivered his most creative literary work. John Stauffer has contended that these sketches present "an image of a nation in which blacks are neither heroes nor villains but humans—complicated men and women struggling to survive in a retrograde society that has rejected them." Stauffer goes on to claim that Smith's characters "define themselves ... in terms of their work, which ... brings autonomy."[34] Derrick Spires has offered a compelling alternative, placing these sketches in dialogue with William J. Wilson's contemporaneous contributions to *Frederick Douglass' Paper*. In opposition to Wilson's contentions that economic elites offered the best form of representation for the free Black community at large—an opinion akin to Douglass's—Smith, in Spires's words, "invokes an ethos of commonwealth republicanism, a polity based on the middling sorts and focused on cultivating a 'public spirit' that cherishes liberty and freedom as its highest end."[35] While this form of "economic citizenship" presents an alternative to the traditional liberal version that was in practice excluding free Black people, it presumes a consistent ideological and aesthetic thread in Smith's thinking and across the sketches. Read in succession, though, the sketches betray numerous inconsistencies, suggesting an alternative aesthetics of representation that averred Douglass's example of and expectations for order, neatness, and good form. In other words, Smith's ever-evolving, vernacular sketches are very much the stuff of misfits.

These disorderly texts foregrounded individual figures who, like many others in this book, would seem ill equipped for the responsibilities of democratic self-rule. Focusing on figures involved in physical labor (the Boot-Black, the Washerwoman, the Whitewasher), service positions (the Sexton, the Steward), print culture (the News-Vender, the Editor), and the intelligentsia (the Inventor, the Schoolmaster), the portraits run the gamut of different types along the socioeconomic food chain. It would seem that Smith came to understand the series as serving exceedingly different purposes at different times. Early on, it seemed largely an opportunity to do just what Stauffer contends: present workers of all types and validate all varieties of labor.[36] But the macabre Sexton and the smuggling Steward hardly revel in the joys of labor. Moreover, with the latter four entries that followed Douglass's rebuke, Smith meditates less on working types and more on the intellectual merit (or lack thereof) of racist ideas. Such disparities in the essays, though all were gathered under the title *The Heads of the Colored People*, demonstrate something like what we see in Lippard's *The Quaker City*, Kirkland's *A New Home*, and Clappe's *The Shirley Letters*. The series was very much an experimental work in progress, and thus evidence of yet another variety of what I have been tracking as vernacular aesthetics.

Importantly, these texts more indelibly work against the criticism that Douglass levied against them, that the figures represented were less-than-respectable types. Here we see what Spires has acknowledged—that these sketches were more invested in respect than in the 1850s politics of respectability.[37] I contend that these sketches foreground something beyond respect: a version of civic dignity in their subjectification that did not depend on or project a rights-based self-possession, but rather the materials that promoted civic dignity as a baseline condition for a more radical democratic ethos. In this enterprise they contribute to the establishment of conditions promoting civic dignity—that is, in the words of Josiah Ober, "being socially accepted as fully worthy of political participation and thereby immune from the disabilities of civic humiliation and infantilization."[38] Tracing a clear sense of consistent authorial intention seems an especially difficult task with a serialized text that took on different themes and issues in relatively short doses across more than two years of composition. While scope and tactics change dramatically, confirmation of noninfantilizing and nonhumiliating forms of dignity nevertheless offers a crucial thread that connects portraits of more and less respectable types.

Such evidence appears in the provocative opening of the first entry, dated 25 March 1852. Opening with a jab at Daniel Webster's contemporaneous run for the presidency, Communipaw hails the Greek lyric poet Anacreon in order to secure the "post of door keeper . . . to the outermost enclosure leading to the Republic of Letters." From this position he can enforce the rules of this alternative "republic of letters" as a "commonwealth, perpetually progressive, free from *caste*, and Cass and Fillmores, which smiles upon all her citizens, if they be but true, which holds triumphant sway and is crowned with perennial laurel in the *coming ages*!"[39] With allusions to caste as well as to the national politicians Lewis Cass and Millard Fillmore, who have done even more harm than Webster's notorious compromise by promoting popular sovereignty discourse to make way for slavery in new western states, the narrative suggests that there are plenty who need to be excluded. Those who are admitted are expected to develop conditional, transactional relationships, for the progressive commonwealth will engage all citizens who desire to be involved. In some ways, this sounds like the contractual language of liberalism: the citizens receive benefits "if they be true." But the rewards do not come in the form of property, but rather in the guise of smiles. It seems this republic of letters will differ from both the abstract universal republicanism idealized in the early national period and the contract-based liberal individualism that was coming to hold sway in the 1850s. The smiles hint at what will become more apparent in the latter stages—the conferral of nonpaternalistic dignity for all.

Dignity appears in limited doses in the first three installments of the series and their championing of everyday working-class figures. These three foreground a variety of impressions on issues of freedom and slavery, mobility and stability, individual self-making and composite world-making. In "The Black News-Vender," the main character is limited in his physical mobility due to his legs having been amputated at the knees, but his dignity is nevertheless preserved. "He's none of your nomad criers in the literary world," the narrative declares. "He is a stationed vender, or, perhaps like his class, the colored people, he noiselessly does his mission and leaves it to others to find out who and what he is." The sketch proceeds with heavy doses of sympathy and pity, which would have been familiar to readers in the sentimentalist-soaked 1850s. Repeatedly, the narrative notes all the different types seeking to patronize the disabled News-Vender and to pay with several more coins than the papers cost, which leads the narrative to declare, "Merciful God! What a living fountain of human sympathy hast thou planted on that stone stoop, linking human creature to human creature, in spite of all the bars which society has vainly placed between them."[40] The narrative's presumptions in many ways echo the pity that Douglass records in "The Heroic Slave." They likewise lay the groundwork for the concerns about impressibility as tool of biopower in this era, which Kyla Schuller has insightfully disclosed.[41] But immediately after this moment of undignified infantilization, the narrative shifts to dialogue, with Communipaw addressing the News-Vender. After a series of questions about his past and the cause of his condition, the News-Vender responds positively, insisting that "I—made myself free," that he deals in policies, and that he saves money with hopes of having his own shop. When he shares a vague recollection of the date of his shipwreck and the accident that cost him his legs, Communipaw immediately steers the event back on his own experience, recollecting that the News-Vender lost his legs on the same day that he lost a child. The loss evokes a good bit of pathos, and the sad misfortunes presumably create a new bond that leads Communipaw to declare that the News-Vender "must have a shop. Your story must be printed and sold. A little place must be hired. And your first stock in trade shall be purchased from the sum left behind by the little girl who found rest in heaven, while you manfully met and battled with your severest ill on earth."[42] Communipaw is definitely feeling the sympathy, even if the News-Vender is not. Here we see the conventions of respectability politics and tropes of sentimentalism working overtime. The News-Vender, however, does not seem to be buying it. To what degree these conventions hold up within and beyond this installment is an important question. Given what follows, parody of these literary forms seems the more likely answer.

The next two entries suggest only slight twists on the themes established in the first of these experimental sketches. "The Boot-Black" details the life of a formerly enslaved man of New York's famed Livingston family after being set free on Emancipation Day in 1827. His activities on "finding himself in possession of himself" include a dandyish walk through New York, the courtship of his eventual bride, and the challenge of building an honest bootblacking business in the face of widespread doubt and condescension. In regard to having a denigrated occupation, the narrative confesses, "But wiser than dandy opinion, he found it and has proved it . . . well fitted for him to exercise by means of it all the faculties which make a man useful to his family and a credit to the State."[43] Similarly, "The Washerwoman" offers some conventions of self-possession as the central character recalls her own self-emancipation on the day when, like Douglass famously facing down Edward Covey, she told "her so-called master" that "if you dare touch me with that lash, I will tear you to pieces!" This celebration of liberal conventions of transactional relationships and self-possession prove temporary, though, as the narrative mentions that the Washerwoman has a child, father unknown: "A sort of social Pariah, he had come into the world after the fashion which so stirs up Ethiop's pious honor. And yet genial, forgiving Nature, with a healthy forgetfulness of priests and the rituals, had stamped this boy's face with no lineament particularly hideous, nor yet remarkable."[44] Avoiding any pious disdain for this child born out of wedlock and calling out Ethiop (the pseudonym of William J. Wilson) for his self-righteousness, the narrative fashions new norms built on dignity. Next to "The Boot-Black" and "The News-Vender," readers encounter healthy doses of liberalism, but the placement of alternatives in areas of emphasis suggests there to be much higher value in collectively developed dignity.

The trend away from liberal conventions to a dynamic equilibrium grounded in dignity gathers pace in the next entries. Whereas the first three entries herald the dignity of working-class figures selling newspapers, polishing boots, and washing laundry, Communipaw's fourth and fifth subjects understandably raise concerns not only with Douglass and Wilson but also with general readers of *Frederick Douglass' Paper*. Few literary figures—even in this study of literary misfits—are less attractive than the one featured in "The Sexton." Graced with an unsettling visage and form, he has spent a life working in various jobs for the church but is best remembered for his role as gravedigger and his propensity for overstuffing Black bodies into the cemeteries and disposing of surplus body parts via any means possible—perhaps even cannibalism.[45] In the next installment, the Steward performs many different jobs in his employment on the ship at sea. Once in port, though, he becomes a deft smuggler, working with a variety of "sundry men" who would come aboard and leave with much more bulk beneath their clothes.[46] The Steward also turns out to be quite the rake as well, having children in many different ports on both sides of the Atlantic. The bad behavior of these two figures largely goes without comment, which raises the question of what Communipaw was doing with these two sketches.

Following the narratives of the honest, earnest labors of the first three figures, these two sketches showcase Black men who have gained positions of greater power and authority and yet show little respect for person or property. The sentimentalist cast that colored the first entry was largely abandoned in the second and third, and here we see an even stronger sense of ambiguity and presumable irony. In contrast with the earlier three sketches, numbers four and five lack the conferral of dignity on their subjects. Moreover, given the subjects' exploitation of bodies, property, and labor for their own selfish gains, these depictions of Black men present a cautionary tale for those who might take advantage of certain freedoms to do the same. To some degree, Smith risks delivering an infantilizing construction, but the lack of commentary means he stops short of moralizing. The more subtle critique is a rejection of continued adherence to the bootstraps narrative, which clearly can lead people like the Sexton and Steward to exploitative ends. The sketches implicitly call instead for a more egalitarian democratic empowerment of all people; in terms of basic democracy, that means a rejection of conditions that can readily lead to the humiliation of others.

As the series evolves, the sixth entry offers yet another turn to new principles, with "The Editor" demonstrating a different example of dignity over individualistic, self-possessing achievement. Smith had long been an active leader in promoting a Black national newspaper, most notably as the chair of the Committee on a National Press at the 1847 National Convention of Colored People in Troy, New York.[47] This installment offers Smith an opportunity to laud Black editors and to cite some individuals by name before the column's conclusion. As demonstration of this editorial skill, Communipaw presents some representative samples of his rhetorical savvy in gathering both content as well as subscriptions, toggling between strategies of guilting readers—the Black reading community specifically—into paying for subscriptions and making lofty claims that this paper is read by elected officials in power.[48] Thereafter, Communipaw reveals a rather damning fact about the Editor: his wife takes dictation of his editorials "because our editor *cannot* write; nay, if the whole truth be told, he cannot read! ... Why he does not learn to read, I cannot imagine. It is a singular defect in our colored editor." While he possesses an unquestionably sharp memory and an impeccable sense of style, the inauthenticity of this editor seems especially curious. But readers once again encounter a challenge to conventional norms connected with self-improvement and self-possession. Given the emphasis that Black leaders like Frederick Douglass and William Wells Brown placed on literacy as a primary means of liberation, Communipaw bucks this trend by finding empowered civic action in an illiterate man. Unlike the Sexton and Steward, he does not exploit others for his own gain, but rather works relentlessly, whatever his bona fides, to promote the causes and needs of the Black community. Failing most tests of self-possession in the form of literacy and autonomy, the Editor nevertheless deserves this distinguished position: "Next to the pulpit, and *behind* the chairs, no place has greater charms for colored Americans than a seat *in* the chair editorial."[49]

Three months after this letter was published, Douglass published his alternative account and rebuke of Communipaw's series. Four more months would pass before a seventh entry appeared, during which time Smith's family suffered the death of a child. Smith and his wife would lose three more children between the seventh and eighth entries. These two sketches have a much different voice than the earlier essays, one that has partially but not fully abandoned its project on the limits of liberal conventions and the need for civic dignity to focus more on systemic issues like the politics of race and the necessity of immediate abolition. In "The Inventor," the narrative rebukes Douglass's presumption that Black people should pursue the higher art of handicraft. In this, Communipaw does not insinuate that Black people are incapable of craft; on the contrary, he cites examples of an enslaved architect in Alabama and a carpenter in Brooklyn. Alternatively, he identifies the systemic racism that has created a white monopoly of this form of artisanship.[50] "The Whitewasher" largely returns to the concerns of the first three entries, once again conferring dignity on a group of laborers who "are a cleanly people, men of families, and regular church-goers."[51] In the final two sketches, which appeared more than a year later, both titled "The Schoolmaster," Communipaw moves even farther away from the investments of his earlier sketches and more explicitly into the realm of contemporary news and democratic politics.[52] In these final two entries, Communipaw assumes the subject position of the sketch, but he looks less like a conventional schoolmaster than an intellectual who is challenging both partisan politics and the functional knowledge of his day. Communipaw prefers a self-sacrificial example and finds greater solace in that process than in selfish gain.

With "The Schoolmaster," Smith's experimental sketches reached conclusion. Along the way, the series moves away from mixed representations of lowly workers toward rebukes of exploitative types who privilege selfish gain over the collective good, before finally giving way to a diverse set of complaints against the norms of both knowledge and politics in his day. Such varieties of representation ultimately abjure Douglass's notion of a more politically expedient representation of Black people and their interests, which had come out in his letter rebuking Smith. There is no outright rejection of the era's highly championed ideas of self-improvement and respectability, but the sketches both individually and collectively reject the conviction that individual rights or successful employment would foster more egalitarian democratic conditions. By focusing on these misfit figures—both good and bad—and frequently making the case for new sensibilities with which to determine their value, *Heads of the Colored People* altogether offers a novel projection of a politics ensconced in the need for dignity bestowed on all peoples and thus imagines an alternative form of basic democracy.

Dignity, Discernment, and *The Afric-American Picture Gallery*

At the same time that Smith was producing the *Heads of the Colored People* sketches, William J. Wilson, writing under the pseudonym "Ethiop," argued in the same pages of *Frederick Douglass' Paper* for a very different catalyst for Black uplift. Instead of championing civic dignity as a precondition for more radical democratic possibilities, Ethiop lobbied for the development of a Black aristocracy and its potential to yield a form of trickle-down gains.[53] But when he launched his series of essays titled *The Afric-American Picture Gallery* later that decade in the *Anglo-African Magazine*, he took a different tack.[54] Following a conventional start commenting on paintings of famous Black scenes and portraits of well-known Black men, near the end of the second installment Ethiop offers a profoundly unsettling description of a painting titled *Mount Vernon*. After noting the supposed glory enveloping the first president's home, Ethiop steers away, highlighting the prominence of decay, images of former slaves turned ghosts, and the overall unflattering appearance of the home of the nation's most prestigious founder.[55] As soon as he finishes this description, Ethiop veers in yet another direction as he moves away from ekphrastic descriptions of paintings and sculptures to dramatize his own interactions with "a white gentleman" and "a colored lady" who have entered the imagined gallery. With these visitors he engages in curious metadialogue about the value of both the gallery and a distinctively Black magazine (the *Anglo-African*), while also working to convince the lady that the Afric-American Picture Gallery plays a crucial role in offering "simple reminders of what the people of color were, now are, and will yet be."[56] Ethiop's narrative shifts midway through the second installment reflect the experimental quality and the unrefined vernacular aesthetics of these sketches. While appearing at first glance to render African Americans as a new form of aesthetic subjectivity, the twists and turns in this second entry and the rewriting of history with all actors involved demonstrates an important convergence of historiography, art, representation, and basic democracy for all Black people, regardless of their condition as "African" or "American" or any other arbitrary place-based appellation.

William J. Wilson was no stranger to Frederick Douglass or James McCune Smith. A longtime contributor to *Frederick Douglass' Paper* as the Brooklyn correspondent, Wilson frequently sparred with Smith in a variety of editorials throughout the mid-1850s. Born in New Jersey and living in Brooklyn as an adult, Wilson was a regular contributor to Black print culture and an active participant in African American political life from the late 1830s through the 1860s, taking part in state suffrage movements and several national conventions.[57] In much of his early periodical writings, as Carla Peterson has noted, "his definition of Negro character differed little from those of white liberals[,] ... defining race through a series of essentialist traits. Positive racial traits were simply substituted for negative ones, and racial categories defining black and white remained firmly in place."[58] Like Douglass and Smith, though, his views took a significantly different shape over time. As Radiclani Clytus and Ivy Wilson have both argued, Wilson was deeply invested in the politics of representation in the crossover discourses of art and politics.[59] Regarding *The Afric-American Picture Gallery*, Wilson contends that Ethiop's "description of the arrangement of the works, his curatorial efforts if you will, becomes the means through which he articulates a form of black subjectivity that is hemispheric and transnational."[60] To some degree, Ethiop counters white supremacist notions of his day with an occasional glimpse into a transnational Black subjectivity built on curatorial practice and aesthetic judgment in these imaginative sketches. That said, he likewise raises doubts about the chances of a conventional liberal subjectivity serving the democratic needs of Black people.

Ethiop's installments in *The Afric-American Picture Gallery* distinctively combine ekphrasis and narrative to produce an innovative aesthetic experience. The combination of generic types yields a provocative political statement: representation comes in a variety of forms, and conventional self-possession and transactional relationships make up only two of a great variety of democratic possibilities. The most enduring takeaway in this reflexive commentary—which John Ernest describes as "a serialized dynamic artistic performance that comments on its own creation as it proceeds"—is the failure of claims to rule of law or right, as well as the lack of a triumphal take on individual autonomy.[61] Because of the work's misfit characteristics, I identify a political project that differs only slightly from the type of critical citizenship that Derrick Spires has drawn from these sketches: "Ethiop's movement through the gallery and his method of analysis provide models for how [readers] could approach objects ... to consolidate citizenship as an escape from politics, anxiety, and difference. His meditation on the pedagogical uses of art and his critique of public taste make each sketch a primer on how to read events in time."[62] Spires's arguments depend on acts of autonomy, willfulness, and volition—all carefully developed formal practices of critical citizenship. Yet, the various sketches themselves, unfolding in an ever-changing rush of narrative varieties, suggest a more limited capacity of self-control and autonomy. Indeed, when faced with various forms of indignity, the narrative evades the controls of individual actors and instead intimates the need for a noninfantilized and nonhumiliated collective. Given that individuals hold subject and object positions based on an ever-shifting positionality, Ethiop's shifty narrative engages an extraliberal horizon that accounts for various modes of experience, political or otherwise.

A major component of this feat comes from the unedited vernacular aesthetics of the series. Over the course of seven installments published between February and October 1859, Ethiop takes readers through a variety of aesthetic ventures: ekphrastic and critical commentary of visual art, embodied narrative, reflexive dialogue. The opening number possesses relative coherence, starting with a first-person narrator detailing his love for visual art, his deficiencies in producing it himself, and his tendencies to go on ventures to discover art in the world. Developing a "habit of rambling in search of, and hunting up curious, old, or rare and beautiful pictures," the narrator discovers the Afric-American Picture Gallery. The gallery is filled with art that "if not highly meritorious, still from its wide range of subjects and ingenuity with which many of them are presented ... affords much for amusement, and ...

much that is valuable and interesting."[63] In these prefatory moments, Ethiop establishes that this gallery holds a diverse selection of artistic pieces, imaginatively presented rather than re-presented, and labeled with middling assessments. Moreover, the "first thing noticeable, is the unstudied arrangement of these pictures. They seem rather to have been put up out of the way, many of them, than hung for any effect."[64] Like Communipaw's sketches in *Heads of the Colored People*, Ethiop's portraits do not fit tidily into Douglass's mold to portray in print the best of African American people and experience. The images that follow are not as unflattering as the portraits of the Sexton and the Steward. Nevertheless, they are not selected as representative simply because they are the best, nor are they ordered in a way that suggests the collective sum is something that the individual parts are not. Analogous in ways to individuals within a democratic polity, these artistic figures are available for improvement as well as augmentation, but they do not, in their dignity, require either.

In the remainder of the first installment, Ethiop presents six paintings: *The Slave Ship, The First and Last Editor, The First Martyr of the Revolution, Sunset in Abbeokuta*, and two paintings that in combination make up *The Under Ground Rail Road*. These ekphrastic sketches of a sampling of artwork demonstrate a clear trajectory: detailing representations of the first African enslaved people on American shores, working through the various steps toward freedom for the formerly enslaved, considering ever so briefly the enticements of a return to Africa, and ultimately revealing the nearly ineffable joy of self-emancipation in the Americas. The descriptions of the paintings themselves are conjoined with aesthetic judgments and critical valuations; for instance, the portrait of the first martyr, Crispus Attucks, "is a fine likeness of a bold, vigorous man,—just such, as would be likely to head a revolution to throw off oppression."[65] To be sure, portraiture throughout the gallery depicts Black figures in a noble fashion that counters the prominent derogatory depictions of Black heads by white phrenologists, as Ivy Wilson has noted.[66] Moreover, when read in relation to the landscape paintings and the paired paintings of various events, the development of an alternative Black subjectivity makes formerly disenfranchised figures more worthy of recognition in the mold of rights-bearing citizens. Perhaps this is what William J. Wilson originally had in mind when he started these entries. But subsequent developments suggest a less orderly execution of that design.

With the opening of the second installment, Wilson's open-ended aesthetic judgments take objects into account in different ways, and the ramifications for a democratic subjectivity built on civic dignity prove crucial. It starts thus: "Pictures are teachings by examples. From them we often derive our best lessons." But the artworks offer more than didacticism in rational forms; they provide affective cues, as they arouse "associations and emotions, and produce troops of thought that paint the memory afresh with hues the most beautiful, touching, beneficial and lasting." Ethiop goes on to consider portraits of great men, citing Washington and Jefferson as subjects who might inspire reflection on the unfinished work of the Revolution and the Declaration of Independence. For Ethiop, though, the portrait that prompts these reflections depicts neither of these two historical figures but rather Toussaint L'Overture, whose painting, ironically, evades ekphrastic description: "Far be it from me," Ethiop opines, "to venture for a description of either the picture or the man. I have no pencil and no pen with which I can do it."[67] The apology follows one form of literary convention of the day, but the painting's ineffability also demonstrates the limits of volitional control that undergirds the liberal-oriented transactions of critical citizenship.

Matters turn more critical at the midpoint of this installment with the extended discussion of "Picture IX.—Mount Vernon" and the heated exchanges with two skeptical visitors in the gallery. Capitalizing on the contemporary tension between idealized portraits of Washington's plantation life and the dilapidated condition of Mount Vernon in the 1850s, Ethiop boldly declares "that in the conception of this picture, the Artist has simply failed; if not in faithfulness to the original, certainly in gratifying the popular American feeling."[68] The description details the general state of decay on display in the image and zooms into a specific area that depicts the exhumed tomb of Washington, the ghost of his body servant (most likely referencing Billy Lee), and several living enslaved people bearing For Sale signs. The details do not resist mediation but rather effectively conjoin past and present, almost in effect creating a sense of motion within the still image. This sense of motion spills into the narrative as the focus moves away from ekphrasis into dramatized interactions between Ethiop and two visitors. The judgments of these three different actors do not come together in any form of consensus; no resolution takes place. Interior angst comes out in Ethiop's descriptions of his own feelings, but the actors appear neither autonomous in their judgments nor secure in their takeaways from the interactions. There is no evidence of dignity conferred, and there is no obvious reassurance of self-possession either.

After hitting dead ends in pursuing uplift, respectability, and consensus, first in ekphrastic depictions of portraits and paintings and subsequently in dramatized dialogue, Ethiop delivers a profound figure who forces a new sort of imagining. In an unexpected turn, he abruptly reveals the name of the young male gallery attendant to be Thomas Onward. Having gone unnamed as he simply watched the door in the second paper, in the third installment Tom now enters the gallery with a painting of himself to hang on the walls. Ethiop appreciates the physical form of the portrait: "Sound in limb, symmetrical in form and robust in health, jovial, frank, easy mannered and handsome." In the next sentence, Ethiop attempts to fold him into an abstracted representative figure, one who "has come down to us through nearly three hundred years of hard trial ... whipped into existence, ... robbed ... hated ... dreaded." Despite all the physical and spiritual hardship, Thomas has countered this narrative by emerging "fresh, smiling, and free."[69] Reflecting further on this figure, Ethiop writes, "The American Nation, if it can, may try its hardened hand yet a few centuries longer upon our live little Tom; but it will hardly mould him to their liking."[70] The opening apostrophe of the third installment thus offers yet another twist in the unconventional representations in the collection. A combination of concrete representation and allegorical amalgamation, Tom is molded by none of it. In some ways, he stands as the supreme individual. Yet he requires no improvement. Whether as human subject or subject of a portrait, Thomas Onward bears all the markers of a nonpaternalistic and nonhumiliating dignity, and on this new figure hangs so much of the motivation for the remaining moments of Wilson's experimental enterprise.

A brand-new trajectory becomes clear when a portrait turns into a lengthy venture away from the gallery and out into a world of disturbing conflict. In what starts as a litany of praise for "Picture No. XI.—The Black Forest," the artwork virtually comes to life as Ethiop receives a letter from the artist of that very picture, inviting him to visit the very place depicted in the painting. Ethiop follows through, leading to a meeting with a reclusive ninety-year-old artist named Bernice, who leads him though a cave to behold a wealth of art objects. He spends extended time detailing stone tablets bearing an account from the future titled "Year 4,000: The Amecans, or Milk White Race," which imagines the decline and fall of white people due to their unethical conflation of people and property. Soon after, Ethiop meets the emaciated figure of Bernice's former owner, now held prisoner, and their subsequent exchange includes a litany of grievances. After Bernice rejects the rule of law as a viable principle, each man shares the wrongs committed against the other: "He plead earnestly for his rights. I told him he had no rights that I was bound to respect. He then begged for his liberty.... He made large promises for that liberty. I told him that they were useless that he had now nothing to give; that he no longer possessed even himself."[71] After a brief comment from Ethiop regarding the fate of a man who could demand his rights while tyrannically abusing Black people, the scene abruptly concludes with a strong sense of the unreliability of the tools of conventional rule of law, the absence of rights as something perpetually possessed, and the need for alternative forms of justice. Ethiop's wariness betrays the failures of dignity on full display here.

The disruptions and disturbances of the trip to the Black Forest prove so unsettling as to keep the narrative unmoored. Perhaps as a way to makes sense of it all by returning to first principles, Ethiop initially returns to the work of ekphrastic description, detailing more paintings, but the emphasis has changed from aesthetic excellence to something more foundational. A paired set titled *Preaching* and *After Preaching*, along with a portrait of Phyllis Wheatley, posit dignity as the supreme value that can be rendered, even as they suggest a retreat into the abstractions and individual isolation that art could offer. In a further return to normalcy in this retreat into the art, Ethiop seems to have gained some proprietary interest in the gallery, which is interesting since he had previously stumbled on it and, to that point, had never claimed ownership or curatorial management over it. But these false starts end up being interrupted by Tom's return with a host of cards bearing the names of a variety of cultural figures who have begged entrance. What had started as a return to the original conceit of descriptions and reflections on the artwork is now moving back into a more collective act of staged dialogue that forces Ethiop out of his individual reverie.

Now that he has failed to maintain his individual stance as subjective observer of the artistic objects, Ethiop delivers some of his most radical and aestheticized reflections on dignity in an otherwise hostile debate between a variety of participants making up a rather broad yet offensively egotistical collective. Addressed by a relatively large number of entrants into the gallery, Ethiop remarks on their engagement with a picture titled *Condition*. Most arresting is the central figure: "The subject is a *colored youth*, sitting upon the bank of a rapid river, beneath a huge tree ... much surrounded by abject wretchedness. Rags and their concomitants cover his body; poverty and want stare him in the face—a face marked with ignorance and the indifference of a stolid content. All else is vacancy." The painting had drawn the ambiguous assessment from a "'little lady' in black," who found it "singularly sad ... and yet ... it is susceptible to improvement. Such a condition, though it tax our best energies, should be rendered better."[72] The comment sparks a long debate about the viability of improvement, which also suggests something of a double entendre: are the comments about the painting, or the subject within the painting? If, for Frederick Douglass, aesthetic representation was the key to self-possession, Ethiop's ambiguity here complicates this assertion. The ensuing conversation focuses more on the chances for improvement of the subject represented, but comments from Ethiop like "the artist may be forgiven for over-drawing occasionally" keeps that central question in play. Whether the subject of the art or the composition itself could be improved raises the larger issue of the site of representation within a democratically inclined jurisdiction. To draw a one-to-one correspondence between the representative and the represented—something that Douglass was arguably promoting in his own paper—demands an intentionality and volition that is privileged within liberal democratic discourse. If, on the other hand, the blurring of the lines between art and politics raises new questions about the viability of representative democracy, then Ethiop is doing more than merely subverting the current markers of self-possession and liberal identity.

Through ongoing conversations and arguments between visitors in the sixth number, Ethiop largely remains silent. An "Old Lady" makes several inconsistent comments, complaining repeatedly about undue emphasis on metaphor: "What stuff and nonsense these new-fangled colored folks are putting into the heads of our people. They are worse than white folks."[73] Steeped in incomprehensive takes, this installment ends abruptly. The seventh and final installment has limited consistency with the six previous entries, as it features a story of a twice-escaped fugitive named Bill that promotes self-emancipation rather than dependence on help from white people.[74] An old notion of condition—nature versus nurture—seems to be answered in a long-winded anecdote that lacks much in the way of visual iconography. The curious closing thus turns away from the collective debates, the questions pertaining to the aesthetics of representation, and an emphasis on dignity for subjects and objects, regardless of their positionality. Ethiop's final entry seems to answer the question of condition raised in the sixth paper, but the self-improvement, bootstraps story depends primarily on epic acts of individual heroism. The path that veers from conventional liberal norms, especially in a literary venture of this variety, seems especially difficult.

Yet, the incongruities of the final entry—and the work of the series altogether—underscore the difficulty with seeking totality and coherence in an orderly fashion and determining artistic merit and political efficacy based solely on that coherence. The demand of individual heroism in narratives of the post-Enlightenment United States was relentless, and the greatest political actors who endeavored for more inclusive democracy within procedural politics made impressive gains. Few communities needed that more than pre–Civil War African Americans. Frederick Douglass no doubt led the charge, but others also persisted, as the works of James McCune Smith and William J. Wilson testify. We have often forgotten them altogether, or on occasion have fit them awkwardly into less meaning-filled historical places. In their commonalities with other imaginings of alternative democracies, we can be reminded of the most basic of starting points, in the simple form of dignity conferred on all.

Coda
Literature, History, Populism, Democracy

In their various ways, the literary misfits of the Philadelphia urban scene, the Old Southwest, the Old Northwest, the California gold rush, and New York respectively conflate literary conventions and transgress generic lines. As texts like Lippard's *Quaker City* and Kirkland's *A New Home* variously posit a fictive world that is only vaguely disjointed from the actual social world, they possess a significant amount of material that has often be described as realist; however, each of the texts considered in this book draws from literary genres that in many ways conflict with realist conventions that came to dominate the postbellum decades. Whether sensational or sentimental, these often-romanticized variations of actual living invade the realist space and disrupt these fictions' relation to the actual world. These generic complications, along with the vernacular informalities addressed throughout the chapters, provide even more justification for using these fictions to consider the ways that democratic aspirations both reflect and constitute the actual social and political world. In the most basic sense, social formations operating under democratic paradigms must deal with conflict and difference. While the novel or short story might be inclined to impose a particular form and order on actual materials and thus consolidate conflict and differences under the aegis of consensus and unity, literary misfits provide even better material to consider the complex operations of social living on terrains characterized by difference and irreconcilability, the terrains in greatest need of democratic outlets (that would otherwise risk tyrannical power grabbing or, worse, unfettered violence). Furthermore, because different people live under very different conditions—which are often reduced to binaries of rural/urban, majority/minority, North/South, settlement/frontier, center/periphery, nation/other nation—yet still imagine and pursue ideals of democratic living, then reading constellations of literary misfits that span these divides provides an ideal platform from which to study the potential and limitations of democracy in various instantiations. In other words, instead of grouping these misfits according to easy demographic categorization, they call for readings that transverse these binaries without necessarily folding them into some new abstraction.

Not only do new readings of misfits address the deictic complications within the texts, but they must also confront the currents of dissemination across boundaries that have typically stood as divisive and impassable, regardless of collective interests, or at least the ones that democracy ideally addresses. While these localized fictions align closely with the times and places they depict, their audiences were much more far reaching. Even though some have figured Philadelphia as the political, economic, and cultural center of the early United States, the city would be better perceived as defined by its position as a border town, and thus a point of intersecting interests and desires that offered dynamic material for writers like Robert Montgomery Bird and George Lippard in some, but not all, of their fictive works produced in this period. Southwestern humorists like Augustus Baldwin Longstreet, Johnson Jones Hooper, and George Washington Harris were widely appreciated in both urban and rural reading communities in the South as well as the North, in spite of growing tensions between the two sections in the years leading up to the Civil War; their popularity extended beyond the Civil War and even traveled to the Far West as well. Caroline Kirkland and Metta Fuller Victor lived several years in the Old Northwest, moved east to New York City, and became central contributors to the rapidly developing national literary scene; however, their novels betray no marks of an inevitable, progressive march toward that national center. Coming from the edge of the continent in a complicated moment of transnational alteration, California gold rush literature by John Rollin Ridge and Louise Clappe found its greatest fans on the opposite coast and across the Atlantic, but not before they imagined alternatives to liberal democratic life in a surprisingly isolated space that was hardly amenable to the overlay of US nationalism. James McCune Smith and William J. Wilson were no doubt invested in the national pariah of slavery, and yet their 1850s writings betray strong doubts about the chances for a nationally inspired solution for underlying racism that made slavery possible. Thus, while each of these respective constellations can be construed as explicitly local, they were all caught up in the various flows and currents of a wide-ranging and heterogeneous body politics as well as print culture, both within the nation and beyond its shifting borders.

The paradoxical nature of these mid-nineteenth-century literary misfits—that they were linked to a specific locality, often a locality that was not yet fully linked up to the material networks facilitating national compression, yet they circulated in much broader circuits of print on both national and transnational scales—creates something of a problem for determining that this fictive material was simply bad literature. If we look at these misfits only from the standpoint of their internal material, then we run into problems of representation, especially when their vernacular aesthetics disrupts elite categorical imperatives. This critical judgment leads us to cast these works aside for the material that better suits traditional critical sensibilities. Conversely, if we look at these localized fictions only from the standpoint of their dissemination and audience, then we often make tidy assessments of bourgeois reading audiences. From there, we might conclude that these audiences either delighted in escapist fantasies that distracted them from taking a more active role in their respective political worlds or believed themselves to be romanticized cosmopolitans who could fully appreciate identifications across difference, even if they had little taste for such excesses in the actual social and political world.

My book offers an alternative. Alexis de Tocqueville's characterization of nesting identifications in the United States, ones that prioritized the local before expanding to broader spheres of state, region, and nation, assumes that nineteenth-century individuals lived out identifications under this expanding rubric. The production and consumption of these literary misfits posit something other than a sense of supralocality in which one progresses through ever-expanding spheres of identification all the way up to an idealized cosmopolitan citizen of the world. Instead, they not only portray a particular locality within its fictive dimensions, but also figure a sort of local, democratically inclined reader (or better, collectives of readers). These local readers ascend the various spheres to reach not some sort of cosmopolitan nirvana, but rather one that finds new possibilities of social and political identifications that do not transcend the elements of locality. In other words, these local misfits potentially constitute readers who register multilocal identifications rather than supralocal ones, if we might see them that way. What this might yield, then, are figures that encounter alternative social and political worlds without necessarily dismissing the actual in order to live within the virtual (a problem for a constitutional nation that would preferably operate according to the dictates of virtual representation). Stated another way, a reconceptualization of scalar dimensions and paradigms in both the production and consumption of localized fictions in this period helps us work through this particular archive with new critical sensibilities that uncover the persistence of alternative democracies in the nineteenth century.

May we find valuable substance for the reimaginings that we need in our present day.

Notes

Introduction

1. Matthiessen, *American Renaissance*, ix.
2. Bercovitch, *Rites of Assent*, 46.
3. Jones, *Adventures of Colonel Gracchus Vanderbomb*, 96.
4. Robert Wuthnow's book argues that "marginalized individuals and groups served persistently, repeatedly, and often quite prominently as the contrasting cases, the negative comparisons through which middle-class respectability was defined" (*American Misfits*, 3).
5. Castiglia, *Interior States*, 5–7.
6. Arguing for what he calls "critical regionalism," Douglas Powell has noted that "the idea of region is in many ways categorically different from other conceptualizations of place, like home, community, city, state, and nation, in that region must refer not to a specific site but to a larger network of sites; region is always a relational term.... The boundaries of a region never have the juridical, insulating force of other kinds of governmental decisions" (*Critical Regionalism*, 4).
7. For certain theorists, democracy will never fully sort itself out. Wendy Brown has characterized this condition as the "unfinished principle" of democracy ("We Are All Democrats Now ...," 45). Sheldon Wolin has developed this condition in terms of "fugitive democracy" (*Fugitive Democracy, and Other Essays*, 100–114).
8. Casanova goes on to write, "Only in this way can a modern work be rescued from aging, by being declared timeless and immortal. That classic incarnates literary legitimacy itself, which is to say what is recognized as constituting *Literature*; what, in serving as a unit of measure, supplies the basis for determining the limits of that which is to be considered literary" (*World Republic of Letters*, 92).
9. The Warwick Research Collective has importantly pointed out this discrepancy as part of its larger critique of theories like Casanova's that presume an autonomous space of literary culture—that is, the concept that the politics of literary culture and value operate in one sphere and geopolitical politics happen in another. See Warwick Research Collective, *Combined and Uneven Development*.
10. Literary critics in the early years of this world republic of letters claimed that literature must promote a "national character" in distinction to nations with more established literary reputations. That said, "literatures are therefore not a pure emanation of national identity" as literary nationalists might have it; instead, Casanova writes, "they are constructed through literary rivalries, which are always denied, and struggles, which are always international" (*World Republic of Letters*, 36).
11. Gerald Kennedy has influentially captured the major conflicts of US literary nationalism during this era and the distinctive position that Edgar Allan Poe took amid the boosters and the critics. See Kennedy, *Strange Nation*. My book focuses on alternatives to all that Kennedy cites, Poe included.

12. This brief catalogue draws from Robert Levine's study on competing nationalisms rising in the nineteenth-century United States. See Levine, *Dislocating Race and Nation*.

13. Channing, "Remarks on National Literature," 126.

14. Channing contends that rather than importing literature from Europe, a "people whose government and laws are nothing but the embodying of public opinion, should jealously guard this opinion against foreign dictation" (130).

15. Griswold, *Prose Writers of America*, 14.

16. Griswold, 49.

17. Nelson, "ConsterNation," 560.

18. I refer to Donald Pease's New Americanists book series from Duke University Press, which ran roughly from 1990 to 2010.

19. Many of these studies benefited from the world-systems theory developed most notably by Immanuel Wallerstein. See, for instance, Wallerstein, *World Systems Analysis*. For a recent study on transnational American literary studies and a take on the field more generally, see Goyal, *The Cambridge Companion to Transnational American Literature*.

20. Shumway, *Creating American Civilization*. For an example of a regional literature following a similar trajectory, see Kreyling, *Inventing Southern Literature*.

21. Pratt, *Archives of American Time*, 131.

22. Madison's logic: "The smaller the society, the fewer probably will be the distinct parties and interests composing it; the fewer the distinct parties and interests, the more frequently will a majority be found of the same party; and the smaller the number of individuals composing a majority, and the smaller the compass within which they are placed, the more easily will they concert and execute their plans of oppression. Extend the sphere, and you take in a greater variety of parties and interests; you make it less probable that a majority of the whole will have a common motive to invade the rights of other citizens; or if such a common motive exists, it will be more difficult for all who feel it to discover their own strength, and to act in unison with each other" ("Federalist, Number 10," 127).

23. Drawing from an archive of legal maneuverings in North Carolina and South Carolina between 1800 and 1850, Edwards contends that this local, peace-based legal economy had brought "revolutionary ideals of participatory government and local control to established legal practices, namely, the multiple traditions and overlapping jurisdictions ... [that] emphasized process over principle: each jurisdiction produced inconsistent rulings aimed at restoring the peace." Although local rule retained a traditional patriarchal hegemony that insisted on specific arrangements within a prescribed hierarchy, Edwards reveals that "everyone participated in the identification of offenses, the resolution of conflicts, and the definition of law. Even those without rights—wives, children, servants, and slaves, ... free blacks, unmarried free women, and poor whites, ... —had direct access to localized law [and] also had some influence over it" (*People and Their Peace*, 7).

24. Moreover, as Edwards puts it, "Their voices acquired resonance over time, as historians relied upon their archive, followed their lead, and ignored—even dismissed—legal localism" (8).

25. Poe, "Philosophy of Composition."

26. Nancy Glazener offers this take on aesthetic autonomy: "Aesthetic autonomy was initially put forward to protect art and literature from repression and censorship, even though this protection eventually jammed literature's general transmission of public thoughts and

feelings. However, aesthetic autonomy was also designed to offset the damaging effects of art's circulation in the form of commodities and commercial exhibits" (*Literature in the Making*, 63). This claim supports her larger arguments about the consolidation of literary culture around imaginative literature in the nineteenth century through the four related discourses of aesthetics, print culture, academic history, and public literary culture.

27. Paradoxically, the depoliticization in one fashion led to different kinds of political effects, as Theodor Adorno and like-minded Marxist critics have thoroughly demonstrated. See Adorno, *Aesthetic Theory*.

28. Moi, *Revolution of the Ordinary*, 175–221.

29. Examples include the sentimental novel's attempts to arouse a common sense of national feeling, as Jane Tompkins and Cindy Weinstein have claimed; the historical novel's retroactive establishment of a deep national past, as Jonathan Arac and Winfried Flück have shown; the gothic novel's sublimation of the darker elements of social experience into national identity, as Theresa Goddu has suggested; and the sensational novel's capacity to steer national interests into imperialist ambitions, as Shelly Streeby has argued. See Tompkins, *Sensational Designs*; Weinstein, *Family, Kinship, and Sympathy*; Arac, *Emergence of American Literary Narrative*; Flück, "Historical Novel"; Goddu, *Gothic America*; and Streeby, *American Sensations*.

30. Paul Gilmore, for instance, in his study of materialism and aesthetics in the late eighteenth and nineteenth centuries, reckons aesthetics as a prepolitical activity, expressing reluctance to fully accept Arendt's formulation. See Gilmore, *Aesthetic Materialism*.

31. Arendt, *Lectures on Kant's Philosophy*, 76, 63, 68–69.

32. See Ngai, *Ugly Feelings*; Ngai, *Our Aesthetic Categories*; and Ngai, *Theory of the Gimmick*.

33. Of the recent scholarship on aesthetics in US literary studies, I have found the following to be most helpful. In their introduction to a special issue on aesthetics, Christopher Castiglia and Russ Castronovo work through the political possibilities of aesthetics and cultural studies. See Castiglia and Castronovo, "Hive of Subtlety." A collection of essays edited by Christopher Looby and Cindy Weinstein further works through the political possibilities of aesthetic critique. See Looby and Weinstein, *American Literature's Aesthetic Dimensions*.

34. Jason Frank addresses the frequency of antidemocratic figures of the early national period associating democracy with disgust, concluding that "because democracy enacts a reconfiguration of the sensible that elicits order-preserving disgust, disgust cannot be finally overcome, but politically confronted and tactically engaged" ("Democracy and Disgust," 402).

35. Cahill and Larkin, "Aesthetics, Feeling, and Form," 236, 242.

36. See Stewart, *Space on the Side*.

37. See Kouwenhoven, *Made in America*.

38. For instance, Sieglinde Lemke has foregrounded "vernacular" to describe how noncanonical US literature can be transferred into the ranks of the national canon. The vernacular has historically been "defined in its opposition to the hegemonic," Lemke contends, and it has thus "served as a means to designate what belongs to the semantic field of the outsider, the marginal, the subordinate, or—to put it in postcolonial terminology—the subaltern. All of them have used this signifier to valorize what was at the time considered minor literature." Lemke goes on to write, "By defining what is presumably vernacular about

the literature of a given people, the term has helped to bring about the culturally specific qualities it affirms. By highlighting what is distinct to a particular literary tradition, the vernacular, by way of constructing cultural difference, yields to the validation of what had once been marginal." ("Theories of American Culture," 167). While critics under her examination have shifted their objects of study from marginal to canonical, Lemke's description of this process neutralizes any subversive potential of the vernacular with regards to dominant social, racial, and literary codes of reference.

39. Nelson, *Commons Democracy*, 6.

40. Nelson, 13.

41. Examples include Bouton, *Taming Democracy*; Holton, *Unruly Americans*; and Nash, *Unknown American Revolution*.

42. For the transportation and communications revolutions, see Howe, *What Hath God Wrought*; for the rise of the market economy, see Sellers, *Market Economy*; for competing nationalisms, see Levine, *Dislocating Race and Nation*. Notable exceptions come from political and legal historians, including Edwards, *People and Their Peace*; Formisano, *For the People*; and Novak, *People's Welfare*.

43. See Hofstadter, *Idea of a Party System*; Silbey, *Partisan Imperative*; and Silbey, *Party over Section*.

44. See Anderson, *Imagined Communities*; and Berlant, *Anatomy of Nationalist Fantasy*. In her critique of Anderson's and Berlant's theories, Loughran contends that the initial formation of the US nation under Federalist ideology depended on the dislocation and disjunction of various localities over vast space; however, from the 1820s onward, "the more connected regions appeared to be (in print), the more regionalized (rather than nationalized) their identities became.... A growing sense of simultaneity, in other words, produced not nationalism but an ever more entrenched sectionalism" (*Republic in Print*, 345).

45. Appiah, *Cosmopolitanism*.

46. Lummis, *Radical Democracy*, 21.

47. Lummis, 15.

48. Lummis, 18.

49. Kloppenberg, *Toward Democracy*, 6.

50. Kloppenberg, 280.

51. Within the pages of books, these local fictions promote the type of radical democratic experience that Castronovo and Nelson describe thus: "Not aggregated around a single conceptual or consensual point, the cleavages of disunified community create multiple sites of address that do not feel compelled to speak *for* each other or speak *to* each other by sacrificing the historical accents of specific cultural mediums" (*Materializing Democracy*, 5).

52. Historians have marked the 1828 election of Andrew Jackson as the dawn of mass party mobilization and the modern political era. Voter participation in this historic election was roughly 57 percent, more than doubling the 27 percent rate of the 1824 election. Turnout would hover around this mark for the next two presidential contests before spiking to 80 percent in the 1840 election. In the face of both contemporary and historical claims regarding mass democratic interest in this era, recent historical arguments by Altschuler and Blumin have offered a more tempered reading of the everyday citizens' political engagement, claiming that "neither a universal passion for politics nor a universal indifference accurately describes the United States during the early 1830s" (*Rude Republic*, 16).

53. Studies of the rational public sphere largely draw from the foundational work of Habermas, *The Structural Transformation of the Public Sphere*. On the emotional side, see Waldstreicher, *Perpetual Fetes*. On spectacle, see Greiman, *Democracy's Spectacle*. On counterpublics, see Warner, *Publics and Counterpublics*. On print culture, see Warner, *Letters of the Republic*; and Loughran, *Republic in Print*. On oral culture, see Looby, *Voicing America*; and Gustafson, *Eloquence Is Power*. On deliberative democracy, see Gustafson, *Imagining Deliberative Democracy*. On more radical varieties, see Castiglia, *Interior States*.

54. See Margolis, *Fictions of Mass Democracy*.

55. In the words of Cathy Davidson, "A community of readers (men and women) turned to novels as a way of participating in national debates on a range of problems that were both included and overlooked in the nation's founding documents" (*Revolution and the Word*, 5). For Castiglia, popular literature of the antebellum era offered "articulations of democratic strivings that, however trivialized, refused to disappear." Accordingly, current critical ventures must recognize that "imaginative fiction is not a mere reflection of social values and mores, handy documents of more immediate historical and cultural forces. Rather, imaginative fiction is the archive of the socially possible, an archive of alternatives to the historically or sociologically 'real.' To study literature of the antebellum period, then, is to find not what 'was' but what might have been" (*Interior States*, 11–12). From a different disciplinary angle, political scientist Catherine Holland stakes a similar claim in her study of the political imagination in the first hundred years of the United States: "Contemporary political life seems to demand that we return to the past not to establish the present as our inescapable heritage, but more pressingly to ask how the resources of the past might be turned to a different purpose, enabling us to see politics with new eyes and to envision new ways of organizing and directing public power" (*Body Politic*, ix).

56. See Brown, *Self-Evident Truths*.

57. Baym, "Melodrama of Beset Manhood," 129. Baym establishes this formulation as a counterpoint to the general orientation of Lionel Trilling's aptly named essay collection *The Liberal Imagination*.

58. See Wood, *Radicalism of the American Revolution*; and Appleby, *Inheriting the Revolution*.

59. Wendy Brown puts this point this way: "Democracy as concept and practice has always been limned by a non-democratic periphery and unincorporated substrate that at once materially sustains the democracy and against which it defines itself. Historically, all democracies have featured an occluded inside—whether slaves, natives, women, the poor, particular races, ethnicities, or religions, or (today) illegals and foreign residents. And there is also always a constitutive outside defining democracies—the 'barbarians' first so named by the ancients and iterated in other ways ever after, from communism to democracies' own colonies" ("We Are All Democrats Now . . . ," 51).

60. See Hammond, "Speech of Hon. James H. Hammond."

61. See Cotlar, *Tom Paine's America*; and Jackson, *American Radicals*.

62. In the last decade, such scholars as Christopher Castiglia, Russ Castronovo, Elizabeth Fenton, Jennifer Greiman, Dana Nelson, Timothy Powell, and Ivy Wilson have effectively traced alternative genealogies of democratic thinking in nineteenth-century literature and culture. See Castiglia, *Interior States*; Castronovo and Nelson, *Materializing Democracy*; Fenton, *Religious Liberties*; Greiman, *Democracy's Spectacle*; Powell, *Ruthless Democracy*; and Wilson, *Specters of Democracy*.

63. After the so-called victory of liberal democracy after the fall of the USSR, democracy was evaluated largely in light of an apparent complacency and lack of civic engagement in the United States. Since the 2016 US presidential election, scholars from a range of disciplines have taken up the subject from a very different angle, with myriad books that look more suspiciously at democracy in the United States and around the world. See, for instance, Rosenfeld, *Democracy and Truth*; Miller, *Can Democracy Work?*; Runciman, *How Democracy Ends*; Levitsky and Ziblatt, *How Democracies Die*; Davies, *Nervous States*; and Mounck, *People vs. Democracy*. All seem to respond in some way to the populist/nationalist threats to liberal democracy around the world, yet most take for granted the complexities of democracy in theory and in practice. Unmentioned yet brimming near the surface in these arguments is a phenomenon that Jacques Rancière has characterized this way: "[The] word itself is [typically] an expression of hatred ... the ruin of legitimate order" (though Rancière nevertheless endeavors to restore the subversive potential of *democracy*) (*Hatred of Democracy*, 2).

64. See Rosenblum, *Good Neighbors*; and Talisse, *Overdoing Democracy*.

65. See Allen, "Democracy versus Republic."

66. Erwin Chemerinsky has argued otherwise about the Constitution in his compelling *We the People*.

67. Rancière posits this idea of democracy to counter unachievable variations of democratic governance. See Rancière, "Does Democracy Mean Something," in *Dissensus*, 45–61.

Chapter One

1. Bird, *Sheppard Lee*, 228–29 (hereafter cited in text as *SL*).

2. Philadelphia has garnered the attention of many scholars interested in theories and practices of democracy—and related practices of freedom, equality, dignity, recognition, and belonging—in the nation's first century. Accounts contributing to my thinking in this chapter include Bouton, *Taming Democracy*; Holton, *Unruly Americans*; Rigal, *American Manufactory*; Otter, *Philadelphia Stories*; Waldstreicher, *Perpetual Fetes*; and White, *Backcountry and the City*.

3. Pennsylvania earns this credit for, among other things, having the only popularly elected unicameral state legislature and eliminating property restrictions on voting and office holding (though it kept intact other limitations based on age, gender, servitude, and religious belief, as well as loyalty oaths). See Selsam, *Pennsylvania Constitution of 1776*; and Bouton, *Taming Democracy*, esp. 4–7.

4. For specifics on post-Revolutionary print culture in Philadelphia, see Remer, *Printers and Men of Capital*. On the significance of the oral tradition in the new nation, see Looby, *Voicing America*; and Gustafson, *Eloquence Is Power*. Regarding public events, see Waldstreicher, *Perpetual Fetes*.

5. For the full story of the initial radical element that established the democratic constitution in 1776 and the conservative backlash that delivered a new constitution to Pennsylvania in 1790, see Brunhouse, *Counter-Revolution in Pennsylvania*. For a more recent account of popular agitation in 1776, see Nash, *Unknown American Revolution*, esp. 189–94. Also worth noting is that according to Kloppenberg, "the Pennsylvania model of unicameralism proved fragile, either because it was undermined by a cabal of antidemocratic elitists or

because it was the flawed product of a deck stacked at the outset. Yet, it exerted a degree of influence incommensurate with its brief history" (*Toward Democracy*, 358).

6. Otter, "Philadelphia Experiments," 114.

7. Otter, *Philadelphia Stories*, 4.

8. The term *synecdochic nationalism* was coined in Miller, *Empire of the Eye*. Timothy Sweet borrows this term from Miller's historical study of American visual art in the nineteenth century, in Sweet, "American Land, American Landscape."

9. Examples of this last concern start with Wilentz, *Chants Democratic*. Especially relevant in this account is Wilentz's description of the rapid appropriation of the Working Men's movements in New York and Philadelphia into mass party politics (211–14). The focus on labor movements continues in Wilentz, *Rise of American Democracy*. For the leading labor history on Philadelphia, see Laurie, *Working People of Philadelphia*.

10. An online exhibit at the Library Company of Philadelphia in 2008 and 2009 recovered these authors' texts, partnered them with the turn-of-the-century work of Charles Brockden Brown, and yoked them to the larger figure of Poe. See Fitzgerald, "Philadelphia Gothic."

11. Wright, *Views of the Society*, 58–85. The name change from "State House" to "Independence Hall" occurred around 1824 when, during preparations for a visit from the Marquis de Lafayette, references to "the Hall of Independence" and "Independence Hall" began appearing in local papers. See Mires, "Independence Hall."

12. Wright, *Views of the Society*, 63.

13. Wright, 63–64.

14. Holland, *Body Politic*, 44.

15. On the aesthetic production of the state, see Slauter, *State as Work of Art*; and Cahill, *Liberty of the Imagination*. On the widespread contentiousness of the Revolution, see Taylor, *American Revolutions*.

16. On Ramsay's history, see Messer, "From a Revolutionary History"; and O'Brien, "David Ramsay."

17. Anderson identifies this as the first of three paradoxes that have "perplexed" theorists of nationalism: "(1) The objective modernity of nations to the historian's eye vs. their subjective antiquity in the eyes of nationalists. (2) The formal universality of nationality as a socio-cultural concept . . . vs. the irremediable particularity of its concrete manifestations. . . . (3) The 'political' power of nationalisms vs. their philosophical poverty and even incoherence" (*Imagined Communities*, 5).

18. While other American myths surfaced and faded away over the decades or took on a regional valence, the Revolution, as Kammen puts it, stood firm. For instance, Kammen cites Slotkin, *Regeneration through Violence*, for offering a regional breakdown of different meanings of Daniel Boone myth (*Season of Youth*, 278).

19. Kammen, *Season of Youth*, 27–28.

20. Kammen, 47.

21. For a breakdown of Sparks's influence on Tocqueville's observations about town democracy in *Democracy in America*, see Aiken, "Educating Tocqueville." Jared Sparks also influenced national development and coherence as editor of the *North American Review* and with his publication of the *Life and Writings of George Washington* (which he was preparing at the time of Tocqueville's tour).

22. Bancroft, *History of the United States*, 3. Regarding Bancroft's composition of volumes 4, 5, and 6, which appeared in quick succession between 1852 and 1854 and covered the years 1748 to 1763, 1763, and 1774 to 1776, Lillian Handlin contends that they served as responses to the sectional crises that had reached a new level of intensity from 1850 on (*George Bancroft*, 256).

23. Citizen of New York, *Retrospect of the Boston Tea-Party*; Bostonian, *Traits of the Tea Party*.

24. Young, *Shoemaker and the Tea Party*, 156.

25. Young, 163.

26. Young, 53.

27. Young, 55.

28. Wilentz starts from the position that "democracy appears when some large number of previously excluded, ordinary persons—what the eighteenth century called 'the many'—secure the power not simply to select their governors but to oversee the institutions of government, as officeholders and as citizens free to assemble and criticize those in office" (*Rise of American Democracy*, xix). I contend that democracy can also appear in other, less table-turning kinds of ways.

29. Ryan, *Civic Wars*, 22. Synthesizing the social, cultural, and political markers of democratic life through the local print cultures in three case studies—New York, New Orleans, and San Francisco—Ryan identifies "recurrent cultural and political collisions" in the form of "civic wars" that most clearly demonstrate the "essential feature of modern democracy" (*Civic Wars*, 3).

30. Since the novel's reissue in 2008 by the *New York Review of Books*, twenty-first-century critics have taken up the novel in a variety of ways. See Otter, *Philadelphia Stories*, 95–107; Altschuler, "From Empathy to Epistemology"; Doty, "Satire, Minstrelsy, and Embodiment"; Jaros, "Faculties of Law"; Leavell, "NOT INTENDED EXCLUSIVELY FOR THE SLAVE STATES"; Mansouri, "Properties of the Novel in America"; Rebhorn, "Ontological Drift"; Stein, "Whig Interpretation of Media"; and my own "This is a strange book." Worth noting is that Murison, "Hypochondria and Racial Interiority," appeared prior to the novel's reintroduction to critical concerns.

31. The *Public Ledger* declared the novel an "extraordinary production" and appreciated "the author's power of accurate delineation of character . . . [and] many excellent moral reflections" ("Sheppard Lee," *Public Ledger*, 30 August 1836). The *Philadelphia Mirror* more soberly offered its positive response: "We have not perused the work entire, but we have read enough to satisfy ourselves that the author understands what he is about. There is a boldness and confidence in his style, and a singularity of plot" ("Sheppard Lee," *Philadelphia Mirror*, 22 August 1836). The triweekly *National Gazette and Literary Register* provided a rather ambivalent account: "We do not know that the writer of this mental phantasmagoria has thrown himself out of the pale of criticism, by the dexterity with which he has made his escape from the usages of all sober writing, sporting with the reader in a 'tipsy dance' of fancy, which bids defiance to everything like rule or reason" ("Sheppard Lee," *National Gazette and Literary Register*, 18 August 1836).

32. For an undisclosed reason, the local Philadelphia celebrity decided to go a different route from the Philadelphia publishers of his first three novels, Carey and Lea, and publish *Sheppard Lee* anonymously in New York City with Harper and Brothers. The first edition

of 3,000 copies did not sell well. In a letter dated 23 February 1839, Harper and Brothers wrote to Bird, proposing "to dispose our interest in the stereotype plates of 'Sheppard Lee' and the copies on hand," which amounted to "1100 copies . . . (400 bound & 700 folded)" (Robert Montgomery Bird Papers, Box 2, folder 65, Rare Book and Manuscript Library, University of Pennsylvania). Looking to divest from further obligations to Bird, the Harpers suggested that Bird ask Philadelphia publishers Lea and Blanchard or Carey and Hartto make the purchase in the event that they would like to produce clean copies of his collected works and a reissue of *Sheppard Lee* with Bird's name attached. While a scrap of a drafted letter discloses Bird entertaining the idea of a second edition with his name on the title page, it never came to fruition.

33. "Shepard Lee," *National Atlas* (28 August, 1836): 78.

34. Looby, introduction to *Sheppard Lee*, xx, xxix.

35. Progressive historians and postmodern critics might savor these so-called flaws and criticisms in the novel, but a thorough reassessment of this novel demands a revised hermeneutic that works against the hegemony of national frames of references.

36. Davidson describes the picaresque as "the loosest of narrative forms," one that "conveniently allows a central character (or characters) to wander the margins of an emerging American landscape, to survey it in all its incipient diversity, to sound out its different constituents from the most lowly, uneducated yeoman to those of high birth and great learning" (*Revolution and the Word*, 152).

37. Davidson, 164.

38. Davidson, 153. Davidson's assessment of early US novels has remained extremely influential. Ed White has challenged the radicalism of the writers that Davidson highlights by claiming that the era's novels are better characterized not as a "battle between radicals and social conservatives, [but] more of spat among Federalist intellectuals" ("Divided We Stand," 6). Elizabeth Fenton has argued that one early novel, Royall Tyler's *The Algerine Captive*, expresses doubts about the conservatism of deliberative models, noting how "the novel suggests time and again that the notion of truly equal citizens being productively open to each other's influence may be a quaint political fantasy rather than a productive element of civil society" ("Indeliberate Democracy," 72–73).

39. [Franklin], *Memoirs of the Life*, 1. The text in this 1818 version differs considerably from the manuscript version and recent editions of Franklin's *Autobiography* (e.g., the Norton Critical Edition). The grandson's heavy editing is evidence, to some degree, of the formal and aesthetic norms that made *Sheppard Lee*'s foibles more problematic.

40. Worth noting is that Franklin was writing and heavily editing these opening lines in 1771 as a subject of the British Empire. Also, in his reconstruction of the *Autobiography*'s journey from print to print, Christopher Hunter debunks the myth of authenticity underlying the publication of Franklin's life story, especially in the period from the 1790s to the time when Bird was writing *Sheppard Lee*. See Hunter, "From Print to Print."

41. Founding figures and documents were by no means immune to satire in this era, but some satires fold more easily into the national narrative than others. For examples of satirical takes on the Declaration of Independence, see Kammen, *Season of Youth*, 260–69.

42. In contrast to my arguments about the empowering potential of Revolutionary history here, Murison contends that Bird's spin on the Declaration of Independence's language, which borrows the language of the French Declaration of the Rights of Man, "implies

that a terror-like revolt will follow the spread of abolitionist principles" ("Hypochondria and Racial Interiority," 15–16).

43. Poe, "Critical Notices," 662–63.

44. Davidson, *Revolution and the Word*, 172.

45. For a detailed rendition of character types considered by Bird in his notes, see Looby, introduction to *Sheppard Lee*, xv–xx.

46. Bird, "*Sheppard Lee*: fragments and notes," Robert Montgomery Bird Papers, Rare Book and Manuscript Library, University of Pennsylvania, Ms. Coll. 108, Box 11, Folder 259.

47. Pre-1830s political theorists who assessed the pros and cons of democracy expressed many fears over selfish interest and mob violence as the two most likely pitfalls resulting from empowering everyday people; mass apathy received little consideration. Complacency and apathy would become one of Tocqueville's greatest fears for US democracy, especially in volume 2 (1840).

48. See Gustafson, *Imagining Deliberative Democracy*.

49. Castiglia has characterized a redirection of democratic agency from the Revolutionary era to the antebellum period as having started during the time of the early republic as a consequence of the "federalization of affect," which he defines as "the creation of metaphors of 'innerness' to serve as sites of correspondence between individual bodies (character, personality, and even biology) and state interest" (*Interior States*, 18).

50. As Joyce Appleby puts it, "American commentators . . . [attributed] their material accomplishments to the superiority of their political institutions and constru[ed] their economic progress as testimony to the soundness of the revolution they had inherited" (*Inheriting the Revolution*, 4).

51. Historians have marked the 1828 election of Andrew Jackson as the dawn of mass party mobilization and the modern political era. Altschuler and Blumin have offered a more tempered reading of the everyday citizens' political engagement, claiming that "neither a universal passion for politics nor a universal indifference accurately describes the United States during the early 1830s" (*Rude Republic*, 16).

52. See Howe, *What Hath God Wrought*, 331–34.

53. Many of Sheppard's experiences are evidenced in the strategies of local and national party leaders laid out by Altschuler and Blumin in *Rude Republic* (esp. 47–86).

54. See Waldrep, *Lynching in America*, 31–37.

55. See Waldrep, 29–31; Poe, "Lynchers' Character," 389.

56. On the transition from property protection during the Revolutionary era to the type of racially motivated form of lynching evidenced in *Sheppard Lee* (and as precursor to more widespread racial lynching in the postbellum years), see Pfeifer, *Roots of Rough Justice*.

57. This chapter's commentary is consistent with Tocqueville's contemporaneous statement regarding the most striking feature of the United States being an "equality of social conditions" (*Democracy in America*, 11).

58. Bird, "Correspondence: drafts," *Robert Montgomery Bird Papers*, Rare Book and Manuscript Library, University of Pennsylvania, Ms. Coll. 108, Box 22, Folder 293.

59. For a take on Lippard's developing radical politics in *The Quaker City*, see Reynolds, "Deformance, Performativity, Posthumanism."

60. Lippard was a frequent speaker at the William Wirt Institute, tantalizing many audiences over several years with his lectures on the Revolution, starting as early as 1845. Many

of these were gathered together in *Washington and His Generals: or, Legends of the Revolution*.

61. Kennedy, "Revising the Public Sphere," 592.

62. Denning, *Mechanic Accents*, 100; Looby, "Lippard in Part(s)," 2.

63. With Poe's blessing, Lippard printed the complete letter—negative criticism included—on the back cover of his second novel, *Herbert Tracy* (*Herbert Tracy*, 167).

64. Jackson, "Misunderstood Man of Letters," 381–83.

65. Leslie Fiedler brought out the first twentieth-century edition, titling it *The Monks of Monk Hall* and penning an introduction that considered the text in relation to the works of other popular writers like Eugene Sue and G. M. W. Reynolds. In the following decade, critical readings that valued Lippard's popularity as foil to canonical writers, especially Poe, appeared in Ziff, *Literary Democracy*, and Reynolds, *Beneath the American Renaissance*.

66. For readings that assess the novel beyond its relationship to canonical literature, see Denning, *Mechanic Accents*, 85–117; Ashwill, "Mysteries of Capitalism"; Nelson, *National Manhood*, 135–75; Anthony, "Banking on Emotion"; Castiglia, *Interior States*, 193–211; Unger, "Dens of Iniquity"; Otter, *Philadelphia Stories*, 165–202; a 2015 special issue of *Nineteenth-Century Literature*, convened by Christopher Looby; and Voeller, "Disability, Masculinity, and Sentimentality."

67. Lippard's radical democratic politics took on a prolabor, anticapitalist tone most clearly when he came to run his own periodical, also named *The Quaker City*, from 1848 to 1850. As Shelley Streeby has shown, Lippard posed a powerful if complicated critique of US liberal capitalism and the politics that protected the interests of the privileged few. In this venture he came to esteem that the "solution . . . involve[d] world revolution, not the gradual refinement and perfection of US democracy" ("Haunted Houses," 454).

68. In introductions to the two most recent editions of *The Quaker City*, Fiedler never mentions the serialized publication yet boasts about its impressive sales numbers, and Reynolds cites similar numbers while briefly acknowledging the publication-in-parts. With sales numbers in this era difficult to compute, most scholars have used Lippard's numbers in prefaces appended to complete editions of the novel, converting the publication-in-parts into a singular event.

69. For detailed explanations of the novel's ad hoc composition and publishing history, see Emerson, "George Lippard's *The Quaker City*," and Winship, "In Search of Monk Hall." For a convincing interpretative take on Lippard's choice of cheap serial publishing, see Looby, "Lippard in Part(s)."

70. An advertisement on the last page of the fourth number (December 1844)—from a rare individual copy current held by the Henry E. Huntington Library—reads: "NOTE.— THIS REVELATION OF PHILADELPHIA LIFE, has so grown upon the Author's hands, that he finds it impossible to wind up the story under four additional numbers. These numbers will be published, at an early day, in a compact volume of 192 pages. This 'SEQUEL' to the 'QUAKER CITY,' will contain the very soul and spirit of the whole work" (Anonymous, *Quaker City*, Number 4, ii).

71. Lippard, *Quaker City* (1849), 1 (italics in original).

72. The plot movement into Book the Second, set on "The Day after the Night" and titled "The Forger," actually occurs with fifteen pages left in Number 3, the issue that appeared nearly concurrently with a cancelled theatrical production. In Number 4, the narrative

opens with Fitz-Cowles duping his creditors and conspiring with Dora to bring about Livingstone's death. This runs about twenty pages of the sixty-four-page Number 4, but the final forty pages shift the focus from "The Forger" to a nearly exclusive tracking of Luke Harvey.

73. The theatrical performance was cancelled due to threats of riot. For the most commonly cited contemporary source, see Wemyss, *Twenty-Six Years*. For a romanticized account of Lippard's role, see Bouton, *Choice Writings of George Lippard*. On the recently discovered playbill, see Altschuler and Tobiason, "Playbill for *The Quaker City*."

74. Lippard, *Quaker City* (1847), 174 (hereafter cited in text as QC). I cite the historical text, digitized on Google Books, because of the unique reading experience of the original printing.

75. Lippard, *Quaker City* (1849), 2.

76. As Elizabeth Barnes puts it, "To expose sympathetic young women to powerful stories of unbridled passion, deception, and broken honor was to invite tragedy not only for the individual family but for the new nation.... Just as women's bodies in the early novel correlated to the health and innocence of the body politic, so, too, impressionable women readers represented a potentially seducible American citizenry" ("Novels," 444–45).

77. According to Silverman, "Given the tremendous restrictions placed on face-to-face interactions in the nineteenth-century public sphere ... we might understand reading as providing an alternative route to intimacy" (*Bodies and Books*, 6).

78. For details on Lippard's print battles with local Philadelphia publishers, see Looby, "Lippard in Part(s)," 3–12.

79. Poodle and Petriken briefly appear together in Number 2 when they attend the first bacchanalian feast in Monk Hall, yet they have no direct interaction with one another until this moment in Number 8.

80. Here we see a counter to Benedict Anderson's theories of newspapers producing a sense of simultaneity and thus an imagined national community. See Looby, "Lippard in Part(s)," 29.

81. Nelson, *National Manhood*, 155.

82. Devil-Bug's first murder, of Paul Western, occurred six years prior to the events of the novel, serving as his "pathway to crime, which was his doom and his delight to tread" (QC, 90). At the end of Number 4, he adds a second body to his cast of personal haunts when he slams the surprisingly feisty Widow Smolby against the andirons of the fireplace (QC, 205).

83. Otter focuses on the spatial and architectural dimensions (*Philadelphia Stories*, 177–78). Castiglia reads it as a radically privatized queer sociality suddenly and violently merging with the public sphere (*Interior States*, 204–6). Nelson characterizes the sexualized rhetoric as the hybrid social/sexual critique threatening the purity of the white male national citizenry (*National Manhood*, 147).

84. For Castronovo, "dead bodies ... imply a type of democratic subject produced in the nineteenth-century US public sphere. Guaranteed formal equality and cultural autonomy, the citizen encounters politics as a near-death experience: he or she thus prefers privacy to public life, passivity to active engagement, and forgetting to memory" (*Necro Citizenship*, 3). While these national forms dominate the cultural scene of the antebellum era, several writers—and I would add Lippard to Castronovo's candidates—contested this antidemocratic ideology.

Chapter Two

1. Hooper, *Adventures of Captain Simon Suggs*, 82 (hereafter cited in text as *SS*).
2. Greeson explicitly acknowledges the omission of southwestern humor as one of several exclusions that make her study less than comprehensive, but offers no further rationale for the exclusion (*Our South*, 15).
3. A reference to "southwestern humor" as a literary genre came as early as 1855, in a review of *A Memoir of S.S. Prentiss*: "There are also interspersed in the various chapters of the narrative many amusing passages and incidents of South-western humor sometimes reminding the reader of Mr. Baldwin's 'Flush Times in Alabama'" ("Notes on New Books," *National Intelligencer*, 13 October 1855).
4. Thomas Clark and John Guice have mapped the Southwest within "the great natural envelope south of the Tennessee River, west of the Ocmulgee River in Georgia, east of the Mississippi, and [north] of the Gulf of Mexico" (*Old Southwest*, 1). This geography serves as a useful starting point, but post-1830s settlement west of the Mississippi and economic changes within the region push on the northern and western boundaries in the heyday of southwestern humor. Frederick Law Olmstead's 1850s journeys made a distinction between coastal regions and "the back country." Southwestern humor mostly emerges from these general "back country" areas. See Olmstead, *Journey in the Back Country*.
5. Two years later, Porter expanded his scope with a national scale of reference in his second collection, *A Quarter Race in Kentucky, and Other Sketches, Illustrative of Scenes, Characters, and Incidents, throughout "The Universal Yankee Nation"* (1847). As one mid-twentieth-century critic explained, Porter's second anthology expanded its geographical scope from the earlier *Big Bear of Arkansas* anthology to include "twelve or thirteen Eastern and Midwestern yarns, which gave the volume a nation-wide scope and justified its claim as a work 'illustrative of scenes ... throughout the Universal Yankee Nation'" (Current-Garcia, "Mr. Spirit," 341). For a broader study of Porter's life and work, see Yates, *William T. Porter*.
6. James Justus offers an exemplary version: "Written by males for an appreciative masculine audience, other sketches by lawyers, planters, editors, and preachers characteristically appeared anonymously or pseudonymously in local newspapers and (through the journalistic exchange system) were distributed nationally in lively [regional] sheets as the *New Orleans Picayune* and the *St. Louis Reveille*. The best of them were published in William T. Porter's popular, influential, and long-lasting weekly, the *New York Spirit of the Times*" (*Fetching the Old Southwest*, 2).
7. See Justus, 2; Justus, *Fetching the Old Southwest*, 261; Grammar, "Southwestern Humor," 370; Arac, *American Literary Narrative*, 33; Gunn, "Humor of the Old Southwest," 63.
8. Lynn's oft cited theory importantly separated the "morally irreproachable Gentleman from the tainted life he described" and signified his distaste for the more egalitarian variations of democracy (*Mark Twain and Southwest Humor*, 64).
9. Anderson, "Scholarship in Southwestern Humor"; Lemay, "Text, Traditions, and Themes." More recent critics who have published widely on southwestern humor have tended to take this latter position. See Inge and Piacentino, *Humor of the Old South*; and Justus, *Fetching the Old Southwest*. Twenty-first-century critics who write occasionally on southwestern humorists tend to follow Lynn's theory. See Grammer, "Southwestern Humor," 381–82; and Pratt, *Archives of American Time*, 125–56.

10. Pratt, *Archives of American Time*, 127, 130. For the development and impact of literature beyond southwestern humor performing this type of cultural work, see Nelson, *National Manhood*.

11. Whether we characterize the antebellum period as one of increasingly entrenched sectionalism, as Trish Loughran contends, or as one of many competing nationalisms, as Paul Quigley and Robert Levine have suggested, print culture has been understood as an important component in fostering identifications with a national community. For Loughran, the material developments of US nation building in this period effectively rechanneled local voices into broader, more streamlined communities: "The more connected regions appeared to be (in print), the more regionalized (rather than nationalized) their identities became" (*Republic in Print*, 345). For other competing nationalisms in nineteenth-century literary culture, see Levine, *Dislocating Race and Nation*. For a more historical, comparative approach to nationalisms in the South and Europe, see Quigley, *Shifting Grounds*.

12. Special thanks to Elizabeth Maddock Dillon and fellow participants in our seminar at the Futures of American Studies Institute in 2010 for help with coining and developing this term.

13. Justus, *Fetching the Old Southwest*, 50.

14. For details on books ranging from his own *Autobiography* (1834) to the four counterfeit titles penned in his name, see Hauck, "Man in the Buckskin Hunting Shirt."

15. For a concise depiction of the many different almanacs and an influential take on their cultural work, see Smith-Rosenberg, *Disorderly Conduct*.

16. John Seelye has since proven the Nashville imprint to be a Boston publisher's charade. See Seelye, "Well-Wrought Crockett."

17. As some of the earliest critics framing the conversation around American humor, Constance Rourke and Walter Blair both claimed the genre was born in the backwoods but nevertheless served as the most distinctive of national forms. See Rourke, *American Humor*; and Blair, *Native American Humor*. Both published books on Crockett. Rourke's, *Davy Crockett*, was a biography for children; Blair's, *Davy Crockett, Frontier Hero*, was cowritten with Powers. Kenneth Lynn and Richard Slotkin provided generational updates with the facile conflation between Crockett and the southwestern humorists. See Lynn, *Mark Twain and Southwestern Humor*, 32–45; and Slotkin, *Regeneration through Violence*, 414–17.

18. *Davy Crockett's Almanack*, 2.

19. *Davy Crockett's Almanack*, 3.

20. My geographical critique here could also hold for Porter's first anthology of southwestern humor, *The Big Bear of Arkansas*, which includes two stories that stretch the boundaries of southwestern geography by being set in Michigan and Illinois. Generic similarities seemed more important than geographical integrity, yet Porter's changes in his second anthology, *A Quarter Race in Kentucky*, include a more balanced distribution of settings across the nation.

21. *Davy Crockett's Almanack*, 44.

22. For instance, Richard Slotkin makes this characterization: "The implications of the Crockett figure were fully elaborated in the writings of the 'Southwestern Humorists,' a group of popular writers who devoted their works to the delineation of the character and life-style of the southern Appalachian and trans-Appalachian frontier" (*Regeneration through Violence*, 415). Add in the publishing detail that the *Almanack* was a product of

urban northeastern publishers seeking a white, male, working-class audience, as Lara Langer Cohen has convincingly detailed, and the *Almanack* provides ample evidence of a larger context of literary fraudulence in national print culture. See Cohen, *Fabrication of American Literature*, 65–100.

23. Greeson, *Our South*, 1 (italics in original). Greeson's conception builds on the basic exclusionary principle of modern nations (formulated by Benedict Anderson), yet cannily distinguishes the South's position as one that "lies simultaneously inside and outside the national imaginary constructed in US literature" (*Our South*, 3).

24. Jackson campaigned on old Jeffersonian principles of minimal government and local self-governance, even as he—like Thomas Jefferson before him—refashioned the presidency to assume new levels of power that increased the distance between governmental power and the governed. Jackson benefited from his reputation for championing the common man.

25. Perman, *Pursuit of Unity*, 47.

26. Flint's history, *A Condensed Geography of the Western States*, starts with some generalizations about ecology and history, and then moves to chapters on individual states, starting with Florida, moving west to Alabama, Mississippi, Louisiana, and Arkansas, and then north along the Mississippi and Ohio Rivers. Ingraham's *The South-West* sticks to a more conventional geography. Olmstead's *A Journey in the Back Country* was the third installment of the trilogy that would become *The Cotton Kingdom*.

27. Drawing from various travel narratives of the period, Freehling's account depicts a metaphorical traveler who sets out from St. Louis and follows the Mississippi River south to New Orleans, then cuts east—very slowly and with great trouble—through the states of Mississippi and Alabama to Atlanta and Charleston, then up the coast through the Carolinas to the old Tidewater region of Virginia, then turns west across the border states to finish up in St. Louis (*Road to Disunion*, 1:9–36).

28. See Clark and Guice, *Old Southwest*.

29. Following such an admission, the authors nevertheless find many of the settlers participating in the nation's imperial ambitions (*Old Southwest*, 261, 262).

30. Quoted in Rachels, *Augustus Baldwin Longstreet's Georgia Scenes*, xlviii.

31. Longstreet, *Georgia Scenes*, xxiv (hereafter cited in text as *GS*).

32. Longstreet's two narrators, Lyman Hall and Abram Baldwin, shared names with two of the most famous political figures in Georgia's early national history. Hall signed the Declaration of Independence. Baldwin was one of Georgia's first congressmen following the ratification of the Constitution, spending a decade in the House and nearly ten more in the Senate.

33. According to Castiglia, "Institutionalism not only made a democratic *now* nearly impossible to conceive, it assisted in the divisions of *types* of people depending on whether they were oriented toward the future (biologically and ideologically reproductive) or the past (those 'stuck' in their memories by an unproductive nostalgia or melancholy)" (*Interior States*, 5).

34. Several scholars have attempted to define the structural order. James Meriwether identifies human progress as in need of civilizing norms such as law and order. See Meriwether, "Augustus Baldwin Longstreet." Keith Newlin finds structure in the oscillating targets of satire between upper and lower classes. See Newlin, "Satiric Artistry." James Kibler

cites Baldwin's failure to genuinely engage with the various strains of Georgia society while Hall moves from genteel and disconnected critic to member accepted by all ranks. See Kibler, introduction to *Georgia Scenes*. Scott Romine offers an assessment that keeps in play the dynamics I have been tracing, but concludes that "at the heart of Longstreet's narrative lies, essentially, a discourse of colonization through which those previously external, alien, and chaotic backwoods communities are subsumed within the hegemonic order" (*Narrative Forms of Southern Community*, 25). My only exception to Romine's conclusion lies in this subsumption to the hegemonic order; this might have proven historically true, but I stop short of this teleological conclusion to keep the contingency of the scenes in play.

35. Pratt, *Archives of American Time*, 132.

36. Hoole, *Alias Simon Suggs*, 21.

37. Hooper's early writings harnessed the attention of Porter, who published Hooper's first story, "Taking the Census," in 1843. Splitting time between responsibilities as newspaper editor and circuit-riding lawyer, Hooper hit his literary stride in December 1844 with the publication of his first story featuring Simon Suggs. By the end of the following summer, the Philadelphia firm Carey and Hart had published the first edition of *Some Adventures of Simon Suggs*, which sold quickly, requiring eleven subsequent editions over the next decade.

38. For Kenneth Lynn, this form betrayed Hooper's Whig-oriented disdain for the crudity of Jacksonian democracy, allowing overt jabs at Andrew Jackson and his administration as well as criticizing Democratic party politics (*Mark Twain and Southwest Humor*, 78–85). See also Hopkins, "Simon Suggs."

39. O'Brien, "Writing with a Forked Pen," 95.

40. Gilfoyle, *City of Eros*, 81.

41. See Anderson, *Imagined Communities*; and Bhabha, *Location of Culture*.

42. Drawing mostly on examples in the post–Civil War era, yet casting to the earliest moments of the nation and forward to the present, Gregory Laski identifies numerous writers who contend that the key to more democracy arises in the refusal of the nation's devotion to progressive time. See Laski, *Untimely Democracy*. Similar principles, I contend, appear here in *Simon Suggs*.

43. Bakhtin, *Rabelais and His World*, 3.

44. Bakhtin, 10.

45. Milton Rickels has been one of the few to connect Bakhtin's work on the carnivalesque with southwestern humor. See Rickels, "Grotesque Body."

46. Sut's most common appearances prior to the 1867 collection occurred in the *Nashville Union and American*. Among several uncollected tales were three in which Sut escorts Abraham Lincoln from Illinois to his inauguration in the spring of 1861.

47. Harris, *Sut Lovingood Yarns*, 23 (hereafter cited in text as *Sut*).

48. In an anachronistic application of twentieth-century theories, the frequent conflation of humans and animals anticipates tropes used by Franz Kafka and celebrated by Gilles Deleuze and Félix Guattari. As Deleuze and Guattari have argued, the act of becoming-animal enables a dismantling of the Oedipal triangle and parallel triangular relationships of power, which have prodemocratic consequences. Texts such as Kafka's fiction and *Sut Lovingood* most effectively challenge the territorialization of power through the trope of becoming-animal: "To become animal is to participate in movement, to stake out the path

of escape in all its positivity" (Deleuze and Guattari, *Kafka*, 13). In these terms, we can read *Sut Lovingood*'s recurrence of authority figures becoming-animal as providing the local people with lines of escape from national containment strategies and making it open to democratic play.

49. Bullen's most offensive abuse of power occurs when he catches Sut and an unnamed woman in a compromising position, then informs her mother after having assured her that he would keep the matter to himself. But this is just one of many affronts. Sut hints at other offenses committed by Bullen and his Hard-Shell Baptist cronies, citing their tendency to commit misdeeds and use Sut as a scapegoat: "All git drunk, an' skeer thar fool sefs ni ontu deth, an' then lay hit ontu me" (*Sut*, 49).

50. See Loughran, *Republic in Print*, 303–61.
51. Yates, *William T. Porter*, 53–57.
52. Porter, *Big Bear of Arkansas*, vii.
53. Gunn, "Humor of the 'Old Southwest,'" 68.
54. See McGill, *Culture of Reprinting*.
55. "Simon Suggs, the Shifty Man," *New Hampshire Patriot*, 18 April 1845.
56. "Photograph of Lincoln," *Nashville Union and American*, 28 February 1861.
57. "Photograph of Lincoln," *Los Angeles Star*, 8 June 1861.
58. See Pratt, *Archives of American Time*, 131.

59. Nick Bromell has posited "reading democratically" as a critical venture that uses past literature to help us better understand the challenges and potential for democracy in our current moment. See Bromell, "Reading Democratically," 283.

Chapter Three

1. Kirkland, *New Home, Who'll Follow?*, 48 (hereafter cited in text as *ANH*).
2. The definitive study of the Northwest from the 1780s to the 1850s appears in Onuf, *Statehood and Union*.
3. Following Lincoln's election in 1860 and through 1900, only one elected president—Grover Cleveland—came from a state outside the five that were developed by the Northwest Ordinance. For the legal significance of that influence in relation to the Northwest Ordinance and the Fourteenth Amendment, see Hegreness, "Organic Law Theory."
4. Feller, *Jacksonian Promise*.
5. Turner pitted "the democracy of the Northwest" against "the institution of slavery[,] which threatened to forbid the expansion of the democratic empire in the West ("Contributions of the West to Democracy," 256–57). Since Turner, most historians of the Midwest acknowledge its shift from national development in the nineteenth century to entrenched pastoralism by the early twentieth. See Cayton and Gray, *Identity of the American Midwest*, 1–26.
6. Among myriad historical and cultural studies, the most influential for this chapter have been Saler, *Settler's Empire*, and Rifkin, *Manifesting America*.
7. For a complete take on the transition of the Northwest to the Middle West, see Shortridge, *Middle West*. For the transition of the Northwest Ordinance from constitutional directive to apotheosis, see Onuf, *Statehood and Union*, 133–52.
8. Kloppenberg, *Toward Democracy*, 6.

9. Histories and theories of popular sovereignty discourse run deep. Morgan's is one of the most influential; see *Inventing the People*. Excellent updates on Morgan's analysis in the period from the American Revolution to the Civil War are Fritz, *American Sovereigns*, and Childers, *Failure of Popular Sovereignty*. Among reassessments of popular sovereignty outside procedural governance in colonial America and the early United States, the most influential for my arguments have been Dillon, *New World Drama*, and Nelson, *Commons Democracy*.

10. Even before the debates about replacing the Articles of Confederation, practical questions regarding democracy and popular sovereignty were anchored to the northwestern territories. With the newly acquired trans-Appalachian region, anxious legislators wanted western settlements, but they worried whether the right kind of citizens would move there. They presumed settlers would choose commercial interests over political ones. This presumption proved wrong. See Onuf, *Statehood and Union*, 1–20; Childers, *Failure of Popular Sovereignty*, 9–39; Saler, *Settler's Empire*, 21–22.

11. Most often, these claims came attached to proslavery arguments that scorned Article VI of the ordinance (forbidding slavery in the Northwest Territory), but not always. Antislavery sentiment was not uniform. Most notably, the antislavery clause of the ordinance was directly challenged in Illinois in 1824, when proslavery advocates lost by a narrow margin. See Simeone, *Democracy and Slavery*.

12. This is surprising, considering the Northwest's representative status as the first nationally designed region, as well as the crucial function that the Ohio city of Cincinnati played as the "literary emporium of the west" (Sutton, *Western Book Trade*, 67–87). To date, two influential literary histories of the pre–Civil War Northwest stand out. The first appears in the feminist criticism of Fetterley and Pryse, *Writing Out of Place*. The second comes from Edward Watts's readings through the theoretical lens of settler colonialism. See Watts, *American Colony*.

13. Rosenblum contends, "Just what good neighbor entails is elusive, . . . more so, I believe, than any other significant social relation. Not because neighboring is abstract but rather because it is concrete and nothing is excluded from the wide-open domain of give and take. Reciprocity is open-ended, loose, and permissive." In relation to procedural politics, Rosenblum points out that "neighborly relations operate in the shadow of law and public policy. . . . In many instances appeal to authorities is unavailable" (*Good Neighbors*, 5).

14. Cayton and Gray, *Identity of the American Midwest*, 10.

15. Later published as "Uncle Lot" in *The May-Flower, and Miscellaneous Stories*. Other than the name change, the edits tend to broaden the scale from regional to more national dimensions.

16. Beecher, "New England Sketch," 169 (hereafter cited in text as "NES").

17. Conzen contends that "regionality . . . [is] a coinage useful for its joint connotations of ethnicity and nationality" ("Pi-ing the Type," 92).

18. Gray, *Yankee West*, 2.

19. Lanman, *History of Michigan*, 295.

20. Pryse, "Stowe and Regionalism," 132.

21. Gray, *Yankee West*, 12.

22. The 1783 Treaty of Paris had ceded all British claims to the Mississippi River, doubling the size of US territory. But these areas were also subject to competing sovereign claims from Indigenous tribes as well as France and Spain. The otherwise weak central gov-

ernment faced theoretical questions about its own powers to dictate unilateral terms over expansion. Virginia helped the central government's case for power by ceding its claims to territories west of the Appalachian Mountains. For details on coastal states ceding land to the national government in the 1780s, see Morrison, *Forging of the Union*, 220–44.

23. Jefferson served on two different committees that presented reports that were later refined into ordinances. The "Report of a Plan for the Government of Western Territories" was presented on 1 March 1784 and endured revisions—most notably the elimination of a clause for gradual emancipation of enslaved peoples—before becoming the Ordinance of 1784. The symmetrically imposed grid on the map appeared in the Land Ordinance of 1785.

24. Fisher, "Democratic Social Space."

25. Hsu, *Geography and the Production of Space*, 31.

26. Hsu uses the work of Charles Brockden Brown; Fisher, that of Herman Melville and Walt Whitman.

27. The ordinance and the proposed Constitution famously ended up establishing different powers of federal authority over the issue of slavery, the former claiming federal authority in its ban and the latter repeatedly claiming no explicit powers over it. Yet, both worked to distance the federal government from the governed and thus limited popular sovereignty,

28. Onuf, *Statehood and Union*, 58–59.

29. Just as they had with western uprising known as the Pennsylvania Regulations of 1791 to 1794, theories of popular disinterest in self-governance proved untenable in the Northwest, evidenced prominently in the lead-up to statehood in Ohio in 1803 and later in the proslavery movement in Illinois in the early 1820s. For histories of the Pennsylvania Regulations, see Bouton, *Taming Democracy*, 216–43. For popular sovereignty in Ohio and Illinois, see Onuf, *Statehood and Union*, 67–87, 123–30.

30. With examples of suburbs, cornflakes, and Marlboro cigarettes, Fisher's essay suggests that Jefferson's plan operates in perpetuity.

31. Rohrbough, *Trans-Appalachian Frontier*, 311.

32. See Faber, *Toledo War*.

33. See Onuf, *Statehood and Union*, 85–108.

34. Mason's 2 January 1837 speech to both houses of the Michigan Territorial Legislature shared a lengthier rationale. The speech was fully reprinted in the *Detroit Evening Spectator and Literary Gazette* in the 4 January 1837 issue.

35. "Great Democratic Festival," *Detroit Democratic Free Press*, 17 January 1837.

36. "The Celebration," *Detroit Evening Spectator and Literary Gazette*, 11 February 1837.

37. "Fourth of March," *Detroit Evening Spectator and Literary Gazette*, 4 March 1837.

38. For an example of cultural history that ignores literary elements, see Schwartz, *Conflict on the Michigan Frontier*. For a representative example of a literary scholar applying a national scale of reference by highlighting the clash between eastern sensibilities and western nonsophisticates, see Zagarell, introduction to *A New Home*, xxvii–xxxviii.

39. See Kirkland, *Forest Life*; and Kirkland, *Western Clearings*.

40. William Kirkland's name appears repeatedly in the short run of the *Evening Spectator*, initially as the "Principal of the Female Seminary" in a group of endorsements for *Smith's Geography and Atlas*. Starting in December 1836, his name appeared as a "land agent" selling "1500 acres of land, lying in the south part of Livingston County . . . 3000 acres in the towns of Ecorce and Romulus . . . [and] a lot well situated on Learned Street" (*Detroit Evening*

Spectator and Literary Gazette, 14 December 1836). The ad appeared in every issue through 24 April 1837, which was just prior to the paper going out of business on 20 May 1837.

41. For a thorough list of books and periodical writings as well as historical and contemporary criticism, see Kreger, "Bibliography of Works."

42. For a reading of Kirkland's use of quotation, with and without citation, that argues for the book's situation in the tradition of western promotional literature that she was otherwise trying to critique, see Azima, "Promotion, Borrowing."

43. Mitford's *Our Village* sketches appeared in numerous editions and made up five volumes published in England and the United States from 1824 to 1836. For a full bibliographic record, see Mary Russell Mitford Society, *Digital Mitford*.

44. "Art. VIII"; "Literary Notices"; and Poe, "Caroline Matilda Kirkland."

45. On satire, see Gebhard, "Comic Displacement." On travel literature, see Hotz, "Imagining a New West." On early realism, see Andrews, "Different Kind of Reality."

46. On women's experiences in the West, see Borup, "Bankers in Buckskins"; Aliaga-Buchenau, "Magic Circle"; and Leverenz, *Manhood and the American Renaissance*. On the civilizing gestures, see Merish, "Hand of Refined Taste"; Gniadek, "Outré-mer adventures"; and Watts, *American Colony*, 168–78.

47. Zagarell, introduction to *A New Home*, xiv–xv.

48. Nelson, *Commons Democracy*, 124.

49. Shapiro argues, "In contrast to the liberal consensus model of US literary history, . . . the consolidation of the early US novel *includes* the representation of class inequality and class struggle, and . . . the early US novel helps to consolidate the US bourgeoisie precisely through its representation of class inequality and class struggle. . . . Through the 1840s, several major US novelists fashioned novels that, instead of skirting or dodging or veiling socioeconomic division in the United States, work to naturalize class inequality among whites" (*Illiberal Imagination*, 3–4).

50. Annette Kolodny offers the most details, stating that "her husband had tired of teaching and harbored dreams of buying land and founding a settlement on the Michigan frontier. To that end, he had accepted the post of principal at the new Detroit Seminary and, upon his arrival, he began acquiring parcels of land in the southern part of Livingston County, along Portage Creek (about twenty miles from what is now the university town of Ann Arbor). In less than a year he owned eight hundred acres; and, having invested his father's capital in an adjoining five hundred, by 1836 William Kirkland controlled over thirteen hundred acres of prairie, forest, and swamp, some sixty miles west of Detroit" (*Land before Her*, 131–32).

51. Watts, for instance, cites this passage as one that works against the romanticized promotional literature that depicts the "Northwest as an economic paradise, but her reasons for doing so reveal her domesticating impulse. . . . The creation of 'home feeling,' then, is incompatible with the opportunism and social instability which accompanied land speculation" (*American Colony*, 175).

52. Merish puts it this way: "On the frontier, Kirkland suggests, domestic reform will take place in several ways: through the seemingly uncoercive means of the power of refined example; through the circulation of texts, including her own, which increased consumer demand and saturated the use of domestic commodities with cultural significance; and through the powerful attractions of objects themselves" ("Hand of Refined Taste," 498).

53. Kolodny, *Land before Her*, 132.

54. Merish has read this passage as exemplifying Kirkland's Whiggish hostility to the Jacksonian democracy: "Throughout the text, Kirkland represents Jacksonianism in negative terms, as a form of false consciousness that buttresses her neighbors' resistance to economic progress and material refinement" ("Hand of Refined Taste," 503).

55. Merish sees this feature as evidence of Clavers being an adept Whig politician: "Like a good Whig orator, Mary Clavers comes 'down to the people.' She studies local customs and habits and borrows her neighbors' colloquialisms in order to appeal to them more effectively and win their support" ("Hand of Refined Taste," 501).

56. See Bercovitch, *Rites of Assent*, esp. 29–38.

57. Kolodny reads this scene differently, esteeming Kirkland's appreciation for the Hastings and dubbing them Kirkland's "model frontier couple" (*Land before Her*, 141).

58. Coincidentally, much as in Philadelphia and other places, the fervor for connections to the founding Revolutionaries simmered throughout the new settlements, and the "Ordinance thus shaped continuing discussion over first principles, . . . enabled the people of the Old Northwest to identify the founding of their states with the national founding, [and became a] symbol of regional distinctiveness" (Onuf, *Statehood and Union*, 135–36).

59. Biographical details can be found in Johannsen, *House of Beadle and Adams*; Carr, "Dead Letter (1866) Spotlight"; and Parham, "Metta Victoria Fuller Victor."

60. Acknowledging the putative justice of the principle of popular sovereignty under the terms of the Kansas-Nebraska Act, the preface declares that Utah is preparing an especially heinous offense against the United States with its plans for both slavery and polygamy. She goes on to quote an article in the *North American and United States Gazette*, from which the basic plot of the subsequent narrative draws. Notably, the article condemns "the absurdity of squatter sovereignty" (Fuller, *Mormon Wives*, xi).

61. Denning, *Mechanic Accents*, 5; Brown, *Reading the West*; Streeby, "Dime Novels."

62. Nickerson, *Web of Iniquity*, 29.

63. Nickerson, 26. Victor's *Dead Letter* was published under the pseudonym "Seeley Register" in the very first issue of *Beadle's Monthly, a Magazine of Today*, and it ran for six installments from January to June 1866. Elizabeth Duquette has argued that *The Dead Letter* sidesteps the typical tactics shared by romances of reunion that prioritized the affective, in order to suggest that "the resolution of uncertainty and the reconstruction of law are necessary preconditions for reunion" ("Office of the Dead Letter," 26).

64. Victor, *Alice Wilde*, 13.

65. Victor, 52.

66. Victor, *Backwoods Bride*, 26 (hereafter cited in text as *BB*).

67. Mihm, *Nation of Counterfeiters*.

Chapter Four

1. Dana, *Two Years before the Mast*, 233–34.

2. Ironically, when the final stake of the transcontinental railroad was hammered down in 1869 to forge that link, the new conduit plunged gold-enriched California into economic depression. See Huntley-Smith, "Print Cultures in the American West," 281.

3. Kevin Starr's description of the progressive, equalitarian vision of the First Federal Republic "envisioned a prosperous and fair civil order welcoming all citizens, whatever

their bloodlines or descent" (*California*, 46). For further details on the self-rule of Alta Californians during this time, see Starr, *California*, 45–70.

4. On the functionality of the alcalde system in interregnum California, see Starr, *California*, 73–75.

5. As Susan Lee Johnson's account of gold rush California social life has shown, Taylor's narrative whitewashes actual life in the vast majority of camps, but Taylor likely found enough evidence of democratic practice to make such a claim. Although cited as a primary source, Taylor's account receives very little attention in Johnson's invaluable social history. See Johnson, *Roaring Camp*.

6. The phrase first appeared in 1839 in the anonymously written article "The Great Nation of Futurity," published in the *United States Magazine and Democratic Review*. It made its second appearance in a July 1845 article titled "Annexation," where it specifically applied to unsettled spaces across the continent "allotted by Providence for the free development of our yearly multiplying millions" ([Cazneau], "Annexation," 7). While many have attributed the phrase to the magazine's editor, John L. O'Sullivan, more recent scholars now credit Jane McManus Storm Cazneau (under the pseudonym Cora Montgomery). See Hudson, *Mistress of Manifest Destiny*.

7. O'Sullivan, "True Title," 1.

8. In the words of Amy Greenberg, "Most Americans believed that expansionism would spread progress and enlightenment to all of mankind . . . [and] that America's territorial destiny would unfold in a natural and peaceful process. . . . By the 1840s, however, Manifest Destiny's discourse had largely become martial in tone" (*Manifest Manhood*, 21).

9. For arguments challenging national narratives that have influenced the arguments in this chapter, see Greenberg, *Manifest Manhood*; Rifkin, *Manifesting America*; Streeby, *American Sensations*; Alemán and Streeby, *Empire and the Literature of Sensation*; and Bramen, *American Niceness*.

10. For instance, Amy Kaplan has focused on the intersections of expansionist rhetoric and domestic and sentimental literature by eastern types like Catherine Beecher and Sara Josepha Hale. See Kaplan, "Manifest Domesticity."

11. Cultural historians like Stephanie LeMenager, Anne Hyde, and Michele Navakas have offered important works that continue to chip away at the narratives of a readily cohering nation. See LeMenager, *Manifest and Other Destinies*; Hyde, *Empires, Nations, and Families*; and Navakas, *Liquid Landscape*.

12. Wecter, *Literary Lodestone*, 9.

13. Historical accounts have accounted poorly for what Benjamin Madley has characterized as the genocide of Indigenous peoples from the time of Russo-Hispanic colonization through the early decades of US acquisition and California statehood. See Madley, *American Genocide*.

14. The crystallization of the often whitewashed cultural memory has led a social historian like Susan Lee Johnson to seek out and to recuperate, "alternative plot lines, stories not customarily nourished by the dominant culture, broadly defined, or even by historical scholarship" (*Roaring Camp*, 27).

15. As one example challenging this convention, Janet Neary has claimed that *The Life and Adventures of James Williams*, a gold rush–era fugitive slave narrative, should "be read as

a reflection of the incoherence or unsettled nature of the position of California in relation to the expanding nation." Neary also states that Williams's narrative employs an "important 'racial vernacular' which reflects the specific regional pressures exerted on it by Williams's experiences as a fugitive—then free—black man" ("Mining the African American Literary Tradition," 341).

16. The arrangement of a recent anthology of gold rush writing and the introductory framing are evidence that this tendency continues. See Kowalewski, introduction to *Gold Rush*.

17. *Contingency* is a helpful term in a couple of senses. In the sense of two entities touching one another, the use is ironic. Unlike the contiguous states of the eastern portion of the nation, California is repeatedly characterized as disconnected from the rest of "the States." With regard to contingent as nonfated, *contingency* demonstrates the failure of national prescriptions and teleology to latch on, for progressive temporalities to take hold. Although in time, the authors might have seen the California experiment becoming folded into national space and its liberal democratic political system, the texts themselves repeatedly betray this sense of inevitability and latency.

18. Taylor, *Eldorado*, 119.

19. Taylor, 120.

20. This latter ban drew the chief objection and became the motivation for the Conventions of Colored Citizens of California held in the mid-1850s. Achieving the power to testify in court was seen by African Americans in the state as the first step to gaining equal political and social rights. See Gardner, "Early African American Print Culture."

21. Taylor, *Eldorado*, 135.

22. Urgo, "Capitalism, Nationalism," 341.

23. For instance, Gary Scharnhorst writes, "Bret Harte has rarely been accused of expressing ideas in his fiction. Instead, he is typically regarded as at best a slipshod and sentimental local colorist and at worst a writer of popular romances who pandered to bourgeois readers unfamiliar with the American West" ("Bret Harte's Naturalism," 144).

24. Kolb, "Outcast of Literary Flat," 55–56.

25. Tara Penry has characterized Harte as one who most successfully "dramatizes and even critiques his own position as inheritor, critic, and adaptor of sentimental western stories" ("Tennessee's Partner," 149).

26. See, for instance, Morrow, "Bret Harte, Popular Fiction." Such readings must overlook the misogynistic and racial politics on display, which target the camp's sole female inhabitant, Cherokee Sal, who dies just after giving birth.

27. Nissen, "Queer Short Story," 186.

28. Harte, "Luck of Roaring Camp," 20 (hereafter cited in text as "Luck").

29. Urgo makes this case across the genre in "Capitalism, Nationalism, and the American Short Story."

30. J. David Stevens has contended alternatively that Harte's reputation of sidestepping social diversity in his stories is largely unearned, arguing that "what most critics have labeled as sentimental excess is actually Harte's method of exploring certain hegemonic cultural paradigms taken for granted in other Western narratives" ("She war a woman," 572).

31. Johnson, *Roaring Camp*, 335.

32. Ridge, *Life and Adventures of Joaquín Murieta* (1955), 7 (hereafter cited in text as *JM*).

33. The incongruities throughout the novel are matched by the writer's biography. As the son of a Cherokee slave-owner, Ridge first suffered removal to Arkansas, only to confront factional discord that culminated in his flight from a potential murder trial to the wilds of the gold rush. For details on Ridge's biography, see Parins, *John Rollin Ridge*.

34. Loney, introduction to *California Gold Rush Plays*, 14. Loney's introduction notes the many versions depicting some version of Joaquín Murieta, but ignores Ridge's version, wrongly claiming the *California Police Gazette*'s was the first.

35. The most prominent of these is Pablo Neruda's 1967 play *Fulgor y Muerte de Joaquín Murieta* (*The Splendor and Death of Joaquín Murieta*).

36. See, for instance, Windell, "Sanctity in Our Suffering World"; Merish, "Print, Cultural Memory"; and Goeke, "Yellow Bird and the Bandit."

37. Rowe, "Highway Robbery," 154–55.

38. Rowe, 159.

39. Winter, "Culture-Tectonics," 260.

40. Unlike Rowe, Cynthia Walker has argued that because Ridge is interested in producing "a vision of national character as essentially contentless, post-modern, in its chameleon-like tendency to act according to circumstances rather than inherent nature or cultural background . . . [it] behooves us to examine the man and his novel as pondering questions of law and nation" (*Indian Nation*, 122). For Walker, law has much more of an emancipatory capacity than in Rowe's assessment.

41. In Alemán's words, "Cherokee history, Rollin Ridge's family history, and Ridge's fictional Murieta thus all demonstrate the power of American ideology—be it individualism, capitalism, or liberal democracy—to disjoint and fragment racial subjects who espouse American nationalist discourses never meant to include racial others in the first place" ("Assimilation," 75).

42. In his introduction to the 1955 edition, Joseph Henry Jackson writes, "Both took their Murieta from Ridge's fiction. Bancroft used the Ridge 'Third Edition" straight, added some even more fanciful dialog and a few quotations from newspapers accounts of the time Captain Love produced the pickled head. Hittell, writing more carefully, admitted that the sources on Murieta were 'to a great extent unreliable,' but nevertheless quoted Ridge as his authority, with exact page references to the 'Third Edition.' That did it. In spite of Hittell's cautionary remarks, people saw only that Murieta had got into the histories" (Jackson, introduction to *Life and Adventures of Joaquín Murieta*, xxxviii).

43. Ridge, *Life and Adventures of Joaquin Murieta* (1871), 5 (italics added).

44. Ridge, 5–6.

45. Ridge, 74.

46. Clappe, *The Shirley Letters*, 56. Further citations are cited parenthetically in text as *Shirley*.

47. Joseph Henry Jackson has claimed that Ridge "was a familiar visitor to in the office of the *Pioneer* at the time [that *The Shirley*] *Letters* would have been in proof on the editor's desk, and some students believe that Ridge did indeed see the Shirley material" and appropriated some for himself. See Jackson, introduction to *Life and Adventures of Joaquín Murieta*, xxxi.

48. Royce, *California*, 271.

49. Lockhart goes on to write, "Similarly, she recorded details of mining life that male writers tended either to miss or ignore ("Legacy Profile," 143).

50. Smith-Baranzini, introduction to *Shirley Letters*, xxxiii.

51. "Introductory," 1.

52. "Introductory," 2.

53. Havens, "America as it was"; Brooks, "State Rights."

54. Downer, "What California Wants."

55. Scott, "Education We Want."

56. For instance, Lockhart writes, "Shirley apparently wrote her report of life in the early mines as events transpired, but clearly intended them to form a single cohesive narrative rather than merely a naïve report of events to her sister at home in 'the States'" ("Legacy Profile," 144).

57. Recent work on the cultural work of seriality—mostly in the case of novels rather than sketches like *The Shirley Letters*—includes Soderberg, "One More Time with Feeling"; Gniadek, "Seriality and Settlement"; and Chiles, "Within and without Raced Nations"; Looby, "Southworth and Seriality"; and Okker, *Social Stories*.

58. Except for the first letter published across the first two issues of *The Pioneer*, the remaining twenty-two letters appeared in the next twenty-two months. But the dates on the letters tell a different story. The first nine overall were allegedly written between 13 September and 29 October 1851. Letters 10 through 21 came about once per month between November 1851 and September 1852. The last three once again came in quicker succession, between late October and November 1852.

59. Sandra Lockhart writes that "Hubert Howe Bancroft, among others, noted that Bret Harte was indebted to Dame Shirley for the firsthand report of life in the mines, which his own experience lacked" ("Legacy Profile," 146).

60. Clappe, *Shirley Letters*, 13.

61. Royce, *California*, 272; Levy, *They Saw the Elephant*, 60.

62. Roberts, *American Alchemy*, 248–55.

63. Bancroft, *Popular Tribunals*; Hittell, *History of the City*.

64. Royce, *California*, 297–366.

65. Culberson, *Vigilantism*, 2.

66. Among others, see Senkewicz, *Vigilantes in Gold Rush San Francisco*; and Taniguchi, *Dirty Deeds*. Taniguchi's convincing account benefits from the recent discovery of several new documents, including Hittell's copy of the previously unpublicized minutes from the 1856 committee meetings.

Chapter Five

1. Grimes, *Life of William Grimes*, 68. In a 2008 reissue, editors William Andrews and Regina Mason point out the misfit qualities of Grimes's *Life* in relation to earlier and later fugitive slave narratives. See Grimes, Andrews, and Mason, *Life of William Grimes, the Runaway Slave*.

2. As Patrick Rael has noted, "By the 1850s, even rejections of black separatisms stood captive to the principles of nationalism. It had become increasingly difficult to discuss any issue without becoming subsumed by the discourse of nationalism." Because of their

exclusion from participation in the Anglo-Saxon narratives of American nationalism, though, "black nationalists crafted an ideology that departed from its American original in important ways.... Black takes on American nationalism constructed the African-descended as a people, united in purpose in destiny." Rael goes on to cite two primary variations of this discourse, the first dipped in a religiously inflected mission-styled discourse and the other turned to racial science and the "logic of uplift and elevation" (*Black Identity and Black Protest*, 239, 241).

3. On the Liberty Party's platform of denationalizing slavery, see Sewell, *Ballots for Freedom*, 90–94.

4. See Foster, "Narrative of the Interesting Origins"; Santamarina, "Are We There Yet?"; and Gardner, *Unexpected Places*.

5. Hartman, *Scenes of Subjection*, Ernest, *Liberation Historiography*, and Ernest, *Chaotic Justice* set very high bars. More recent work has expanded the field. See Foreman, *Activist Sentiments*; Neary, *Fugitive Testimony*; Wright, *Black Girlhood*; and Fielder, *Relative Races*. The edited volume by Cohen and Stein, *Early African American Print Culture*, has been both influential and controversial. Addressing a longer history of print and media culture is Fielder and Senchyne, *Against a Sharp White Background*. Tompkins, *Racial Indigestion*, Rusert, *Fugitive Science*, and Schuller, *Biopolitics of Feeling* have been three of the most insightful and influential interdisciplinary works in the field.

6. Wilson examines the dynamics by which mid-nineteenth-century Black aesthetics reframed the terms of representative democracy, attending specifically to the ways that "African Americans manipulated aurality and visuality in art that depicted images of national belonging not only as a mode of critique but as an iteration of democratic representation itself" (*Specters of Democracy*, 6). Pratt argues that the selected writings of Frederick Douglas and the free men of color in the first African American anthology of poetry, *Les Cenelles*, moved beyond attempts to achieve recognition of Black humanity and instead found a third way between an outdated civic republicanism and the rapidly entrenching liberal individualism, claiming that these works conceptualized a "stranger humanism" that "envisioned a racially integrated democracy" (*Stranger Book*, 7). Spires explores the critical and reparative theorizations of democratically oriented citizenship, making the case for citizenship as posited by Black thinkers "not as common identity as such but rather as a set of common practices: political participation, mutual aid, critique and revolution, and the myriad daily interactions between people living in the same spaces" (*Practice of Citizenship*, 3).

7. Ober, *Demopolis*, esp. 1–17.

8. Ober, "Democracy's Dignity," 827.

9. Jones, *Birthright Citizens*, 11.

10. This argument untethers democracy from what Bonnie Honig has argued is the quintessential democratic task: the taking of liberal-ordered rights and privileges (*Democracy and the Foreigner*, 98–106). It likewise draws on Walter Johnson's arguments about the ways that historians' focus on agency has "shoved to the side ... a consideration of human-ness lived outside the conventions of liberal agency" ("On Agency," 115).

11. Ober, *Demopolis*, 6.

12. Blight, *Frederick Douglass*, xv.

13. Levine, "Uncle Tom's Cabin."

14. For more on the connections between Douglass's journalism and "The Heroic Slave," see Fishkin and Peterson, "We hold these truths."

15. A representative selection of these essays has been included in the 2015 critical edition of Douglass, *Heroic Slave*.

16. As Krista Walter has noted, "The Heroic Slave" is dripping with nationalism, from the choice of character names (Madison Washington) to Tom Grant's declaration that the revolt aboard the *Creole* is inspired by the principles of 1776. See Walter, "Trappings of Nationalism." Ivy Wilson has argued for the transnational scope of the novella. See Wilson, "On Native Ground."

17. In the words of Carrie Hyde, "As much as Douglass might idealize the ocean as an extranational utopian space (which if not 'nowhere' is still foremost not the nation), his ultimate objective is not properly transnational or cosmopolitan[.] Instead, Douglass prescriptively uses the universalizing rhetoric of natural law as a model for political reform in the United States" ("Climates of Liberty," 494).

18. Douglass, *Heroic Slave*, 4 (hereafter cited in text as *HS*).

19. On the numerous events and writings connected to Douglass's turn away from Garrisonian moral suasion to political abolition and an antislavery reading of the US Constitution in the late 1840s, see Blight, *Frederick Douglass*, 178–227.

20. This has been repeatedly noted, leading to correctives like the volume *Beyond Douglass*, edited by Michael Drexler and Ed White.

21. Robert Stepto reads this moment as an effective riddle that conjoins a Revolutionary hero and an enslaved man of the same name. See "Storytelling in Early Afro-American Fiction," 361–62.

22. See, for instance, see Stepto, 361–62; Andrews, "Novelization of Voice," 29; and Sale, *Slumbering Volcano*, 179–80.

23. Ernest, *Liberation Historiography*, 5.

24. Ernest, 83; Castronovo, *Necro Citizenship*, 61; Pratt, *Strangers Book*, 100–113.

25. For Robert Stepto and William Andrews, Douglass's innovations drew on and enhanced traditions of fugitive narratives of the formerly enslaved. Douglass's text demonstrates such changes by dramatizing the ways that listeners of the right kind of stories might transform listeners into actors, as well as the need to establish a self-authenticating voice that demonstrated the equal attributes and humanity of a Black author. See Stepto, "Storytelling in Early Afro-American Fiction"; and Andrews, "Novelization of Voice." For other critics, though, Douglass's narrative and aesthetic choices suggest an inability to work outside the dominant white, male, individualist dogmas that dominated the era. Richard Yarborough, for instance, has noted that Douglass is unable to move beyond his preoccupations with self-reliance and heroic male individualism in this story and thus has fallen victim to a variety of weaknesses. See Yarborough, "Race, Violence, and Manhood," 176. Yarborough quotes Valerie Smith, who writes, "Within his critique of American cultural practices [of slavery], then, is an affirmation of its definitions of manhood and power," which means that his "indictment of mainstream practice actually authenticates one of its fundamental assumptions" (*Self-Discovery and Authority*, 42–43).

26. Stauffer continues, "The sublime power of the imagination could be used to create a performative self that would help usher in a new world of interracial equality.... His

aesthetic vision was sublime, darkly Romantic, and apocalyptic. It embodied both the fulfillment of the nation's sacred ideals, and the desolation that would accompany this transformation. It was a millennial vision defined in nationalist terms." Stauffer goes on to detail Douglass's consistency with Burkean and Kantian conceptions of the sublime and to demonstrate his embrace of Blackness as the sublime ("Aesthetics of Freedom," 115, 117).

27. Stepto, "Storytelling in Early Afro-American Fiction," 365.

28. The closing scene offers the only ambivalence when it comes to my assessment. The fourth part brings the tale to a close with two white men discussing the events, which seems consistent with the cordon sanitaire theory in readings of southwestern humor. But Grant's version of events comes to a rather abrupt end, suggesting something more fragmented, less orderly. Instead of a tidy bow that ties up loose ends, the last line offers little closure. Herein lies one moment in which the historical record seems insufficient.

29. At letter's end, Douglass explicitly cites the contributor of "the heads of the colored people" (Smith) as chief offender. This comment about the vacuous representations of dandyish Black culture on Broadway suggests a criticism of some of William J. Wilson's contributions to *Frederick Douglass' Paper*, an issue that Radiclani Clytus elucidates in "Visualizing in Black Print."

30. F. D., "Letter from the Editor," *Frederick Douglass' Paper*, 27 May 1853.

31. In his introduction to *My Bondage and My Freedom*, Smith praised Douglass's self-creation largely in conventionally nationalistic and liberal terms; for instance, he writes, "He is a Representative American man—a type of his countrymen. . . . To the fullest extent, has Frederick Douglass passed through every gradation of rank comprised of our national make-up, and bears his person and upon his soul everything that is American" (xxv–xxvi). The introduction, along with a host of other published material from Smith, demonstrates an extremely distinctive political philosophy and rhetoric at play in this misfit text.

32. For biographical details, see Stauffer, *Works of James McCune Smith*, xiii–xl.

33. Stauffer describes this choice as "derived from a colonial settlement in what is now Jersey City, New Jersey, made legendary by Washington Irving as an interracial community of blacks, Indians, and Dutch settler who resisted British invaders" (*Works of James McCune Smith*, xxxi).

34. Stauffer, 188.

35. Spires, *Practice of Citizenship*, 143.

36. Jacob Crane has qualified this notion with his recent work on Smith's representation of the antihero. See Crane, "Razed to the Knees."

37. Spires, *Practice of Citizenship*, 146.

38. Ober goes on to note, "Dignity provides an answer, lacking in Hobbes's theory, for how a government can induce pro-social behavior from individuals who, as a matter of ingrained character (aka, the ordinal ranking of their preferences), gain greater utility from asserting their own superiority and having that superiority acknowledged by others than they do from other aspects of life" (*Demopolis*, 103).

39. Communipaw, "Done with a Whitewash Brush," 2.

40. Communipaw, 2.

41. For Schuller, "*impressibility* denotes the capacity of a substance to receive impressions from external objects that thereby change its characteristics. Impressibility signals the ca-

pacity of matter to be alive to movements made on it, to retain and incorporate changes rendered in its material over time.... The notion of impressibility fills a crucial gap in theories of biopower: how bodies were understood to bind together into the organic phenomenon of population" (*Biopolitics of Feeling*, 7–8).

42. Communipaw, "Done with a Whitewash Brush," 2.

43. Communipaw, "Boot-Black," 3.

44. Communipaw, "Washerwoman," 1.

45. Communipaw, "Sexton," 3.

46. Communipaw, "Steward," 3.

47. Benjamin Fagan opens his book with analysis of the 1847 national convention and McCune Smith's advocacy of a national press. See *Black Press and the Chosen Nation*, 1–3.

48. Communipaw's words, "In the transition state of colored-Americandom, the editor must be an amphibious animal, half orator, half editor; he must tear the fibres of his own brain one way to adorn his columns for the inspection of the most fastidious and merciless newspaper critics in the world—I mean colored Americans; and then, he must tear the fibres of his brain another way to coax, beg, or wheedle money enough out of chance audiences to print his paper and keep a coat on his back" (Communipaw, "Editor," 3).

49. Communipaw, "Editor," 4.

50. Communipaw, "Inventor," 3.

51. Communipaw, "Whitewasher," 3.

52. Without explicit signs of a schoolmaster here, it appears that Communipaw assumes this persona while addressing the politics of the Crimean War and recent events involving a Black heroine, Anna Downer, who had gained fame trying to rescue others from a sinking ship. In the second installment, he goes in yet another direction. Picking up a geology book, he shares his disappointment with the author's "cruel abuse and misrepresentation of the free colored people of our free States!" Using his own data, statistics, and reasoning, Communipaw rebuts the book's faulty scientific claims. After lengthy rebuttal, he finally turns to a specific schoolmaster, who resides in a quiet village of New Hampshire. "He was about forty years old, with bushy hair; A STOOP IN HIS SHOULDERS; of middle height, an average forehead, and eyes of that inlooking absent cast, common to abstract thinkers or men pained with lifelong grief" (Communipaw, "Schoolmaster (No. X)," 2–3).

53. Derrick Spires details these columns in *Practice of Citizenship*, 131–43.

54. For an invaluable history of the extraordinary periodical production that was the *Anglo-African Magazine*, see Wilson, "Brief Wondrous Life."

55. The scene here very much calls up Russ Castronovo's idea of necro citizenship and echoes of Devil-Bug's dream in *The Quaker City*, which I discussed in chapter 1.

56. Ethiop, "Second Paper," 90.

57. Biographical details on Wilson are limited, but scholars have pieced together details. See Wilder, *Covenant with Color*, 72–74; Peterson, *Black Gotham*, 165–74; and Spires, *Practice of Citizenship*, 131.

58. Peterson, *Black Gotham*, 218.

59. Clytus, "Visualizing in Black Print"; Wilson, *Specters of Democracy*, 145–68.

60. Wilson, *Specters of Democracy*, 146. Wilson goes on to write, "As much as the story is about imagining a figurative space where blacks can have their own works presented, the story also becomes a metaliterary site where Wilson's readers are challenged with imagining

an African American subjectivity that encompasses and subsumes a black politics that moves beyond the history and borders of the United States" (147).

61. Ernest, *Liberation Historiography*, 326.
62. Spires, *Practice of Citizenship*, 186.
63. Ethiop, "Afric-American Picture Gallery," 52–53.
64. Ethiop, 53.
65. Ethiop, 54.
66. Employing liberalist convention, Wilson goes on to write that Ethiop's portraiture "compels readers to think about the synecdochic representation whereby the head might be able to represent the whole of the body (as well as the body politic) and engage the politics of recognition by having Ethiop come head-to-head with these faces" (*Specters of Democracy*, 161).
67. Ethiop, "Second Paper," 87.
68. Ethiop, 88.
69. Ethiop, "Third Paper," 100.
70. Ethiop, 101.
71. Ethiop, 177.
72. Ethiop, "Sixth Paper," 243.
73. Ethiop, 246.
74. Ethiop only mentions the gallery twice in this installment, first in the opening, when Bill has burst in declaring that he will shoot a man in the streets, and then again at the closing with the line, "The portrait of our sable hero, in all the flush of manhood, hangs on the north side of the Gallery, for the inspection of the curious" (Ethiop, "Seventh Paper," 324).

Bibliography

Primary Sources

ARCHIVES

American Antiquarian Society (Worcester, MA)
Bancroft Library at University of California Berkeley
Historical Society of Pennsylvania
The Huntington Library (San Marino, CA)
Library Company of Philadelphia (PA)
Rare Book and Manuscript Library, University of Pennsylvania

PERIODICALS

Anglo-African Magazine (New York, NY)
California Police Gazette (San Francisco, CA)
Democratic Free Press (Detroit, MI)
Detroit Evening Spectator and Literary Gazette (MI)
Frederick Douglass' Paper (Rochester, NY)
Godey's Lady's Book (Philadelphia, PA)
Graham's Magazine (Philadelphia, PA)
Los Angeles Star (CA)
Nashville Union and American (TN)
National Atlas and Sunday Morning Mail (Philadelphia, PA)
National Gazette and Literary Register (Philadelphia, PA)
National Intelligencer (Washington, DC)
New Hampshire Patriot (Concord, NH)
New York Morning News (NY)
Philadelphia Mirror (PA)
The Pioneer, or California Monthly Magazine (San Francisco, CA)
Public Ledger (Philadelphia, PA)
Southern Literary Messenger (Richmond, VA)
United States Magazine and Democratic Review (Washington, DC)
The Western Monthly Magazine, and Literary Journal (Cincinnati, OH)

PUBLISHED PRIMARY SOURCES

"Art. VIII.—*A New Home, Who'll Follow? or, Glimpses of Western Life*. By Mrs. Mary Clavers, an Actual Settler." *North American Review* 50 (1840): 206–23.
Bancroft, George. *History of the United States of America, from the Discovery of the Continent*. Vol. 4. New York: D. Appleton, 1892.
Bancroft, Hubert Howe. *Popular Tribunals*. Vols.1 and 2. San Francisco: History Company, 1887.
Beecher, Harriet E. "A New England Sketch." *Western Monthly Magazine, and Literary Journal* 3, no. 16 (1834): 169–92.
Bird, Robert Montgomery. *Sheppard Lee: Written by Himself*. 1836. New York: New York Review of Books, 2008.

A Bostonian [Benjamin Bussey Thatcher]. *Traits of the Tea Party; Being a Memoir of George R. T. Hewes, One of the Last of Its Survivors; With a History of That Transaction; Reminiscences of the Massacre, and the Siege, and Other Stories of Old Times*. New York: Harper and Brothers, 1835.

Bouton, John Bell. *The Life and Choice Writings of George Lippard*. New York: H. H. Randall, 1855.

Brooks, B. S. "State Rights." *The Pioneer, or California Monthly Magazine* 3, no. 1 (1855): 1–15.

[Cazneau, Jane McManus Storm]. "Annexation." *United States Magazine and Democratic Review* 17, no. 1 (1845): 5–10.

Channing, William E. "Remarks on National Literature." In *The Works of William E. Channing, D. D.*, 124–38. Boston: American Unitarian Association, 1890.

A Citizen of New York [James Hawkes]. *A Retrospect of the Boston Tea-Party, with a Memoir of George R. T. Hewes, a Survivor of the Little Band of Patriots Who Drowned the Tea in Boston Harbour in 1773*. New York: S. Bliss, 1834.

Clappe, Louise Amelia Knapp Smith. *The Shirley Letters from the California Mines, 1851–1852*. Edited by Marlene Smith-Baranzini. Berkeley, CA: Heyday Books, 1998.

Communipaw. "'Heads of the Colored People,' Done with a Whitewash Brush." *Frederick Douglass' Paper*, 25 March 1852, 2.

———. "Heads of the Colored People—No. VI. The Editor." *Frederick Douglass' Paper*, 18 February 1853, 3–4.

———. "Heads of the Colored People—No. VII. The Inventor." *Frederick Douglass' Paper*, 9 September 1853, 3.

———. "Heads of the Colored People—No. VIII. The Whitewasher." *Frederick Douglass' Paper*, 30 September 1853, 3.

———. "Heads of the Colored People—No. X. The Schoolmaster." *Frederick Douglass' Paper*, 3 November 1854, 3.

———. "Heads of the Colored People—No. X. The Schoolmaster." *Frederick Douglass' Paper*, 17 November 1854, 2–3.

———. "Heads of the Colored People—No. 2. The Boot-Black." *Frederick Douglass' Paper*, 15 April 1852, 3.

———. "Heads of the Colored People—No. 3. The Washerwoman." *Frederick Douglass' Paper*, 17 June 1852, 1.

———. "Heads of the Colored People—No. 4. The Sexton." *Frederick Douglass' Paper*, 16 July 1852, 3.

———. "Heads of the Colored People—No. 5. The Steward." *Frederick Douglass' Paper*, 24 December 1852, 3.

Dana, Richard Henry, Jr. *Two Years before the Mast: A Narrative of Life at Sea*. 1840. New York: Penguin, 1986.

Davy Crockett's Almanack, of Wild Sports in the West, Life in the Backwoods, Sketches of Texas, and Rows on the Mississippi. Nashville, TN: Heirs of Col. Crockett, 1838.

Douglass, Frederick. *The Heroic Slave: A Cultural and Critical Edition*. 1854. Edited by Robert S. Levine, John Stauffer, and John R. McKivigan. New Haven, CT: Yale University Press, 2015.

Downer, S. A. "What California Wants." *The Pioneer, or California Monthly Magazine* 2, no. 2 (1854): 80–85.

Ethiop. "Afric-American Picture Gallery." *Anglo-African Magazine* 1, no. 2 (1859): 52–55.
———. "Afric-American Picture Gallery.—Second Paper." *Anglo-African Magazine* 1, no. 3 (1859): 87–90.
———. "Afric-American Picture Gallery.—Third Paper." *Anglo-African Magazine* 1, no. 4 (1859): 100–104.
———. "Afric-American Picture Gallery.—Third Paper." *Anglo-African Magazine* 1, no. 6 (1859): 173–77.
———. "Afric-American Picture Gallery. Fifth Paper." *Anglo-African Magazine* 1, no. 7 (1859): 216–19.
———. "Afric-American Picture Gallery. Sixth Paper." *Anglo-African Magazine* 1, no. 8 (1859): 243–47.
———. "Afric-American Picture Gallery. Seventh Paper. The Early Days of the Underground Railroad." *Anglo-African Magazine* 1, no. 10 (1859): 321–24.
Flint, Timothy. *A Condensed Geography of the Western States, or the Mississippi Valley*. Cincinnati: E. F. Flint, 1828.
Foust, Clement E. *The Life and Dramatic Works of Robert Montgomery Bird*. New York: Knickerbocker Press, 1919.
[Franklin, Benjamin]. *Memoirs of the Life and Writings of Benjamin Franklin, Written by Himself*. Edited by William Temple Franklin. Philadelphia: T. S. Manning, 1818. Internet Archive. https://archive.org/details/memoirslifeandwo5frangoog/page/n33/mode/2up.
Grimes, William. *Life of William Grimes, the Runaway Slave. Written by Himself*. New York: W. Grimes, 1825.
Griswold, Rufus Wilmot. *The Prose Writers of America. With a Survey of the Intellectual History, Condition, and Prospects of the Country*. 3rd ed. Philadelphia: Carey and Hart, 1849.
Hammond, James Henry. "Speech of Hon. James H. Hammond, of South Carolina, On the Admission of Kansas, Under the Lecompton Constitution: Delivered in the Senate of the United States, March 4, 1858." *Northern Visions of Race, Region and Reform*, an American Antiquarian Society Online Exhibition curated by Lucia Z. Knoles. 2006. https://www.americanantiquarian.org/Freedmen/Manuscripts/cottonisking.html.
Harris, George Washington. *Sut Lovingood Yarns*. 1867. Memphis: St. Lukes Press, 1987.
Harte, Bret. *The Luck of Roaring Camp and Other Writings*. New York: Penguin, 2001.
Havens, C. E. "America as it was to America as it will be." *The Pioneer, or California Monthly Magazine* 2, no. 1 (1854): 16–21.
Hittell, Theodore. *A History of the City of San Francisco, and Incidentally of the State of California*. San Francisco: A. L. Bancroft, 1878.
Hooper, Johnson Jones. *Adventures of Captain Simon Suggs*. 1845. Nashville, TN: J. S. Sanders, 1993.
Ingraham, Joseph Holt. *The South-West*. New York: Harper and Brothers, 1835.
"Introductory." *The Pioneer, or California Monthly Magazine* 1, no. 1 (1854): 1.
Jones, John Beauchamp. *The Adventures of Colonel Gracchus Vanderbomb of Sloughcreek, in Pursuit of the Presidency: also, the Exploits of Mr. Numerius Plutarch Kipps, His Private Secretary*. Philadelphia: A. Hart, 1852.
[Kirkland, Caroline]. *Forest Life. By the Author of "A New Home."* New York: James W. Judd, 1842.

———. *A New Home, Who'll Follow?* 1839. Edited by Sandra A. Zagarell. New Brunswick, NJ: Rutgers University Press, 1996.
[———.]. *Western Clearings.* New York: Wiley and Putnam, 1845.
Lanman, James. *History of Michigan, Civil and Topographical, in a Compendious Form, with a View of the Surrounding Lakes.* New York: E. French, 1839.
Lippard, George. *Herbert Tracy: A Romance of the Battle of Germantown.* Philadelphia: R. G. Berford, 1844.
———. *The Quaker City.* Philadelphia: Published by the author, 1849.
———. *The Quaker City; or, the Monks of Monk-Hall.* Philadelphia: Published by the author, 1847. Google Books. Accessed July 2014. https://books.google.com/books?id=aTs4AAAAYAAJ&source=gbs_slider_cls_metadata_7_mylibrary.
———. *Washington and His Generals: or, Legends of the Revolution.* Philadelphia: G. B. Zieber, 1847.
"Literary Notices." *The Knickerbocker, or, New-York Monthly Magazine* 14 (1839): 452–56.
Longstreet, Augustus Baldwin. *Georgia Scenes.* 1835. Nashville, TN: J. S. Sanders, 1992.
Madison, James. "Federalist, Number 10: The Same Subject Continued (the Union as a Safeguard against Domestic Faction and Insurrection)." In *The Federalist Papers*, 122–27. New York: Penguin, 1987.
Olmstead, Frederick Law. *A Journey in the Back Country.* New York: Mason Brothers, 1860.
[O'Sullivan, John L.] "The Great Nation of Futurity." *United States Magazine and Democratic Review* 6, no. 23 (1839): 426–30.
———. "The True Title." *New York Morning News*, 27 December 1845, 1.
Poe, Edgar A. "Caroline Matilda Kirkland." In "The Literati of New York City, No. IV," *Godey's Lady's Book* 33 (1846): 75–76.
———. "Critical Notices." *Southern Literary Messenger* 2, no. 10 (1836): 662–63.
———. "Lynchers' Character." *Southern Literary Messenger* 2, no. 6 (1836): 389.
———. "Philosophy of Composition." *Graham's Magazine* 28, no. 4 (1846): 163–67.
Porter, William Trotter, ed. *The Big Bear of Arkansas, and Other Sketches, Illustrative of Characters and Incidents in the South and South-West.* Philadelphia: Carey and Hart, 1846.
———, ed. *A Quarter Race in Kentucky, and Other Sketches, Illustrative of Scenes, Characters, and Incidents, throughout "The Universal Yankee Nation."* Philadelphia: Carey and Hart, 1847.
Ridge, John Rollin [Yellow Bird]. *The Life and Adventures of Joaquín Murieta, the Celebrated California Bandit.* 1854. Norman: University of Oklahoma Press, 1955.
———. *The Life and Adventures of Joaquin Murieta, the Celebrated California Bandit.* 3rd ed. San Francisco: Frederick MacCrellish, 1871.
Scott, W. A. "The Education We Want." *The Pioneer, or California Monthly Magazine* 4, no. 6 (1855): 359–75.
Smith, James McCune. Introduction to *My Bondage and My Freedom*, by Frederick Douglass, xvii–xxxi. Edited by James McCune Smith. New York: Miller, Orton, and Mulligan, 1855.
Taylor, Bayard. *Eldorado.* 1850. Santa Clara, CA: Haymarket Books, 2002.
Thorpe, Thomas Bangs. "The Big Bear of Arkansas." In *The Big Bear of Arkansas, and Other Sketches, Illustrative of the Characters and Incidents in the South and South-West*, edited by William T. Porter, 13–31. Philadelphia: Carey and Hart, 1846.

———. *The Hive of the "Bee-Hunter": A Repository of Sketches, including Peculiar American Character, Scenery, and Rural Sports*. New York: D. Appleton, 1854.
Victor, Metta V. *Alice Wilde: The Raftsman's Daughter. A Forest Romance*. New York: Beadle, 1860.
———. *The Backwoods Bride: A Romance of Squatter Life*. New York: Beadle, 1860.
———. *Mormon Wives: A Narrative of Facts Stranger than Fiction*. Cincinnati, OH: H. W. Derby, 1856.
Wemyss, Francis Courtney. *Twenty-Six Years of the Life of an Actor and Manager*. New York: Burgess, Stringer, 1846.
Wright, Frances. *Views of the Society and Manners in America; in a Series of Letters from the Country to a Friend in England during the Years 1818, 1819, and 1820*. New York: Printed for E. Bliss and E. White, 1821.

Secondary Sources

Adorno, Theodor W. *Aesthetic Theory*. Edited and translated by Robert Hullot-Kentor. Minneapolis: University of Minnesota Press, 1997.
Aiken, Guy. "Educating Tocqueville: Jared Sparks, the Boston Whigs, and Democracy in America." *Tocqueville Review / La revue Tocqueville* 34, no. 1 (2014): 169–92.
Alemán, Jesse. "Assimilation and the Decapitated Body Politic in *The Life and Adventures of Joaquín Murieta*." *Arizona Quarterly* 60, no. 1 (2004): 71–98.
Alemán, Jesse, and Shelley Streeby, eds. *Empire and the Literature of Sensation: An Anthology of Nineteenth-Century Popular Fiction*. New Brunswick, NJ: Rutgers University Press, 2007.
Aliaga-Buchenau, Ana-Isabel. "'The Magic Circle': Women and Community Formation of a Frontier Village in Caroline Kirkland's *A New Home—Who'll Follow?*" *Critical Survey* 16, no. 3 (2004): 62–77.
Allen, Danielle. "Democracy versus Republic." In *Democracies in America: Keywords for the Nineteenth Century and Today*, edited by D. Berton Emerson and Gregory Laski, 17–23. Oxford: Oxford University Press.
Altschuler, Glenn C., and Stuart M. Blumin. *Rude Republic: Americans and Their Politics in the Nineteenth Century*. Princeton, NJ: Princeton University Press, 2000.
Altschuler, Sari. "From Empathy to Epistemology: Robert Montgomery Bird and the Future of the Medical Humanities." *American Literary History* 28, no. 1 (2016): 1–26.
Altschuler, Sari, and Aaron M. Tobiason. "Playbill for George Lippard's *The Quaker City*." *PMLA* 129, no. 2 (2014): 267–73.
Anderson, Benedict. *Imagined Communities: Reflections on the Origin and Spread of Nationalism*. Rev. ed. London: Verso, 2006.
Anderson, John Q. "Scholarship in Southwestern Humor—Past and Present." *Mississippi Quarterly* 17 (1963–1964): 67–84.
Andrews, Jennifer. "A Different Kind of Reality: Reading the Humor of Caroline Kirkland's *A New Home, Who'll Follow?*" *Studies in American Humor* 3, no. 10 (2003): 5–20.
Andrews, William L. "The Novelization of Voice in Early African American Narrative." *PMLA* 105, no. 1 (1990): 23–34.

Anthony, David. "Banking on Emotion: Financial Panic and the Logic of Male Submission in the Jacksonian Gothic." *American Literature* 76, no. 4 (2004): 719–47.
Appiah, Kwame Anthony. *Cosmopolitanism: Ethics in a World of Strangers*. New York: W. W. Norton, 2007.
Appleby, Joyce. *Inheriting the Revolution: The First Generation of Americans*. Cambridge, MA: Harvard University Press, 2004.
Arac, Jonathan. *The Emergence of American Literary Narrative, 1820–1860*. Cambridge, MA: Harvard University Press, 2005.
Arendt, Hannah. *Lectures on Kant's Philosophy*. Edited by Ronald Beiner. Chicago: University of Chicago Press, 1992.
Armitage, David. *The Declaration of Independence: A Global History*. Cambridge, MA: Harvard University Press, 2007.
Ashwill, Gary. "The Mysteries of Capitalism in George Lippard's City Novels." *ESQ: A Journal of the American Renaissance* 40, no. 4 (1994): 293–317.
Azima, Rachel. "Promotion, Borrowing, and Caroline Kirkland's Literary Labors." *ESQ: A Journal of the American Renaissance* 57, no. 4 (2011): 390–426.
Bakhtin, Mikhail. *Rabelais and His World*. Translated by Hélène Iswolsky. Bloomington: Indiana University Press, 1984.
Barnes, Elizabeth. "Novels." In *History of the Book in America, An Extensive Republic: Print, Culture, and Society in the New Nation, 1790–1840*. Vol. 2, edited by Robert A. Gross and Mary Kelley, 440–49. Chapel Hill: The University of North Carolina Press, 2010.
Baym, Nina. "Melodramas of Beset Manhood: How Theories of American Fiction Exclude Women Authors." *American Quarterly* 33, no. 2 (1981): 123–39.
Bercovitch, Sacvan. *Rites of Assent: Transformations in the Symbolic Construction of America*. New York: Routledge, 1993.
Berlant, Lauren. *The Anatomy of Nationalist Fantasy: Hawthorne, Utopia, and Everyday Life*. Chicago: University of Chicago Press, 1991.
Bhabha, Homi. *The Location of Culture*. London: Routledge, 1994.
Blair, Walter. *Native American Humor (1800–1900)*. Cincinnati, OH: American Book Company, 1937.
Blair, Walter, and Richard M. Powers. *Davy Crockett, Frontier Hero: The Truth as He Told It—the Legend as Friends Built It*. New York: Coward-McCann, 1955.
Blight, David W. *Frederick Douglass: Prophet of Freedom*. New York: Simon and Schuster, 2018.
Borup, Rachel. "Bankers in Buckskins: Caroline Kirkland's Critique of Frontier Masculinity." *American Transcendental Quarterly* 18, no. 4 (2004): 230–46.
Bouton, Terry. *Taming Democracy: "The People," the Founders, and the Troubled Ending of the American Revolution*. Oxford: Oxford University Press, 2007.
Bramen, Carrie Tirado. *American Niceness: A Cultural History*. Cambridge, MA: Harvard University Press, 2017.
Bromell, Nick. "Reading Democratically: Pedagogies of Difference and Practices of Listening in *The House of Mirth* and *Passing*." *American Literature* 81, no. 2 (2009): 281–303.
Brown, Bill, ed. *Reading the West: An Anthology of Dime Westerns*. Boston: Bedford, 1997.

Brown, Richard D. *Self-Evident Truths: Contesting Equal Rights from the Revolution to the Civil War.* New Haven, CT: Yale University Press, 2017.
Brown, Wendy. "We Are All Democrats Now. . . ." In *Democracy in What State?*, by Giorgio Agamben et al. with translations from French by William McCuaig, 44–57. New York: Columbia University Press, 2012.
Brunhouse, Robert L. *The Counter-Revolution in Pennsylvania, 1776–1790.* Harrisburg: Pennsylvania Historical Commission, 1942.
Buffington, Nancy. "Conquering History: The Historical Romances of Robert M. Bird." *Modern Language Studies* 30, no. 2 (2000): 89–117.
Cahill, Edward. *Liberty of the Imagination: Aesthetic Theory, Literary Form, and Politics in the Early United States.* Philadelphia: University of Pennsylvania Press, 2012.
Cahill, Edward, and Edward Larkin. "Aesthetics, Feeling, and Form in Early American Literary Studies." *Early American Literature* 51, no. 2 (2016): 235–54.
Carr, Felicia L. "The Dead Letter (1866) Spotlight." *Nickels and Dimes: From the Collections of Johannsen and LeBlanc.* Northern Illinois University Libraries. Accessed 13 June 2023. https://dimenovels.lib.niu.edu/learn/spotlights/deadletter.
Casanova, Pascale. *The World Republic of Letters.* Translated by M. B. DeBevoise. Cambridge, MA: Harvard University Press, 2004.
Castiglia, Christopher. *Interior States: Institutional Consciousness and the Inner Life of Democracy in the Antebellum United States.* Durham, NC: Duke University Press, 2008.
Castiglia, Christopher, and Russ Castronovo. "A 'Hive of Subtlety': Aesthetics and the End(s) of Cultural Studies." *American Literature* 76, no. 3 (2004): 423–35.
Castronovo, Russ. *Necro Citizenship: Death, Eroticism, and the Public Sphere in the Nineteenth-Century United States.* Durham, NC: Duke University Press, 2001.
Castronovo, Russ, and Dana D. Nelson, eds. *Materializing Democracy: Toward a Revitalized Cultural Politics.* Durham, NC: Duke University Press, 2002.
Cayton, Andrew R. L., and Susan E. Gray, eds. *The Identity of the American Midwest: Essays on Regional History.* Bloomington: Indiana University Press, 2001.
Chemerinsky, Erwin. *We the People: A Progressive Reading of the Constitution for the Twenty-First Century.* New York: Picador, 2018.
Childers, Christopher. *The Failure of Popular Sovereignty: Slavery, Manifest Destiny, and the Radicalization of Southern Politics.* Lawrence: University Press of Kansas, 2012.
Chiles, Katy. "Within and without Raced Nations: Intratextuality, Martin Delany, and *Blake: or the Huts of America.*" *American Literature* 80, no. 2 (2008): 323–52.
Clark, Thomas D., and John D. W. Guice, eds. *The Old Southwest, 1795–1830: Frontiers in Conflict.* Norman: University of Oklahoma Press, 1996.
Clytus, Radiclani. "Visualizing in Black Print: The Brooklyn Correspondence of William J. Wilson, aka 'Ethiop.'" *J19: The Journal of Nineteenth-Century Americanists* 6, no. 1 (2018): 29–66.
Cohen, Lara Langer. *The Fabrication of American Literature: Fraudulence and Antebellum Print Culture.* Philadelphia: University of Pennsylvania Press, 2012.
Cohen, Lara Langer, and Jordan Alexander Stein, eds. *Early African American Print Culture.* Philadelphia: University of Pennsylvania Press, 2012.
Cohen, Michael. *The Social Lives of Poems in Nineteenth-Century America.* Philadelphia: University of Pennsylvania Press, 2015.

Conzen, Kathleen Neils. "Pi-ing the Type: Jane Grey Swisshelm and the Contest of Midwestern Regionality." In *The Identity of the American Midwest: Essay on Regional History*, edited by Andrew R. L. Cayton and Susan E. Gray, 91–110. Bloomington: Indiana University Press, 2001.

Cotlar, Seth. *Tom Paine's America: The Rise and Fall of Transatlantic Radicalism in the Early Republic*. Charlottesville, University of Virginia Press, 2011.

Crane, Jacob. "'Razed to the Knees': The Anti-Heroic Body in James McCune Smith's 'The Heads of Colored People.'" *African American Review* 51, no. 1 (2018): 7–21.

Culberson, William C. *Vigilantism: Political History of Private Power in America*. New York: Greenwood Press, 1990.

Current-Garcia, Eugene. "'Mr. Spirit' and *The Big Bear of Arkansas*: A Note on the Genesis of Southwestern Sporting and Humor Literature." *American Literature* 27, no. 3 (1955): 332–46.

Davidson, Cathy N. *Revolution and the Word: The Rise of the Novel in America*. New York: Oxford University Press, 1986.

Davies, William. *Nervous States: Democracy and the Decline of Reason*. New York: W. W. Norton, 2019.

Deleuze, Gilles, and Félix Guatarri. *Kafka: Toward a Minor Literature*. Translated by Dana Polan. Minneapolis: University of Minnesota Press, 1986.

Denning, Michael. *Mechanic Accents: Dime Novels and Working-Class Culture in America*. London: Verso, 1987.

Dillon, Elizabeth Maddock. *New World Drama: The Performative Commons in the Atlantic World, 1649–1849*. Durham, NC: Duke University Press, 2014.

Doty, Benjamin L. "Satire, Minstrelsy, and Embodiment in *Sheppard Lee*." *Early American Literature* 51, no. 1 (2016): 131–56.

Drexler, Michael J., and Ed White, eds. *Beyond Douglass: New Perspectives on Early African-American Literature*. Lewisburg, PA: Bucknell University Press, 2008.

Duquette, Elizabeth. "The Office of the Dead Letter." *Arizona Quarterly* 69, no. 4 (2013): 25–58.

Edwards, Laura F. *The People and Their Peace: Legal Culture and the Transformation of Inequality in the Post-Revolutionary South*. Chapel Hill: The University of North Carolina Press, 2009.

Emerson, D. Berton. "George Lippard's *The Quaker City*: Disjointed Text, Dismembered Bodies, Regenerated Democracy." *Nineteenth-Century Literature* 70, no. 1 (2015): 102–30.

———. "'This is a strange book': Re-Membering Local Democratic Agency in Bird's *Sheppard Lee*." *ESQ: A Journal of the American Renaissance* 61, no. 2 (2015): 222–61.

Emerson, D. Berton, and Gregory Laski, eds. *Democracies in America: Keywords for the Nineteenth Century and Today*. Oxford: Oxford University Press, 2023.

Ernest, John. *Chaotic Justice: Rethinking African American Literary History*. Chapel Hill: The University of North Carolina Press, 2009.

———. *Liberation Historiography: African American Writers and the Challenge of History*. Chapel Hill: The University of North Carolina Press, 2004.

Faber, Don. *The Toledo War: The First Michigan-Ohio Rivalry*. Ann Arbor: University of Michigan Press, 2008.

Fagan, Benjamin. *The Black Press and the Chosen Nation*. Athens: University of Georgia Press, 2016.
Feller, Daniel. *The Jacksonian Promise: America, 1815–1840*. Baltimore: Johns Hopkins University Press, 1995.
Fenton, Elizabeth. "Indeliberate Democracy: The Politics of Religious Conversion in Royall Tyler's *The Algerine Captive*." *Early American Literature* 51, no. 1 (2016): 71–100.
———. *Religious Liberties: Anti-Catholicism and Liberal Democracy in Nineteenth-Century U.S. Literature and Culture*. New York: Oxford University Press, 2011.
Fetterley, Judith, and Marjorie Pryse. *Writing out of Place: Regionalism, Women, and American Literary Culture*. Urbana-Champaign: University of Illinois Press, 2002.
Fielder, Brigitte. *Relative Races: Genealogies of Interracial Kinship in Nineteenth-Century America*. Durham, NC: Duke University Press, 2020.
Fielder, Brigitte, and Jonathan Senchyne, eds. *Against a Sharp White Background: Infrastructures of African American Print*. Madison: University of Wisconsin Press, 2019.
Fisher, Philip. "Democratic Social Space: Whitman, Melville, and the Promise of American Transparency." *Representations* 24 (1988): 60–101.
Fishkin, Shelly Fisher, and Carla Peterson. "'We hold these truths to be self-evident': The Rhetoric of Frederick Douglass's Journalism." In *Frederick Douglass: New Literary and Historical Essays*, edited by Eric J. Sundquist, 189–204. New York: Cambridge University Press, 1990.
Fitzgerald, Neil K. "Philadelphia Gothic: Murders, Mysteries, Monsters, and Mayhem Inspire American Fiction, 1798–1854." Library Company of Philadelphia. 2008–2009. https://librarycompany.lcpimages.org/gothic/.
Flück, Winfried. "The Historical Novel." In *Cambridge History of the American Novel*, edited by Leonard Cassuto, Clare Virginia Eby, and Benjamin Reiss, 117–34. Cambridge: Cambridge University Press, 2011.
Foreman, P. Gabrielle. *Activist Sentiments: Reading Black Women in the Nineteenth Century*. Urbana-Champaign: University of Illinois Press, 2009.
Formisano, Ronald P. *For the People: American Populist Movements from the Revolution to the 1850s*. Chapel Hill: The University of North Carolina Press, 2008.
Foster, Frances Smith. "A Narrative of the Interesting Origins and (Somewhat) Surprising Development of African American Print Culture." *American Literary History* 17, no. 4 (2005): 714–40.
Frank, Jason. "Democracy and Disgust." *J19: A Journal of Nineteenth-Century Americanists* 5, no. 2 (2017): 396–403.
Freehling, William H. *The Road to Disunion*. Vol. 1, *Secessionists at Bay*. Oxford: Oxford University Press, 1990.
Fritz, Christian G. *American Sovereigns: The People and America's Constitutional Tradition before the Civil War*. Oxford: Cambridge University Press, 2008.
Gardner, Eric. "Early African American Print Culture and then American West." In *Early African American Print Culture*, edited by Lara Langer Cohen and Jordan Alexander Stein, 75–89. Philadelphia: University of Pennsylvania Press, 2012.

———. *Unexpected Places: Relocating Nineteenth-Century African American Literature.* Jackson: University Press of Mississippi, 2009.

Gebhard, Caroline. "Comic Displacement: Caroline M. Kirkland's Satire of Frontier Democracy in *A New Home, Who'll Follow?*" In *Women, America, and Movement: Narratives of Relocation,* edited by Susan L. Roberson, 157–75. Columbia: University of Missouri Press, 1998.

Gilfoyle, Timothy. *City of Eros: New York City, Prostitution, and the Commercialization of Sex, 1790–1920.* New York: W. W. Norton, 1992.

Gilmore, Paul. *Aesthetic Materialism: Electricity and American Romanticism.* Stanford, CA: Stanford University Press, 2009.

Glazener, Nancy. *Literature in the Making: A History of U.S. Literary Culture in the Long Nineteenth Century.* Oxford: Oxford University Press, 2016.

Gniadek, Melissa. "'Outré-mer adventures': Caroline Kirkland's *A New Home, Who'll Follow?* and the Maritime World." *Legacy: A Journal of American Women Writers* 32, no. 2 (2015): 196–213.

———. "Seriality and Settlement: Southworth, Lippard, and *The Panorama of the Monumental Grandeur of the Mississippi Valley.*" *American Literature* 86, no. 1 (2014): 31–59.

Goddu, Theresa. *Gothic America: Narrative, History, and Nation.* New York: Columbia University Press, 1997.

Goeke, Joe. "Yellow Bird and the Bandit: Minority Authorship, Class, and Audience in John Rollin Ridge's *The Life and Adventures of Joaquín Murieta.*" *Western American Literature* 37, no. 4 (2003): 453–78.

Goyal, Yogita, ed. *The Cambridge Companion to Transnational American Literature.* Cambridge: Cambridge University Press, 2017.

Grammar, John M. "Southwestern Humor." In *A Companion to the Literature and Culture of the American South,* edited by Richard Gray and Owen Robinson, 370–87. Malden, MA: Blackwell, 2004.

Gray, Susan E. *The Yankee West: Community Life on the Michigan Frontier.* Chapel Hill: The University of North Carolina Press, 1996.

Greenberg, Amy. *Manifest Manhood and the Antebellum American Empire.* New York: Cambridge University Press, 2005.

Greeson, Jennifer Rae. *Our South: Geographic Fantasy and the Rise of National Literature.* Cambridge, MA: Harvard University Press, 2010.

Greiman, Jennifer. *Democracy's Spectacle: Sovereignty and Public Life in Antebellum American Writing.* New York: Fordham University Press, 2010.

Grimes, William, William L. Andrews, and Regina E. Mason. *Life of William Grimes, the Runaway Slave.* 1855. New York: Oxford University Press, 2008.

Gunn, Robert. "The Humor of the Old Southwest and National Regionality." In *Mapping Region in Early American Writing,* edited by Edward Watts, Keri Holt, and John Funchion, 62–80. Athens: University of Georgia Press, 2015.

Gustafson, Sandra M. *Eloquence Is Power: Performance and Oratory in Early America.* Chapel Hill: The University of North Carolina Press, 2000.

———. *Imagining Deliberative Democracy in the Early American Republic.* Chicago: University of Chicago Press, 2011.

Habermas, Jürgen. *The Structural Transformation of the Public Sphere: An Inquiry into a Category of Bourgeois Society*. Cambridge, MA: MIT Press, 1991.
Handlin, Lillian. *George Bancroft: The Intellectual as Democrat*. New York: Harper and Row, 1984.
Harris, Susan K. "'But is it any good?': Evaluating Nineteenth-Century American Women's Fiction." *American Literature* 63, no. 1 (1991): 43–61.
Hartman, Saidiya V. *Scenes of Subjection: Terror, Slavery, and Self-Making in Nineteenth-Century America*. New York: Oxford University Press, 1997.
Hauck, Richard Boyd. "The Man in the Buckskin Hunting Shirt: Fact and Fiction in the Crockett Story." In *Davy Crockett: The Man, the Legend, the Legacy, 1786–1986*, edited by Michael A. Lofaro, 3–20. Knoxville: University of Tennessee Press, 1985.
Hegreness, Matthew J. "An Organic Law Theory of the Fourteenth Amendment: The Northwest Ordinance as the Source of Rights, Privileges, and Immunities." *Yale Law Journal* 120, no. 7 (2011): 1820–84.
Hofstadter, Richard. *The Idea of a Party System: The Rise of Legitimate Opposition in the United States, 1780–1840*. Berkeley: University of California Press, 1969.
Holland, Catherine A. *The Body Politic: Foundings, Citizenship, and Difference in the American Political Imagination*. London: Routledge, 2001.
Holton, Woody. *Unruly Americans and the Origins of the Constitution*. Oxford: Oxford University Press, 2007.
Honig, Bonnie. *Democracy and the Foreigner*. Princeton, NJ: Princeton University Press, 2001.
Hoole, W. Stanley. *Alias Simon Suggs: The Life and Times of Johnson Jones Hooper*. Westport, CT: Greenwood Press, 1970.
Hopkins, Robert. "Simon Suggs: A Burlesque Campaign Biography." *American Quarterly* 15, no. 3 (1963): 459–63.
Hotz, Jeffrey. "Imagining a New West, a Midwest, in Caroline Kirkland's *A New Home, Who'll Follow?*" *Midwestern Miscellany* 38 (2010): 8–23.
Howe, Daniel Walker. *What Hath God Wrought: The Transformation of America, 1815–1848*. Oxford: Oxford University Press, 2007.
Hsu, Hsuan L. *Geography and the Production of Space in Nineteenth-Century American Literature*. Cambridge: Cambridge University Press, 2010.
Hudson, Linda S. *Mistress of Manifest Destiny: A Biography of Jane McManus Storm Cazneau, 1807–1878*. Austin: University of Texas Press, 2001.
Hunter, Christopher A. "From Print to Print: The First Complete Edition of Benjamin Franklin's *Autobiography*." *Papers of the Bibliographical Society of America* 101, no. 4 (2007): 481–505.
Huntley-Smith, Jen A. "Print Cultures in the American West." In *Perspectives on American Book History: Artifacts and Commentary*, edited by Scott Casper, Joanne D. Chaison, and Jeffrey D. Groves, 255–84. Amherst: University of Massachusetts Press, 2002.
Hyde, Anne. *Empires, Nations, and Families*. Lincoln: University of Nebraska Press, 2011.
Hyde, Carrie. "The Climates of Liberty: Natural Rights in the *Creole* Case and 'The Heroic Slave.'" *American Literature* 85, no. 3 (2013): 475–504.
Inge, M. Thomas, and Edward J. Piacentino, eds. *The Humor of the Old South*. Lexington: University Press of Kentucky, 2001.

Jackson, Holly. *American Radicals: How Nineteenth-Century Protest Shaped the Nation.* New York: Crown, 2019.

Jackson, Joseph. "George Lippard: Misunderstood Man of Letters." *Pennsylvania Magazine of History and Bibliography* 59 (1935): 376–91.

Jackson, Joseph Henry. Introduction to *The Life and Adventures of Joaquín Murieta, the Celebrated California Bandit*, by John Rollin Ridge. Norman: University of Oklahoma Press, 1955.

Jaros, Peter. "The Faculties of Law: Robert Montgomery Bird's *Sheppard Lee* as Legal Fiction." *J19: The Journal of Nineteenth-Century Americanists* 3, no. 2 (2015): 307–35.

Johannsen, Albert. *The House of Beadle and Adams and Its Dime and Nickel Novels: The Story of a Vanished Literature.* Vol. 2. Norman: University of Oklahoma Press, 1950.

Johnson, Susan Lee. *Roaring Camp: The Social World of the California Gold Rush.* New York: W. W. Norton, 2000.

Johnson, Walter. "On Agency." *Journal of Social History* 37, no. 1 (2003): 113–24.

Jones, Martha S. *Birthright Citizens: A History of Race and Rights in Antebellum America.* Cambridge: Cambridge University Press, 2018.

Justus, James. *Fetching the Old Southwest: Humorous Writing from Longstreet to Twain.* Columbia: University of Missouri Press, 2004.

Kammen, Michael. *A Season of Youth: The American Revolution and the Historical Imagination.* New York: Alfred A. Knopf, 1978.

Kaplan, Amy. "Manifest Domesticity." *American Literature* 70, no. 3 (1998): 581–606.

Kennedy, Dustin. "Revising the Public Sphere: George Lippard, Class, and U.S. Nationalism." *ESQ: A Journal of the American Renaissance* 59, no. 4 (2013): 585–617.

Kennedy, J. Gerald. *Strange Nation: Literary Nationalism and Cultural Conflict in the Age of Poe.* Oxford: Oxford University Press, 2016.

Kibler, James. Introduction to *Georgia Scenes*, by Augustus Baldwin Longstreet, vii–xxii. Nashville, TN: J. S. Sanders, 1992.

Kloppenberg, James T. *Toward Democracy: The Struggle for Self-Rule in European and American Thought.* New York: Oxford University Press, 2016.

Kolb, Harold H. "The Outcast of Literary Flat: Bret Harte as Humorist." *American Literary Realism* 23, no. 2 (1991): 52–63.

Kolodny, Annette. *The Land before Her: Fantasy and Experience of the American Frontiers, 1630–1860.* Chapel Hill: The University of North Carolina Press, 1984.

Kouwenhoven, John A. *Made in America: The Arts in Modern Civilization.* New York: Doubleday, 1948.

Kowalewski, Michael. Introduction to *Gold Rush: A Literary Exploration*, xi–xxix. Berkeley, CA: Heyday Books, 1997.

Kreger, Erica M. "A Bibliography of Works by and about Caroline Kirkland." *Tulsa Studies in Women's Literature* 18, no. 2 (1999): 299–350.

Kreyling, Michael. *Inventing Southern Literature.* Jackson: University Press of Mississippi, 1998.

Laski, Gregory M. *Untimely Democracy: The Politics of Progress after Slavery.* New York: Oxford University Press, 2018.

Laurie, Bruce. *Working People of Philadelphia, 1800–1850.* Philadelphia: Temple University Press, 1980.

Leavell, Lori. "'NOT INTENDED EXCLUSIVELY FOR THE SLAVE STATES': Antebellum Recirculation of David Walker's *Appeal*." *Callaloo* 38, no. 3 (2015): 679–95.
Lemay, J. A. Leo. "The Text, Traditions, and Themes of 'The Big Bear of Arkansas.'" *American Literature* 17, no. 3 (1975): 321–42.
LeMenager, Stephanie. *Manifest and Other Destinies: Territorial Fictions of the United States*. Lincoln: University of Nebraska Press, 2006.
Lemke, Sieglinde. "Theories of American Culture in the Name of the Vernacular." *Yearbook of Research in English and American Literature* 19 (2003): 139–59.
Leverenz, David. *Manhood and the American Renaissance*. Ithaca, NY: Cornell University Press, 1989.
Levine, Robert. *Dislocating Race and Nation: Episodes in Nineteenth-Century American Literary Nationalism*. Chapel Hill: The University of North Carolina Press, 2008.
———. "Uncle Tom's Cabin in Frederick Douglass' Paper: An Analysis of Reception." *American Literature* 64, no. 1 (1992): 71–93.
Levitsky, Steven, and Daniel Ziblatt. *How Democracies Die*. New York: Broadway Books, 2019.
Levy, JoAnn. *They Saw the Elephant: Women in the California Gold Rush*. Norman: University of Oklahoma Press, 1990.
Lockhart, Sandra. "Legacy Profile: Louise Amelia Knapp Smith Clappe (Dame Shirley) (1819–1906)." *Legacy: A Journal of American Women Writers* 8, no. 2 (1992): 141–48.
Loney, Glenn. Introduction to *California Gold Rush Plays*, 7–19. New York: Performing Arts Journal Publications, 1983.
Looby, Christopher. Introduction to *Sheppard Lee: Written by Himself*, by Robert Montgomery Bird, xv–xliii. New York: New York Review of Books, 2008.
———. "Lippard in Part(s): Seriality and Secrecy in *The Quaker City*." *Nineteenth-Century Literature* 70, no. 1 (2015): 1–35.
———. "Southworth and Seriality." *Nineteenth-Century Literature* 59, no. 2 (2004): 179–211.
———. *Voicing America: Language, Literary Form, and the Origins of the United States*. Chicago: University of Chicago Press, 1996.
Looby, Christopher, and Cindy Weinstein. *American Literature's Aesthetic Dimensions*. New York: Columbia University Press, 2012.
Loughran, Trish. *The Republic in Print: Print Culture in the Age of US Nation Building, 1770–1870*. New York: Columbia University Press, 2007.
Lummis, C. Douglas. *Radical Democracy*. Ithaca, NY: Cornell University Press, 1996.
Lynn, Kenneth M. *Mark Twain and Southwest Humor*. Boston: Little, Brown, 1959.
Madley, Benjamin. *An American Genocide: The United States and the California Indian Catastrophe, 1846–1873*. New Haven, CT: Yale University Press, 2016.
Mansouri, Leila. "*Sheppard Lee* and Properties of the Novel in America." *Novel: A Forum on Fiction* 49, no. 1 (2016): 49–64.
Margolis, Stacey. *Fictions of Mass Democracy in Nineteenth-Century America*. New York: Cambridge University Press, 2015.
Mary Russell Mitford Society. *Digital Mitford: The Mary Russell Mitford Digital Archive*. Last modified 23 May 2023. https://digitalmitford.org/.
Matthiessen, F. O. *American Renaissance: Art and Expression in the Age of Emerson and Whitman*. 1941. New ed. London: Oxford University Press, 1968.

McGill, Meredith. *American Literature and the Culture of Reprinting, 1834–1853.* Philadelphia: University of Pennsylvania Press, 2003.

Merish, Lori. "'The Hand of Refined Taste' in the Frontier Landscape: Caroline Kirkland's *A New Home, Who'll Follow?* and the Feminization of American Consumerism." *American Quarterly* 45, no. 4 (1993): 485–523.

———. "Print, Cultural Memory, and John Rollin Ridge's *The Life and Adventures of Joaquín Murieta, the Celebrated California Bandit.*" *Arizona Quarterly* 59, no. 4 (2003): 31–70.

Meriwether, James. "Augustus Baldwin Longstreet: Realist and Artist." *Mississippi Quarterly* 35, no. 4 (1982): 351–64.

Messer, Peter C. "From a Revolutionary History to a History of Revolution: David Ramsay and the American Revolution." *Journal of the Early Republic* 22, no. 2 (2002): 205–33.

Mihm, Stephen. *A Nation of Counterfeiters: Capitalists, Con Men, and the Making of the United States.* Cambridge, MA: Harvard University Press, 2007.

Miller, Angela. *The Empire of the Eye: Landscape Representation and American Cultural Nationalism.* Ithaca, NY: Cornell University Press, 1993.

Miller, James. *Can Democracy Work? A Short History of a Radical Idea, from Ancient Athens to Our World.* New York: Farrar, Strauss and Giroux, 2018.

Mires, Charlene. "Independence Hall." *The Encyclopedia of Greater Philadelphia.* Mid-Atlantic Regional Center for the Humanities, Rutgers University–Camden. Last modified 2012. http://philadelphiaencyclopedia.org/archive/independence-hall/.

Moi, Toril. *Revolution of the Ordinary: Literary Studies after Wittgenstein, Austin, and Cavell.* Chicago: University of Chicago Press, 2017.

Morgan, Edmund. *Inventing the People: The Rise of Popular Sovereignty in England and America.* New York: W. W. Norton, 1985.

Morrison, Richard B. *The Forging of the Union, 1781–1789.* New York: Harper and Row, 1987.

Morrow, Patrick. "Bret Harte, Popular Fiction, and the Local Color Movement." *Western American Literature* 8, no. 3 (1973): 123–31.

Mounck, Yascha. *The People vs. Democracy: Why Our Freedom Is in Danger and How to Save It.* Cambridge, MA: Harvard University Press, 2018.

Murison, Justine. "Hypochondria and Racial Interiority in Robert Montgomery Bird's *Sheppard Lee.*" *Arizona Quarterly* 64, no. 1 (2008): 1–25.

Nash, Gary B. *The Unknown American Revolution: The Unruly Birth of Democracy and the Struggle to Create America.* New York: Penguin, 2006.

Navakas, Michele Currie. *Liquid Landscape: Geography and Settlement at the Edge of Early America.* Philadelphia: University of Pennsylvania Press, 2017.

Neary, Janet. *Fugitive Testimony: On the Visual Logic of Slave Narratives.* New York: Fordham University Press, 2017.

———. "Mining the African American Literary Tradition: James Williams's *Fugitive Slave in the Gold Rush* and the Contours of a 'Black Pacific.'" *ESQ: A Journal of the American Renaissance* 59, no. 2 (2013): 329–74.

Nelson, Dana D. *Commons Democracy: Reading the Politics of Participation in the Early United States.* New York: Fordham University Press, 2015.

———. "ConsterNation." In *Futures of American Studies*, edited by Donald E. Pease and Robyn Wiegman, 559–79. Durham, NC: Duke University Press, 1998.

———. *National Manhood: Capitalist Citizenship and the Imagined Fraternity of White Men*. Durham, NC: Duke University Press, 1998.
Newlin, Keith. "*Georgia Scenes*: The Satiric Artistry of Augustus Baldwin Longstreet." *Mississippi Quarterly* 41, no. 1 (1987): 21–37.
Ngai, Sianne. *Our Aesthetic Categories: Zany, Cute, Interesting*. Cambridge, MA: Harvard University Press, 2012.
———. *Theory of the Gimmick: Aesthetic Judgment and Capitalist Form*. Cambridge, MA: Harvard University Press, 2020.
———. *Ugly Feelings*. Cambridge, MA: Harvard University Press, 2005.
Nickerson, Catherine Ross. *The Web of Iniquity: Early Detective Fiction by American Women*. Durham, NC: Duke University Press, 1998.
Nissen, Axel. "The Queer Short Story." In *The Art of Brevity: Excursions in Short Fiction Theory and Analysis*, edited by Per Winther, Jakob Lothe, and Hans H. Skei, 181–90. Columbia: University of South Carolina Press, 2004.
Novak, William J. *The People's Welfare: Law and Regulation in Nineteenth-Century America*. Chapel Hill: The University of North Carolina Press, 1996.
Ober, Josiah. "Democracy's Dignity." *American Political Science Review* 106, no. 4 (2012): 827–46.
———. *Demopolis: Democracy before Liberalism in Theory and Practice*. Cambridge: Cambridge University Press, 2017.
O'Brien, Karen. "David Ramsay and the Delayed Americanization of American History." *Early American Literature* 29, no. 1 (1994): 1–18.
O'Brien, Shelia Ruzycki. "Writing with a Forked Pen: Racial Dynamics and Johnson Jones Hooper's Twin Tale of Swindling Indians." *American Studies* 35, no. 2 (1994): 95–113.
Okker, Patricia. *Social Stories: The Magazine Novel in Nineteenth-Century America*. Charlottesville: University of Virginia Press, 2003.
Onuf, Peter S. *Statehood and Union: A History of the Northwest Ordinance*. Bloomington: Indiana University Press, 1987.
Otter, Samuel. "Philadelphia Experiments." *American Literary History* 16, no. 1 (2004): 103–16.
———. *Philadelphia Stories: America's Literature of Race and Freedom*. Oxford: Oxford University Press, 2010.
Parham, Katharine. "Metta Victoria Fuller Victor." In *Nineteenth-Century American Women Writers*, edited by Denise Knight, 433–37. Westport, CT: Greenwood Press, 1997.
Parins, James W. *John Rollin Ridge: His Life and Works*. Lincoln: University of Nebraska Press, 1991.
Pattee, Fred Lewis. *The First Century of American Literature: 1770–1870*. New York: Appleton-Century, 1935.
Penry, Tara. "'Tennessee's Partner' as Sentimental Western Metanarrative." *American Literary Realism* 36, no. 2 (2004): 148–65.
Perman, Michael. *Pursuit of Unity: A Political History of the American South*. Chapel Hill: The University of North Carolina Press, 2010.
Peterson, Carla L. *Black Gotham: A Family History of African Americans in Nineteenth-Century New York City*. New Haven, CT: Yale University Press, 2011.
Pfeifer, Michael J. *The Roots of Rough Justice: Origins of American Lynching*. Urbana-Champaign: University of Illinois Press, 2011.

Powell, Douglas Reichert. *Critical Regionalism: Connecting Politics and Culture in the American Landscape*. Chapel Hill: The University of North Carolina Press, 2007.
Powell, Timothy. *Ruthless Democracy: A Multicultural Interpretation of the American Renaissance*. Princeton, NJ: Princeton University Press, 2000.
Pratt, Lloyd. *Archives of American Time: Literature and Modernity in the Nineteenth Century*. Philadelphia: University of Pennsylvania Press, 2009.
———. *The Stranger Book: The Human of African American Literature*. Philadelphia: University of Pennsylvania Press, 2016.
Pryse, Marjorie. "Stowe and Regionalism." In *The Cambridge Companion to Harriet Beecher Stowe*, edited by Cindy Weinstein, 131–53. Cambridge: Cambridge University Press, 2004.
Quigley, Paul. *Shifting Grounds: Nationalism and the American South, 1848–1865*. Oxford: Oxford University Press, 2012.
Rachels, David, ed. *Augustus Baldwin Longstreet's Georgia Scenes Completed*. Athens: University of Georgia Press, 1998.
Rael, Patrick. *Black Identity and Black Protest in the Antebellum North*. Chapel Hill: The University of North Carolina Press, 2001.
Rancière, Jacques. *Dissensus: On Politics and Aesthetics*. Translated by Steven Corcoran. London: Continuum, 2010.
———. *Hatred of Democracy*. Translated by Steve Corcoran. 2005. London: Verso, 2014.
Rebhorn, Matthew. "Ontological Drift: Medical Discourse and Racial Embodiment in Robert Montgomery Bird's *Sheppard Lee*." *ESQ: A Journal of the American Renaissance* 61, no. 2 (2015): 262–96.
Remer, Rosalind. *Printers and Men of Capital: Philadelphia Book Publishers in the New Republic*. Philadelphia: University of Pennsylvania Press, 1996.
Reynolds, David S. *Beneath the American Renaissance: The Subversive Imagination in the Age of Emerson and Melville*. New York: Knopf, 1988.
———. "Deformance, Performativity, Posthumanism: The Subversive Style and Radical Politics in George Lippard's *The Quaker City*." *Nineteenth-Century Literature* 70, no. 1 (2015): 236–64.
———. Introduction to *The Quaker City; or, The Monks of Monk Hall*, by George Lippard, vii–xliv. Edited by David S. Reynolds. Amherst: University of Massachusetts Press, 1995.
Rickels, Milton. "The Grotesque Body of Southwestern Humor." In *Critical Essays on American Humor*, edited by William Bedford Clark and W. Craig Turner, 155–66. Boston: Hall, 1984.
Rifkin, Mark. *Manifesting America: The Imperial Construction of U.S. National Space*. Oxford: Oxford University Press, 2009.
Rigal, Laura. *The American Manufactory: Art, Labor, and the World of Things in the Early Republic*. Princeton, NJ: Princeton University Press, 1998.
Roberts, Brian. *American Alchemy: The California Gold Rush and Middle-Class Culture*. Chapel Hill: The University of North Carolina Press, 2000.
Rohrbough, Malcolm J. *The Trans-Appalachian Frontier: People, Societies, and Institutions, 1775–1850*. 3rd ed. Bloomington: Indiana University Press, 2008.

Romine, Scott. *The Narrative Forms of Southern Community*. Baton Rouge: Lousiana State University Press, 1999.

Rosenblum, Nancy L. *Good Neighbors: The Politics of Everyday Life in America*. Princeton, NJ: Princeton University Press, 2016.

Rosenfeld, Sophia. *Democracy and Truth: A Short History*. Philadelphia: University of Pennsylvania Press, 2018.

Rourke, Constance. *American Humor: A Study of the National Character*. New York: Harcourt Brace Jovanovich, 1931.

———. *Davy Crockett*. New York: Harcourt Brace Jovanovich, 1931.

Rowe, John Carlos. "Highway Robbery: 'Indian Removal,' the Mexican-American War, and American Identity in *The Life and Adventures of Joaquín Murieta*." *Novel: A Forum on Fiction* 31, no. 2 (1998): 149–73.

Royce, Josiah. *California: A Study of the American Character*. 1886. Berkeley, CA: Heyday Books, 2002.

Runciman, David. *How Democracy Ends*. New York: Basic Books, 2018.

Rusert, Britt. *Fugitive Science: Empiricism and Freedom in Early African American Print Culture*. New York: New York University Press, 2017.

Ryan, Mary P. *Civic Wars: Democracy and Public Life in the American City during the Nineteenth Century*. Berkeley: University of California Press, 1999.

Sale, Maggie Montesinos. *The Slumbering Volcano: American Slave Ship Revolts and Rebellious Masculinity*. Durham, NC: Duke University Press, 1997.

Saler, Bethel. *The Settler's Empire: Colonialism and State Formation in the Old Northwest*. Philadelphia: University of Pennsylvania Press, 2015.

Santamarina, Xiomara. "'Are We There Yet?': Archives, History, and Specificity in African American Literary Studies." *American Literary History* 20, nos. 1–2 (2008): 304–16.

Scharnhorst, Gary. "Bret Harte's Naturalism." *Studies in American Naturalism* 1, nos. 1–2 (2006): 144–51.

Schuller, Kyla. *Biopolitics of Feeling: Race, Sex, and Science in the Nineteenth Century*. Durham, NC: Duke University Press, 2018.

Schwartz, James Z. *Conflict on the Michigan Frontier: Yankee and Borderland Cultures, 1815–1840*. DeKalb: Northern Illinois University Press, 2009.

Seelye, John. "A Well-Wrought Crockett: or, How the Fake-lorists Passed through the Credibility Gap and Discovered Kentucky." In *Davy Crockett: The Man, The Legend, the Legacy, 1786–1986*, edited by Michael A. Lofaro, 21–45. Knoxville: University of Tennessee Press, 1985.

Sellers, Charles. *The Market Economy: Jacksonian America, 1815–1846*. Oxford: Oxford University Press, 1994.

Selsam, Paul. *The Pennsylvania Constitution of 1776: A Study in Revolutionary Democracy*. New York: Octagon, 1971.

Senkewicz, Robert M. *Vigilantes in Gold Rush San Francisco*. Palo Alto, CA: Stanford University Press, 1985.

Sewell, Richard H. *Ballots for Freedom: Anti-Slavery Politics in the United States, 1837–1860*. New York: Oxford University Press, 1976.

Shapiro, Joe. *The Illiberal Imagination: Class and the Rise of the U.S. Novel*. Charlottesville: University of Virginia Press, 2017.

Shortridge, James R. *The Middle West: Its Meaning in American Culture*. Lawrence: University Press of Kansas, 1989.

Shumway, David. *Creating American Civilization: A Genealogy of American Literature as a Discipline*. Minneapolis: University of Minnesota Press, 1994.

Silbey, Joel H. *The Partisan Imperative: The Dynamics of American Politics before the Civil War*. New York: Oxford University Press, 1985.

———. *Party over Section: The Rough and Ready Presidential Election of 1848*. Lawrence: University Press of Kansas, 2009.

Silverman, Gillian. *Bodies and Books: The Fantasy of Communion in Nineteenth-Century Literature*. Philadelphia: University of Pennsylvania Press, 2012.

Simeone, James. *Democracy and Slavery in Frontier Illinois*. Dekalb: University of Illinois Press, 2000.

Slauter, Eric. *The State as Work of Art: The Cultural Origins of the Constitution*. Chicago: University of Chicago Press, 2010.

Slotkin, Richard. *Regeneration through Violence: The Mythology of the American Frontier, 1600–1860*. Middletown, CT: Wesleyan University Press, 1973.

Smith-Baranzini, Marlene. Introduction to *The Shirley Letters from the California Mines, 1851–1852*, xviii–xix. Edited by Marlene Smith-Baranzini. Berkeley, CA: Heyday Books, 1998.

Smith-Rosenberg, Caroll. *Disorderly Conduct: Visions of Gender in Victorian America*. New York: Knopf, 1985.

Smith, Valerie. *Self-Discovery and Authority in Afro-American Narrative*. Cambridge, MA: Harvard University Press, 1987.

Soderberg, Laura. "One More Time with Feeling: Repetition, Reparation, and the Sentimental Subject in William Wells Brown's Rewritings of *Clotel*." *American Literature* 88, no. 2 (2016): 241–67.

Spires, Derrick R. *The Practice of Citizenship: Black Politics and Print Culture in the Early United States*. Philadelphia: University of Pennsylvania Press, 2019.

Starr, Kevin. *California*. New York: Modern Library, 2005.

Stauffer, John. "Frederick Douglass and the Aesthetics of Freedom." *Raritan* 25, no. 1 (2005), 114–36.

———, ed. *The Works of James McCune Smith: Black Intellectual and Abolitionist*. Oxford: Oxford University Press, 2006.

Stein, Jordan Alexander. "The Whig Interpretation of Media: *Sheppard Lee* and Jacksonian Paperwork." *History of the Present* 3, no.1 (2013): 29–56.

Stepto, Robert. "Storytelling in Early Afro-American Fiction: Frederick Douglass' 'The Heroic Slave.'" *Georgia Review* 36, no. 2 (1982): 355–68.

Stevens, J. David. "'She war a woman': Family Roles, Gender, and Sexuality in Bret Harte's Western Fiction." *American Literature* 69, no. 3 (1997): 571–93.

Stewart, Kathleen. *A Space on the Side of the Road: Cultural Poetics in an "Other" America*. Princeton, NJ: Princeton University Press, 1996.

Stowe, Harriet Beecher. *The May-Flower, and Miscellaneous Stories*. Boston: Phillips, Sampson, 1855.

Streeby, Shelley. *American Sensations: Class, Empire, and the Production of Popular Culture.* Berkeley: University of California Press, 2002.

———. "Dime Novels and the Rise of Mass-Market Genres." In *Cambridge History of the American Novel*, edited by Leonard Cassuto, Clare Virginia Eby, and Benjamin Reiss, 586–99. Cambridge: Cambridge University Press, 2011.

———. "Haunted Houses: George Lippard, Nathaniel Hawthorne, and Middle-Class America." *Criticism* 38, no. 3 (1996): 443–72.

Sutton, Walter. *The Western Book Trade: Cincinnati as a Nineteenth-Century Publishing and Book-Trade Center.* Columbus: Ohio State University Press, 1961.

Sweet, Timothy. "American Land, American Landscape, American Novels." In *The Cambridge History of the American Novel*, edited by Leonard Cassuto, Clare Virginia Eby, and Benjamin Reiss, 88–102. Cambridge: Cambridge University Press, 2011.

Talisse, Robert B. *Overdoing Democracy: Why We Must Put Democracy in Its Place.* New York: Oxford University Press, 2019.

Taniguchi, Nancy J. *Dirty Deeds: Land, Violence, and the 1856 San Francisco Vigilance Committee.* Norman: University of Oklahoma Press, 2016.

Taylor, Alan. *American Revolutions: A Continental History: 1750–1804.* New York: W. W. Norton, 2015.

Tompkins, Jane. *Sensational Designs: The Cultural Work of American Fiction, 1790–1860.* Oxford: Oxford University Press, 1986.

Tompkins, Kyla Wazana. *Racial Indigestion: Eating Bodies in the 19th Century.* New York: New York University Press, 2012.

Trilling, Lionel. *The Liberal Imagination: Essays on Literature and Society.* New York: Scribners, 1940.

Turner, Frederick Jackson. "The Significance of the Mississippi Valley in American History." *Proceedings of the Mississippi Valley Historical Association* 3 (1909–1910): 159–84.

Unger, Mary. "'Dens of Iniquity and Holes of Wickedness': George Lippard and the Queer City." *Journal of American Studies* 43, no. 2 (2009): 319–39.

Urgo, Joseph. "Capitalism, Nationalism, and the American Short Story." *Studies in Short Fiction* 35, no. 4 (1998): 339–53.

US Census Bureau. "Through the Decades." US Census Bureau. Accessed 27 July 2019. https://www.census.gov/history/www/through_the_decades/.

Voeller, Carey R. "Disability, Masculinity, and Sentimentality in Lippard's *The Quaker City*." *Studies in American Fiction* 32, no. 1 (2016): 1–25.

Volk, Kyle G. *Moral Minorities and the Making of American Democracy.* Oxford: Oxford University Press, 2014.

Waldrep, Christopher, ed. *Lynching in America: A History in Documents.* New York: New York University Press, 2006.

Waldstreicher, David. *In the Midst of Perpetual Fetes: The Making of American Nationalism, 1776–1820.* Chapel Hill: The University of North Carolina Press, 1997.

Walker, Cynthia. *Indian Nation: Native American Literature and Nineteenth-Century Nationalisms.* Durham, NC: Duke University Press, 1997.

Wallerstein, Immanuel. *World Systems Analysis: An Introduction.* Durham, NC: Duke University Press, 2004.

Walter, Krista. "Trappings of Nationalism in Frederick Douglass's 'The Heroic Slave.'" *African American Review* 34, no. 2 (2000): 233–47.
Warner, Michael. *The Letters of the Republic: Publication and the Public Sphere in Eighteenth-Century America.* Cambridge, MA: Harvard University Press, 1990.
———. *Publics and Counterpublics.* New York: Zone Books, 2005.
Warwick Research Collective. *Combined and Uneven Development: Towards a New Theory of World-Literature.* Liverpool: Liverpool University Press, 2015.
Watts, Edward. *An American Colony: Regionalism and the Roots of Midwestern Culture.* Athens: Ohio University Press, 2001.
Wecter, Dixon. *Literary Lodestone: One Hundred Years of California Writing.* Palo Alto, CA: Stanford University Press, 1950.
Weinstein, Cindy. *Family, Kinship, and Sympathy in Nineteenth-Century American Literature.* New York: Cambridge University Press, 2004.
White, Ed. *The Backcountry and the City: Conflict and Colonization in Early America.* Minneapolis: University of Minnesota Press, 2005.
———. "Divided We Stand: Emergent Conservatism in Royall Tyler's *The Algerine Captive.*" *Studies in American Fiction* 37, no. 1 (2010): 5–27.
Wilder, Craig Steven. *A Covenant with Color: Race and Social Power in Brooklyn, 1636–1990.* New York: Columbia University Press, 2000.
Wilentz, Sean. *Chants Democratic: New York City and the Rise of the American Working Class, 1788–1850.* New York: Oxford University Press, 1984.
———. *The Rise of American Democracy: From Jefferson to Lincoln.* New York: W. W. Norton, 2005.
Wilson, Ivy G. "The Brief Wondrous Life of the *Anglo-African Magazine*; or, Antebellum African American Editorial Practices and Its Afterlives." In *Publishing Blackness: Textual Constructions of Race since 1850*, edited by George Hutchinson and John K. Young, 18–38. Ann Arbor: University of Michigan Press, 2013.
———. "On Native Ground: Transnationalism, Frederick Douglass, and 'The Heroic Slave.'" *PMLA* 121, no. 2 (2005): 453–68.
———. *Specters of Democracy: Blackness and the Aesthetics of Politics in the Antebellum US.* Oxford: Oxford University Press, 2011.
Windell, Maria A. "Sanctity in Our Suffering World with Tears: Transamerican Sentimentalism in *Joaquín Murieta.*" *Nineteenth-Century Literature* 63, no. 2 (2008): 170–96.
Winship, Michael. "In Search of Monk Hall: A Publishing History of George Lippard's *The Quaker City.*" *Nineteenth-Century Literature* 70, no. 1 (2015): 132–49.
Winter, Molly Crumpton. "Culture-Tectonics: California Statehood and John Rollin Ridge's *Joaquín Murieta.*" *Western American Literature* 43, no. 3 (2008): 259–76.
Wolin, Sheldon S. *Fugitive Democracy, and Other Essays.* Edited by Nicholas Xenos. Princeton, NJ: Princeton University Press, 2016.
Wood, Gordon. *The Radicalism of the American Revolution.* New York: Vintage, 1993.
Wright, Nazera Sadiq. *Black Girlhood in the Nineteenth Century.* Urbana: University of Illinois Press, 2016.
Wuthnow, Robert. *American Misfits and the Making of Middle-Class Respectability.* Princeton, NJ: Princeton University Press, 2017.

Yarborough, Richard A. "Race, Violence, and Manhood: The Masculine Ideal in Frederick Douglass's 'The Heroic Slave.'" In *Frederick Douglass: New Literary and Historical Essays*, edited by Eric J. Sundquist, 166–88. Cambridge: Cambridge University Press, 1990.

Yates, Norris W. *William T. Porter and the "Spirit of the Times": A Study of the Big Bear School of Humor*. Baton Rouge: Louisiana State University Press, 1957.

Young, Alfred F. *The Shoemaker and the Tea Party: Memory and the American Revolution*. Boston: Beacon, 1999.

Zagarell, Sandra A. Introduction to *A New Home, Who'll Follow?*, by Caroline Mathilda Kirkland, xi–xlvi. Edited by Sandra A. Zagarell. New Brunswick, NJ: Rutgers University Press, 1996.

Ziff, Larzer. *Literary Democracy: The Declaration of Independence in America*. New York: Viking, 1981.

Index

abolition, 8, 28, 42–43, 47, 147, 154, 157, 163, 203n19
Adams, John, 6
Adams, Samuel, 25, 37
Adorno, Theodor, 179n27
aesthetic autonomy, 3, 18–19, 178n26
African American(s), 8, 11, 28, 32, 75, 147–72 passim, 199n20
African Free School (Brooklyn), 157
Alemán, Jesse, 133, 200n41
Allen, Danielle, 29
Altschuler, Glenn, 180n52, 186n51, 186n53
Anacreon, 159
Anderson, Benedict, 23, 35, 77, 183n17, 188n80, 191n23
Andrews, William, 201n1, 203n25
Anglo-African Magazine, 164, 165, 205n54
Appiah, Kwame Anthony, 24
Appleby, Joyce, 27, 186n50
Arac, Jonathan, 179n29
Arendt, Hannah, 21; *Lectures on Kant's Political Philosophy*, 21
Articles of Confederation, 90, 96, 194n10
Atlantic, The, 123
Attucks, Crispus, 167
autonomy, 25, 48, 86, 90, 96, 106, 158, 163, 166

Bakhtin, Mikhail, 79; *Rabelais and His World*, 79
Bancroft, George, 8, 36–37, 40, 47, 51, 106, 143, 152, 184n22; *History of the United States*, 36
Bancroft, Hubert Howe, 121, 134, 143, 200n42, 201n59
Barnes, Elizabeth, 188n76
Baym, Nina, 27, 181n57
Beadle Dime Novels, 10, 92, 109–11
Beecher, Catherine, 198n10

Beecher, Harriet. *See* Stowe, Harriet Beecher
Bercovitch, Sacvan, 2, 4, 106
Berlant, Lauren, 23
Bhabha, Homi, 77
Bird, Robert Montgomery, 4, 16, 30–33, 38, 174, 184–185n32, 185n40, 186n45, 186n56; *Calavar*, 40; *The Hawks of Hawk-Hollow*, 40; *The Infidel*, 40; *Sheppard Lee*, 4, 9, 30–33, 38–49, 60, 184nn30–32
Blair, Walter, 190n17
Blight, David, 150
Blumin, Stuart, 180n52, 186n51, 186n53
Boone, Daniel, 183n18
Bromell, Nick, 193n59
Brooks, B. S., 138
Brotherhood of the Union, 49
Brown, Bill, 110
Brown, Charles Brockden, 67, 96, 183n10, 195n26
Brown, Richard, 27
Brown, Wendy, 177n7, 181n59
Brown, William Wells, 163
Bumppo, Natty, 27

Cahill, Edward, 21
California, 8, 10, 28, 117, 118–46 passim, 148, 173, 174, 198n13, 199n17
California Police Gazette, 128, 134, 200n34. *See also* Ridge, John Rollin
canon, 2, 7, 19, 33, 179n38
Carey and Hart, 192n39
Carey and Lea, 184n32
carnivalesque, 65, 79–80, 192n45
Casanova, Pascale, 11–13, 15, 62, 177nn8–10
Cass, Lewis, 97, 159
Castiglia, Christopher, 7, 26, 70, 179n33, 181n55, 181n62, 186n49, 188n83, 191n33

Castronovo, Russ, 59, 153, 179n33, 180n51, 181n62, 188n84, 205n55
Cayton, Andrew, 92
Cazneau, Jane McManus Storm, 198n6
Channing, William Ellery, 13–15, 17, 18, 22, 178n14; "Remarks on National Literature," 13
Chemerinsky, Erwin, 182n66
Childers, Christopher, 194n9
Cincinnati, 10, 91, 93, 96, 194n12
citizenship: African American quests for, 148–49; critical, 166, 168, 202n6; democratic, 89; economic, 158; nascent, 37; necro, 59, 188n84, 205n55
Civil War, 5, 8, 83, 111, 174
Clappe, Louise, 4, 11, 121–122, 136–46, 174, 200n46; *The Shirley Letters*, 4, 11, 121–22, 132, 136–46, 159, 200n47
Clark, Thomas D., 68, 189n4
Clavers, Mary, 6, 88–91, 99–108, 140, 141, 145, 197n55. *See also* Kirkland, Caroline
Clay, Henry, 53
Cleveland, Grover, 193n3
Clytus, Radiclani, 165, 204n29
Cohen, Lara Langer, 191n22, 202n5
Colton, Walter, 119; *Three Years in California*, 119
common man, 8, 10, 48, 62, 63, 91, 191n24
Common Sense, 37
Communipaw, 157–64, 167, 205n52. *See also* Smith, James McCune
Compromise of 1850, 148
Congregational Methodist Church (New York), 156
Congress, Continental, 34, 36, 89, 95–97
Congress, US, 47, 92, 97–98, 111, 113, 115–16, 123
Constitution, US, 14–15, 22, 29, 32, 35, 36, 49, 90, 123, 182n66, 191n32, 195n27, 203n19
constitutional nation, 3, 14, 24, 35, 70, 150, 175
Convention of Colored Citizens of California, 199n20
Conzen, Kathleen Neils, 93, 194n17
Cooper, James Fenimore, 7, 12, 35

Cotlar, Seth, 27
Crane, Jacob, 204n36
Creek Indians, 61, 78, 80
critical regionalism, 9, 177n6
Crockett, Davy, 8, 10, 63, 65–68, 124; *Davy Crockett's Almanack*, 65–68, 83, 84, 190n22
Culberson, William C., 143

Dana, Richard Henry, Jr., 118–19, 121, 138; *Two Years Before the Mast*, 118–19
Davidson, Cathy, 26, 40, 43, 181n55, 185n36, 185n38
Declaration of Independence, 31, 34, 35, 42, 49, 96, 145, 168, 185n41, 191n32
Delany, Martin, 147; *Blake*, 147
Deleuze, Gilles, 192n48
deliberation, 25, 142
democracy: alternative, 8, 20, 23–29, 72, 105, 125, 136, 139, 148, 154, 172, 175; basic, 11, 146, 147–72 passim; centralized, 24; deliberative, 3, 6, 8, 39, 44, 49; direct, 44, 49, 61; frontier, 63; fugitive, 177n7; localized, 29, 48, 61, 122; nationalized, 33, 61–62; neighborly, 10, 48, 92, 99–117, 194n13; possibilities of, 2; radical, 9, 24, 33, 52, 125, 146, 159, 182n3; vernacular, 23. *See also* liberal democracy
democratic: affect, 44–49, 186n49; citizens, 4, 6, 14, 89, 148; play, 10, 64–65, 68, 71–87 passim, 193n48; space, 86, 91, 102–3, 109, 111, 112, 120, 143
Democratic Review, The, 120
demos, 4, 7, 73, 145
Denning, Michael, 50, 110
Detroit Evening Spectator and Literary Gazette, 99, 195n34
Devil-Bug, 27, 57–59, 188n82, 205n55. *See also* Lippard, George
Dick and Fitzgerald, 80
dignity, 11, 15, 20, 149–72 passim, 204n38
Dillon, Elizabeth Maddock, 190n12, 194n9
Douglas, Steven, 89
Douglass, Frederick, 8, 11, 17, 149–72 passim, 203n14, 203n17, 203n19, 203n25, 204n29;

Douglass (cont.)
"The Heroic Slave," 11, 150–56, 203n16;
My Bondage and My Freedom, 157, 204n31;
Narrative of the Life of Frederick Douglass, 155
Drexler, Michael, 203n20
Duquette, Elizabeth, 197n63

economic determinism, 48, 141
Edwards, Laura, 17–18, 23, 178nn23–24; *The People and Their Peace*, 17, 178nn23–24
Emancipation Day (New York), 157, 161
Emerson, Ralph Waldo, 2, 35, 138; *Representative Men*, 2
equality, 13, 15, 25, 48, 58, 76–77, 90, 96, 102, 149, 186n57
Era of Good Feelings, 12
Erie Canal, 97
Ernest, John, 153, 166
Ethiop, 27, 161, 164–72. See also Wilson, William J.
Ewer, F. C., 138, 139

Fagan, Benjamin, 205n47
Federalist Papers, 10, 17, 118
Federalist Party, 3, 9, 48
Feller, Daniel, 89
Female Seminary (Detroit), 99
Fenton, Elizabeth, 181n62, 185n38
Fetterley, Judith, 194n12
Fiedler, Leslie, 121, 187n65, 187n68
Fielder, Brigitte, 202n5
Fillmore, Millard, 144, 159
Fisher, Philip, 96, 195n26, 195n30
Flint, Timothy, 68, 191n26; *A Condensed Geography of the Western States*, 68, 191n26
Flück, Winfried, 179n29
Foster, Frances Smith, 148
Frank, Jason, 22, 179n34
Franklin, Benjamin, 41, 185nn39–40; *Autobiography*, 41
Frederick Douglass' Paper, 151, 156–58, 161, 164–65, 204n29
Freehling, William H., 68, 191n27
Fritz, Christian, 194n9

fugitive slave narratives, 147, 153, 198n15, 201n1, 203n25
Futures of American Studies Institute, 190n12

Gardner, Eric, 148, 199n20
Garnet, Henry Highland, 148
Garrisonian abolitionism, 157, 203n19
Gilfoyle, Timothy, 76
Gilmore, Paul, 179n30
Glazener, Nancy, 18, 178n26
Goddu, Theresa, 179n29
gold rush, 8, 11, 28, 117, 120–26 passim, 137–38, 146, 173, 198n5, 199n16
gothic, 20, 28, 33, 179n29
Grabhorn Press, 139
Gray, Susan, 92, 93, 95
Greeley, Horace, 119
Greenberg, Amy, 198n8
Greeson, Jennifer Rae, 67, 87, 189n2, 191n23
Greiman, Jennifer, 181n62
Griffith, Julia, 151; *Autographs for Freedom*, 151
Grimes, William, 147, 149, 201n1; *Life of William Grimes, the Runaway Slave*, 147, 201n1
Griswold, Rufus Wilmot, 14, 15, 16, 17, 18, 22; *The Prose Writers of America*, 14
Guattari, Félix, 192n48
Guice, John D. W., 68, 189n4
Gunn, Robert, 84
Gustafson, Sandra, 44

Haiti, 148
Hale, Sara Josepha, 198n10
Hall, James, 101, 103; *Letters from the West*, 101
Hamilton, Alexander, 17
Hammond, James Henry, 27
Hancock, John, 37
Handlin, Lillian, 184n22
Harper and Brothers, 69, 184n32
Harris, George Washington, 10, 16, 62–64, 74, 80–83, 174; *Sut Lovingood*, 10, 62–64, 80–83, 84, 85–86, 87, 193n48. See also Lovingood, Sut

Harrison, William Henry, 89
Harte, Bret, 8, 11, 121–24, 136, 139, 150, 199n23, 199n25, 201n59; "The Legend of Monte Diablo," 123; "The Luck of Roaring Camp," 124–25; "The Outcasts of Poker Flat," 124; "Tennessee's Partner," 124
Havens, C. E., 138
Hawthorne, Nathaniel, 2, 5, 17, 27, 35, 37; *The Scarlet Letter*, 19
Henry, Patrick, 152
Hewes, George Robert Twelves, 36–38, 40, 43–44, 48, 119
Heydey Press, 139
historical romances, 3, 7, 20, 179n29
Hittell, Theodore, 134, 143, 200n42
Hoffman, Charles Fenno, 101, 103; *A Winter in the Far West*, 101
Holland, Catherine, 35, 181n55
Honig, Bonnie, 202n10
Hooper, Johnson Jones, 10, 61–64, 74–80, 84, 124, 174, 192n37; *Some Adventures of Simon Suggs*, 10, 61–64, 74–80, 84, 85, 87, 124, 144, 192n37; "Taking the Census," 192n37
Howe, Charles E. B., 127; *A Dramatic Play Entitled Joaquín Murieta de Castillo*, 127
Hsu, Hsuan, 96, 195n26
Hunter, Christopher, 185n40
Hyde, Anne, 198n11
Hyde, Carrie, 203n17

Independence Hall, 34–35, 55–56, 58, 183n11
Indian removal, 61, 87
Ingraham, Joseph Holt, 68, 191n26; *The South-west*, 68, 191n26
institutionalism, 7, 70
Ishmael (*Moby-Dick*), 27

Jackson, Andrew, 8, 48, 49, 61, 63, 65, 67, 78, 97–98, 144, 180n52, 186n51, 191n24, 192n38
Jackson, Holly, 27
Jackson, Joseph, 50
Jackson, Joseph Henry, 200n42, 200n47

Jacksonian democracy, 65, 105, 192n38, 197n54
Jacksonian Democrats, 37
Jefferson, Thomas, 42, 47, 95–96, 152, 168, 191n24, 195n23
Johnson, Susan Lee, 121, 126, 198n5, 198n14
Johnson, Walter, 202n10
Jones, John Beauchamp, 3–4; *The Adventures of Col. Gracchus Vanderbomb*, 3–4, 9
Jones, Martha, 149; *Birthright Citizens*, 149
Justus, James, 64, 189n6

Kafka, Franz, 192n48
Kammen, Michael, 35, 183n18
Kansas-Nebraska Act, 110, 197n60
Kaplan, Amy, 198n10
Kendall, Amos, 61
Kennedy, Dustin, 50
Kennedy, Gerald, 177n11
Kibler, James, 191n34
Kirkland, Caroline, 10, 88–89, 92, 99–108, 112, 122, 124, 141, 159, 173–74, 196n42, 196n52; *A New Home, Who'll Follow?*, 10, 88, 99–108, 118, 122, 159, 173. See also Clavers, Mary
Kirkland, William, 195n40, 196n50
Kloppenberg, James, 25, 90, 182n5
Knickerbocker Magazine, The, 12, 100, 138
Kolb, Harold, 124
Kolodny, Annette, 104, 196n50, 197n57
Kouwenhoven, John A., 22

labor movements, 9, 33, 39, 49–50, 183n9, 187n67
Lafayette, Marquis de, 144
Lanman, James, 94; *History of Michigan*, 94
Larkin, Edward, 21
Laski, Gregory, 192n42
Lee, Billy, 168
Lee, Sheppard, 16
LeMenager, Stephanie, 198n11
Lemke, Sieglinde, 179n38
Levine, Robert, 151, 178n12, 190n11
Levy, JoAnn, 142

liberal: individualism, 27, 156, 160, 200n41, 202n6; subjectivity, 166; tradition, 3, 4, 139, 153
liberal democracy: critiques of, 39, 109, 122, 149, 196n49; law and order, 127, 130–34, 144; contemporary threats to, 182n63; norms of, 3, 26–27, 63, 66, 91, 128, 134, 142, 150, 152, 171. See also democracy
liberalism, 25, 101, 151–52, 159, 161
Liberty of the Press, 55–56
Liberty Party, 148, 202n3
Library Company of Philadelphia, 183n10
Lincoln, Abraham, 17, 63, 85–86, 89, 192n46, 193n3
Lippard, George, 4, 27, 32–33, 49–60, 136–37, 139, 141, 159, 173, 174, 186n60, 187n63; 187n67; *Herbert Tracy*, 187n63; *Ladye Annabel*, 50; *The Quaker City* (novel), 4, 9, 27, 32–33, 49–60, 139, 159, 173; *The Quaker City* (periodical), 187n67
local color, 5
Lockhart, Sandra, 137, 201n49, 201n56, 201n59
Locofocos, 49
Loney, Glenn, 200n34
Longstreet, Augustus Baldwin, 7, 10, 62–64, 68–74, 114, 174, 192n34; *Georgia Scenes*, 7, 10, 62–64, 68–74, 84, 87, 114
Looby, Christopher, 39, 43, 50, 179n33, 186n45, 187n66, 188n78
Los Angeles Star, 85–86
Loughran, Trish, 23, 83, 180n44, 190n11
L'Overture, Toussaint, 168
Lovingood, Sut, 6, 16. See also Harris, George Washington
Loyalists, 3
Lummis, C. Douglas, 24–25
lynching, 47, 114–15, 129–32, 141, 186n56
Lynn, Kenneth, 63, 189n8, 190n17, 192n38

MacCrellish, Frederick, 128
Madison, James, 17, 118, 178n22; *Federalist* 10, 17, 118, 178n22
Madley, Benjamin, 198n13

manifest destiny, 8, 10, 101, 117, 118–46 passim, 198n6, 198n8
Margolis, Stacey, 26
market capitalism, 89, 101, 128, 180n42
Mason, Stevens, 98, 195n34
mass party politics, 44–49, 180n52, 186n53
material transformations: communications revolution, 5, 18, 23, 180n42; transportation revolution, 5, 18, 23, 180n42
Matthiessen, F. O., 2, 4; *American Renaissance*, 2
Melville, Herman, 2, 17, 67, 96, 195n26
Memoir of S.S. Prentiss, A, 189n3
Merish, Lori, 104, 196n52, 197nn54–55
Mexico: alcalde governance, 119, 198n4; challenges for democracy in, 118–19, 126
Michigan, 6, 10, 59, 66, 88–117
Mihm, Stephen, 115
misfits: aesthetic, 5–8, 19, 173–75; California, 121, 126, 134; democratic, 25, 27–29; New York, 148, 158, 161, 164, 204n31; Northwestern, 91 101; Philadelphia, 38; Southwestern, 62–63, 75
Mitford, Mary Russell, 100, 196n43; *Our Village*, 100, 196n43
Moi, Toril, 19
Morgan, Edmund, 90, 194n9
Murison, Justine, 184n30, 185n42

Napoleon Bonaparte, 144
Nashville Union and American, 85, 192n46
nation, US, 2, 14–15, 21, 29, 31, 35, 51, 62, 89, 101, 118, 151, 180n44, 190n11
national: cohesion, 5; compression, 174; consolidation, 59; imperatives, 64; incorporation, 84; manhood, 57; prescriptions, 37, 51, 121, 122, 126, 127, 131, 149, 199n17
National Convention of Colored People (1847), 162, 205n47; Committee on a National Press, 162, 205n47
National Gazette and Literary Register, The, 184n31
nationalisms, 13, 35, 95, 150, 174, 177n11, 180n42, 201n2, 203n16

Navakas, Michele, 198n11
Neary, Janet, 198n15
Nelson, Dana D., 14, 23, 26, 56–57, 101, 180n51, 181n62, 188n83
Neruda, Pablo, 200n35; *Fulgor y Muerte de Joaquín Murieta*, 200n35
New Critics, 7
New England: townships of, 1, 36; emigrants from, 93–95
New Hampshire Patriot, 85
New Historicists, 7
Newlin, Keith, 191n34
New Orleans Picayune, 62, 189n6
New York, 8, 11, 28, 92, 94, 100, 103, 109, 138, 146, 147–72 passim, 173, 174
New York Tribune, 119
Ngai, Sianne, 21
Nickerson, Catherine Ross, 110
Nissen, Axel, 124
North American Review, 12, 100, 183n21
Northwest Ordinance of 1787, 90, 91, 96, 109, 193n3, 193n7, 194n11, 195n23, 195nn27–28

Ober, Josiah, 149, 159, 204n38
O'Brien, Shelia, 75
O'Connor, Flannery, 5; "A Good Man is Hard to Find," 5
Old Northwest, 28, 70, 87, 88–117, 118, 148, 173, 197n58
Old Southwest, 6, 62, 91, 148, 173, 174
Olmstead, Frederick Law, 68, 189n4, 191n26; *A Journey in the Back Country*, 68, 189n4, 191n26; *The Cotton Kingdom*, 191n26
Onuf, Peter, 96, 109, 193n2
O'Sullivan, John L., 10
Otis, James, 25, 37
Otter, Samuel, 32, 188n83; *Philadelphia Stories*, 32

Panic of 1837, 26, 67, 74, 84, 97, 99
Paulding, James Kirke, 65; *Lion of the West*, 65
Peale, Charles Willson, 34

Pease, Donald, 178n18
Pennsylvania Regulations of 1791–1794, 195n29
Penry, Tara, 199n25
periodical press, 52, 55–56
Perman, Michael, 67
Peterson, Carla, 165
Philadelphia, 9, 28, 30–60, 89, 152, 173–74, 182n2, 182n4, 197n58
Philadelphia Mirror, The, 184n31
picaresque, 9, 30, 39–40, 43–44, 185n36
Pioneer, The, 122, 137–38, 200n47, 201n58
pluralism, 15, 25
Poe, Edgar Allan, 5, 17, 18, 22, 43, 47, 50, 67, 100, 177n11, 183n10, 187n63, 187n65
Polk, James K., 144
popular sovereignty, 8, 25, 90–99, 102, 108, 113–17 passim, 159, 194nn9–10, 195n27, 195n29, 197n60
Porter, William T., 62, 80, 84, 189n5, 190n20, 192n37; *Big Bear of Arkansas, The*, 62, 189n5, 190n20; *A Quarter Race in Kentucky*, 189n5, 190n20; *The Spirit of the Times*, 62, 80, 189n6
Powell, Douglas, 177n6
Powell, Timothy, 181n62
Pratt, Lloyd, 16, 74, 86, 148, 153, 202n6
Pryse, Marjorie, 95, 194n12
Public Ledger, The, 184n31

Quigley, Paul, 190n11

Radical Abolitionist Party, 157
Rael, Patrick, 201n2
Ramsay, David, 34, 183n16; *History of the American Revolution*, 34
Rancière, Jacques, 29, 182n63, 182n67
reciprocity, 15, 25, 101, 106, 107, 114
Reconstruction Amendments, 148, 149
regionalism, 5, 9, 13
republicanism: rhetoric of, 1, 3; tradition of, 25, 160
Republican Party, 157
republic of letters, 11–12, 15–16, 19, 62, 159–60, 177n10

Revolution, American: legacy of, 8, 9, 152, 153, 186n50; heroes of, 152; history of, 143; memory of, 33–38, 47, 66, 72, 197n58; monuments to, 28, 35, 38, 41; promises of, 147; radicalism of, 42
Reynolds, David, 187n68
Reynolds, G. M. W., 187n65
Rickels, Milton, 192n45
Ridge, John Rollin, 4, 11, 121–22, 126–36, 146, 174, 200n33, 200nn40–41; *The Adventures of Joaquín Murieta* (1854), 4, 11, 121–22, 126–36, 137, 139, 140, 143, 146; *The Adventures of Joaquín Murieta, Third Edition* (1871), 134–36, 200n42
Rifkin, Mark, 193n6
Riley, Benet, 123
Roberts, Brian, 142
Robinson, Alfred, 119; *Life in California Before the Conquest*, 119
Rohrbough, Malcolm, 97
Romantic era, 6
Romine, Scott, 192n34
Rosenblum, Nancy, 29, 92, 194n13
Rourke, Constance, 190n17
Rowe, John Carlos, 128
Royce, Josiah, 137, 142, 143
Rusert, Brit, 202n5
Russell, Thomas C., 139
Ryan, Mary, 38, 184n29

Saler, Bethel, 193n6
Santamarina, Xiomara, 148
Scharnhorst, Gary, 199n23
Schuller, Kyla, 160, 202n5, 204n41
Seelye, John, 190n16
Senchyne, Jonathan, 202n5
Senkewicz, Robert M., 143
sentimental novels, 3, 7, 20, 179n29
Shakespeare, William, 136
Shapiro, Joe, 102, 196n49
Shumway, David, 16
Silverman, Gillian, 54, 188n77
Slotkin, Richard, 190n17, 190n22
Smith, Gerit, 157
Smith, Henry Nash, 121

Smith, James McCune, 7, 16, 149, 150, 156–64, 165, 174, 204n31, 204n36, 205n48; *Heads of the Colored People*, 7, 16, 149, 156–64, 167. *See also* Communipaw
Smith, Valerie, 203n25
Smith-Baranzini, Marlene, 138, 139
social protest, 9, 28
southwestern humor, 10, 28, 61–87, 124, 144–45, 189nn2–4, 190n22, 204n28
Sparks, Jared, 36, 183n21
Spires, Derrick, 148, 158, 159, 166, 202n6, 205n53
Starr, Kevin, 119, 197n3
Stauffer, John, 153, 158, 203n26, 204n33
Stein, Jordan, 202n5
Stepto, Robert, 203n21, 203n25
Stevens, J. David, 199n29
Stewart, Kathleen, 22
St. Louis Reveille, 62, 189n6
Stowe, Harriet Beecher, 7, 8, 10, 17, 91, 93–97, 100, 105, 108, 112, 138, 143, 150, 151; "A New England Sketch," 10, 91, 93–97, 100, 105, 112; "Uncle Lot," 93, 194n15; *Uncle Tom's Cabin*, 7, 51, 151
Streeby, Shelly, 110, 179n29, 187n67
Sue, Eugene, 187n65
Suggs, Simon, 6
Sweet, Timothy, 183n8
synecdochic representativeness, 2, 20, 32, 183n8

Talisse, Robert, 29
Taniguchi, Nancy J., 143, 201n66
Taylor, Bayard, 119, 121–23, 134, 136, 198n5; *Eldorado*, 119, 121–23
Tejon Indians, 129
Thoreau, Henry David, 2, 27
Tocqueville, Alexis de, 1–2, 4, 5, 6, 13, 15, 17, 22, 26, 36, 127, 175, 183n21, 186n47, 186n57; *Democracy in America*, 1, 2, 26
Toledo War, 97–98
Tompkins, Jane, 179n29
Tompkins, Kyla Wazana, 202n5
transcendentalist essays, 3

transcontinental railroad, 197n2
transnational studies, 7, 15, 16, 20, 178n19
Treaty of Guadalupe Hidalgo, 120
Turner, Frederick Jackson, 89, 91, 121, 193n5
Twain, Mark, 12, 62, 65, 139; *The Adventures of Huckleberry Finn*, 12, 19

Universal Yankee Nation, 70, 92, 94–95, 99, 109, 156. *See also* Yankee West
University of Glasgow, 157
University of Pennsylvania, 43
Urgo, Joseph, 123, 199n29
US-Mexican War, 10, 120–121, 145

Van Buren, Martin, 49, 99
Vanderbomb, Gracchus, 6. *See also* Jones, John Beauchamp
vernacular aesthetics: in California gold rush literature, 122, 130, 136; as a concept, 8, 19–23, 175; in New York periodicals, 159, 165, 166; in northwestern settlement narratives, 106, 115; in Philadelphia novels, 33, 39, 41, 48, 51; in southwestern humor, 69, 71–72
Victor, Metta Fuller, 4, 10, 27, 92, 108–17, 174; *Alice Wilde*, 92, 111–13; *The Backwoods Bride*, 4, 10, 27, 92, 109, 111, 113–17; *The Dead Letter*, 110, 197n63; *The Last Days of Tul*, 110; *Mormon Wives*, 1110; "The Silver Lute," 110
Victor, Orville, 109
Vigilance Committee of San Francisco in 1851, 143
vigilance committees: in *Joaquín Murieta*, 132–33; in *The Shirley Letters*, 142–43, 145
Virginia, 152
voting rights, 3

Walker, Cynthia, 200n40
Walker, David, 13; *Appeal*, 13
Wallerstein, Immanuel, 178n19
Walter, Krista, 203n16
Warwick Research Collective, 177n9
Washington, DC, 116
Washington, George, 6, 42, 58, 72, 144, 168
Watts, Edward, 194n12, 196n51
Webster, Daniel, 159
Wecter, Dixon, 120
Weinstein, Cindy, 179n29, 179n33
Western Monthly Magazine, 93, 95
Wheatley, Phyllis, 170
Whig Party, 37, 49, 53, 62, 192n38, 197n55
White, Ed, 185n38, 203n20
Whitman, Walt, 2, 17, 27, 67, 96, 195n26; *Leaves of Grass*, 2
Wilentz, Sean, 38, 183n9, 184n28
Wilson, Ivy G., 148, 165, 167, 181n62, 202n6, 203n16, 205n60, 206n66
Wilson, William J., 4, 27, 149, 150, 158, 161, 164–72, 174, 205n57; *Afric-American Picture Gallery*, 4, 27, 149, 164–71. *See also* Ethiop
Winter, Molly Crumpton, 129
Wolin, Sheldon, 177n7
Wood, Gordon, 27
world-systems analysis, 20, 178n19
Wright, Frances, 34–36, 40, 47, 51
Wuthnow, Robert, 177n4

Yankee West, 93, 96. *See also* Universal Yankee Nation
Yarborough, Richard, 203n25
Young, Alfred, 37–38
Young America, 12

Zagarell, Sandra, 101

www.ingramcontent.com/pod-product-compliance
Lightning Source LLC
Chambersburg PA
CBHW032037300426
44117CB00009B/1096